WITHDRAWN

Three Catholic Writers
of the Modern South

# Three Catholic Writers of the Modern South

by
Robert H. Brinkmeyer, Jr.

UNIVERSITY PRESS OF MISSISSIPPI
JACKSON

**Library of Congress Cataloging in Publication Data**

Brinkmeyer, Robert H.
    Three Catholic writers of the modern South.

    Bibliography: p.
    Includes index.
    1. American literature—Catholic authors—History and
criticism.   2. American literature—Southern States—
History and criticism.   3. American literature—20th
century—History and criticism.   4. Tate, Allen,
1899–      —Criticism and interpretation.   5. Gordon,
Caroline, 1895–      —Criticism and interpretation.
6. Percy, Walker, 1916–      —Criticism and interpretation.   7. Theology, Catholic, in literature.   8. Southern
States in literature.   I. Title.
PS153.C3B75    1985        810'.9'382        84-19641
ISBN 0-87805-246-1

The University Press of Mississippi thanks the following publishers and copyright holders for permission to reprint material
used in this book:

Excerpts abridged and adapted from "Remarks on the Southern Religion" by Allen Tate in *I'll Take My Stand: The South and the Agrarian
Tradition* by Twelve Southerners. Copyright © 1930, by Harper and
Row, Publishers, Inc.; renewed 1958 by Donald Davidson. Reprinted by
permission of the publishers.

Excerpts from *The Moviegoer* by Walker Percy. Copyright © 1961,
Alfred A. Knopf, Inc. Reprinted by permission of the publisher.

Excerpts from *Allen Tate: A Literary Biography* by Radcliffe Squires, ©
1971, The Bobbs-Merrill Company, Inc., Indianapolis. Reprinted with
permission of the publisher.

Excerpts from *The Literary Correspondence of Donald Davidson and Allen
Tate* edited by John Fain and Thomas Daniel Young. © 1974 by The
University of Georgia Press. Reprinted with permission of The Univer-
sity of Georgia Press.

*To my parents*
*with love*

As social and political men we may, if we choose, select all the provisional absolutes that we desire; as poets we must be selected by some absolute. We may then criticize it or even reject it, but we cannot get rid of it; like Lord Tennyson's God, it is nearer than hands and feet.

**ALLEN TATE**

*The ceremony must be found*
*Traditional, with all its symbols*

**JOHN PEALE BISHOP**

# Contents

# Acknowledgments

This book has been a long time coming, and I would like to thank here a few of the people who have helped me along the way. My first thanks go out to the numerous librarians at Duke University's Perkins Library and East Campus Library who have been so helpful and friendly. As much work as I have done in those libraries and as many books as I have checked out, I know I am a familiar face to them all. Second, I would like to thank John Seelye, C. Carroll Hollis, Giles Gunn, and Louis D. Rubin, Jr., professors at the University of North Carolina at Chapel Hill whose friendship, advice, and support have been so important all along to me and my work. Next, my thanks go to my typist, Muriel Dyer, who did an excellent job with a not-so-neat manuscript. Her patience and professionalism were much appreciated. My editor at the University Press of Mississippi, Seetha Srinivasan, has also been most helpful and patient. I am thankful for all the ways she has helped shape this book.

Finally there is my family, who deserve by themselves a paragraph—and more!—for all their support. I know I have put them through a lot. My three daughters, Mary, Eliza, and Emma, have had, on those days when my work was not going well, to put up with a sometimes cranky daddy. My wife Chris, of course, suffered a similar fate—a sometimes cranky husband. She more than anyone else deserves my thanks, for both her moral support and her editorial assistance. I am glad that she and my daughters, along with my parents, can now all share in my joy in seeing my work become a book.

# Introduction

In her essay "The Catholic Novelist in the Protestant South," Flannery O'Connor writes that "the writer whose themes are religious particularly needs a region where these themes find a response in the life of the people." "The American Catholic," she goes on to say, "is short on places that reflect his particular religious life and his particular problems. This country isn't exactly cut in his image." Two exceptions come to her mind—J. F. Powers's midwestern parishes and Edwin O'Connor's South Boston. For the rest of America, O'Connor observes, the Catholic Church stands far from the mainstream of life, and this fact has assuredly affected the nature and volume of American Catholic fiction: "If the Catholic faith were central to life in America, Catholic fiction would fare better, but the Church is not central to this society."[1]

O'Connor of course knew that in her own homeland—both middle Georgia and the South in general—Catholics were far removed from the mainstream culture, a culture dominated by evangelical Protestantism whose influence cut across both religious and social realms. Yet she was also aware of the seemingly odd fact that the South nourished not only her but also a number of writers who were converts to the Catholic Church. The literary careers of three of these converts—Allen Tate, Caroline Gordon, and Walker Percy—form the heart of this study.

As a born Catholic, O'Connor knew that her intellectual development was markedly different from that of the converts. Though all were brought up in small town Southern communities, O'Connor, unlike the converts, experienced the Church as a force that interpreted and ordered the experiences of her formative years. This, she understood, was crucial both to her personal and her artistic development. "The convert does not get to experience his convictions in the years that experience forms the imagination," she wrote (13 February 1960) to a friend in Atlanta who was a convert.[2] She drove home the point of the all-embracing nature of her faith in a letter (6 November 1955) to John Lynch: "I feel that if I were not a Catholic, I would have no reason to write, no reason to see, no reason to feel horrified or even to enjoy anything. I am a born Catholic, went to Catholic schools in my early years, and have never left or wanted to leave the Church" (*HB*, 114).

I don't mean to downplay O'Connor's "southernness" here. One needs only to read a page or two from her fiction to realize how much she opened herself up to her homeland, allowing its traditions, beliefs, and modes of thought to inform her consciousness and art. Indeed, as she well knew, she owed much of her greatness as a writer to the cultural and philosophical interplay of her southern and Catholic sensibilities. "To my way of thinking," she wrote (15 September 1955) to Andrew Lytle, "the only thing that keeps me from being a regional writer is being a Catholic and the only thing that keeps me from being a Catholic writer (in the narrow sense) is being a Southerner" (*HB*, 104). Nonetheless, this healthy tension was always weighted in favor of the Church. It is clear from her essays and letters that the Church and her faith—rather than her southern heritage— were the elements to which O'Connor gave her deepest thoughts and over which she agonized most intensely. Overstating her case perhaps a bit, she wrote to John Lynch in the letter just cited, "I write the way I do because and only because I am a Catholic" (*HB*, 114).

If the primary shaping force of O'Connor's imagination was her Catholicism, that which molded Tate, Gordon, and Percy was the heritage of Old South tradition and community. All three grew up in out-of-the-way communities where the modern world had made few inroads. Classical ideals of decorum and honor shaped their moral vision; community ideals of kinship and tradition forged their social values. None had a strict religious upbringing of any sort, though each imbibed a deep sense of humanity's flawed and fallen nature. This realization, however, probably stemmed more from the pessimism that lay at the heart of the Old South's Stoic vision than from any specific religious training, although what they may have heard in church would likely have underscored this dark vision of human nature.

When Tate, Gordon, and Percy grew up and entered the

rapidly changing world of modern society, they found their value systems, indeed, their identities, under extreme challenge. In what to them must have seemed a shockingly short time, they stepped from a society rooted in myth and tradition into one preoccupied with history and science. The order and stability of their community-based world view gave way before new theories of psychology and sociology that spurned traditional values and morality. Positivism pervaded almost all levels of thinking, even theology. Here was Nietzsche's "weightless" society, bereft of supernatural frameworks of meaning and strict moral guideposts.

Finding a path in such a world was difficult for Tate, Gordon, and Percy—and for many others. As Jackson Lears makes clear in his wide-ranging study, *No Place of Grace: Antimodernism and the Transformation of American Culture 1880–1920,* a great number of Americans in the late nineteenth and early twentieth centuries suffered from the modern malaise which one more often associates with the disillusionment after World War I. Drawing on the observations of sociologist Peter Berger, Lears outlines the difficulties a person has in extracting meaning from life's chaos when his or her society lacks a coherent and transcendent-based order. "As supernatural frameworks of meaning become problematic," writes Lears, "individuals slide into anomie; the sense of a coherent universe wavers; reality seems to slip out of focus and blur into unreality. This was the most profound effect of secularization on late-nineteenth-century Americans: they sensed that familiar frameworks of meaning were evaporating; they felt doomed to spiritual homelessness."[3]

Lears's observation here speaks tellingly to the situation facing Tate and Gordon when they left the South for New York City in the 1920s and to that confronting Walker Percy when he made a similar move in the 1940s. Their alienation and sense of loss assuredly was deeper and more intense than the average citizen's, since they were widely read, self-professed intellectuals and, even more important, writers. They not only suffered from their predicament emotionally but also wrestled with it on planes of thought that made them think and rethink the basic questions of existence and meaning. These probings, these intellectual and emotional grapplings, became the basis for their art and perhaps the greatest source of their powers of expression. Each day spent at the writing table was a time of confrontation and reevaluation, a wrenching challenge to achieve order amidst chaos.

Writing added a deeper dimension to their alienation. Entering into the humanistic realm of letters, Tate, Gordon, and Percy became deeply aware of the dilemmas that were tearing asunder the very fabric of this large tradition. According to Lewis P. Simpson in his brilliant study, *The Brazen Face of History: Studies in the Literary Consciousness in America,* the Third Realm—or the Republic of Letters, the other two realms being Church and State—has since the late Middle Ages been in a protracted process of secularization.[4] What Simpson calls the Great Critique of Church and State occurred in the seventeenth and eighteenth centuries, when a number of intellectuals—Simpson names among many others Francis Bacon, Newton, Locke, Pope, Franklin, Jefferson—explored the nature of existence not by contemplating ideal constructs of order (as Plato, Augustine, and Dante had done) but by testing it according to the processes of the rational and scientific mind. The effects upon humanistic thought were far-reaching. Writes Simpson: "From Descartes on, mind became identified with the introspective, instructional functions of consciousness—with the processes of cognition. Believing solely in its own existence, mind has no knowledge outside its own functioning. Consciousness cannot transcend consciousness."[5]

By the nineteenth century, with the rise of the Romantic and symbolist poets, a literary reaction against the overwhelmingly pervasive rationality set in. Feeling the loss of spiritual and religious transcendence, a number of writers celebrated the ultimate mystery of consciousness against the rational world and looked to their art for the creation of an Absolute. In Simpson's words:

> This phenomenon was accompanied by the opening of the priesthood of the imagination, not only to those writers who were prophets and revealers, like Blake, but to those who were like the symbolist poets in France, radical experimenters with words and fabricators of a new literary language. Literary seers and craftsmen together made an irregular spiritual government, a polity of the literary mind, dedicated, we may say, to creating out of the diverse

contents of the cultural dialectic an irregular myth of creativity, a myth of the artist's self-interpretation and self-fulfillment.[6]

This conception of the artist as a member of a select group, a heroic elite standing opposed to the everyday reality of the rational world, has of course become the central legend of the twentieth-century artist. Any number of literary giants come to mind—Proust, Joyce, Yeats, Faulkner, Hemingway, to name several. The dark underside to this legend is that modern writers, despite their idealized community (itself based on alienation), are solitary figures, exiles from a society whose moral systems lack a transcendent framework. In a world of fragmented and isolated existence, their quests for meaning become pursuits for pure consciousness, the only knowable realm. This is what Allen Tate was so painfully aware of early in his career when he wrote of the modern poet and his poetry: "The external world is a permanent possibility of sign-posts upon which the poet may hang his attitudes, his sensibility. Not the world, but consciousness; hence his difficult abstractness."[7] For Tate and many other modern artists, their art became their religion; through the creative act, they sought to achieve the only order they believed possible in a chaotic world. And they were deadly earnest, this literary priesthood. "Art has its own hagiography and its Book of Martyrs," wrote Malcolm Cowley, to which might be added Hemingway's words: "A writer should be of great probity and honesty as a priest of God."[8]

Throughout the twentieth century, southern writers, by and large, have found it difficult to accept wholeheartedly the role of the artist as literary priest. Searching for order and meaning only through the pursuit of pure consciousness and the creation of art seems to satisfy the southern writer for only a limited time. This has proved particularly true for those southerners who grew up in communities outside the mainstream of modernity where the old, highly structured ways of life still held sway. Although they often go into a self-imposed exile from their homeland and revel, for a while, in the freedom—artistic and otherwise—of the modern world, most southern writers eventually find something missing from their lives: a strong sense of community, a strict morality, a respect for the sacredness of life;

in other words, the society of their childhoods, or at least their conception of that society as they interpret it as adults. For these, a central tension develops: how to reinvigorate their modern identities with the knowledge they bring of their southern heritage, a heritage which to modern eyes seems out of place and reactionary.

This has been the experience of Allen Tate and Caroline Gordon. In the early stages of their careers, both writers embraced their roles as modern artists, thriving in the camaraderie they shared with numerous writers and artists in New York and Europe. For a while they were content not to search for meaning and purpose beyond their art. But before long a sense of loss and disorientation set in, and their enthusiasm for modernity waned.

Allen Tate was especially affected early on by this sense of spiritual homelessness. Haunted in the late 1920s by a desire to add a foundation of morality and faith to his life, Tate explored alternatives both political-historical (Agrarianism) and religious (Roman Catholicism). At the time, neither proved satisfactory. Agrarianism lacked a religious base, an element Tate had come to see as necessary for any transcendence of the philosophy of modern naturalism, which he saw dominating contemporary thought. Catholicism, on the other hand, seemed unduly abstracted from the naturalistic world; to believe in Catholicism, Tate believed, was to cut oneself from the here and now and to deny one's heritage. Tate could not wholeheartedly endorse either system, and for many years he wrestled with what might best be called his "unbelieving belief"; these decades of struggle produced some of his most memorable art. Not until the late 1940s was he able to transform his unbelief into faith, and shortly thereafter he became a Catholic.

Caroline Gordon apparently accepted her role as modern artist for a longer period. She came early under the influence of Ford Madox Ford, who conveyed to her a deep appreciation of the power and mystery of the written word. Moreover, she likened herself as artist to the classical heroes confronting the dark forces of life, thus bolstering her fortitude in facing twentieth-century chaos. While Tate was immersing himself in the Agrarian movement, Gordon remained aloof from political involvement; she was more skeptical of the regenerative powers of the South and its traditions, while at the same time she never abandoned entirely her southern allegiance and her nostalgic love for the home country. Not until the early 1940s did Gordon begin seriously to search for ways other than art to transcend the chaotic nature of modern life. In her fiction from this period she began to suggest tentatively the possibilities of two transcending orders—one built on a classical vision, the other on Christianity. In 1947 she became a Catholic. Even after her conversion, however, she maintained her interest in the classical studies, and, in the final stages of her career, sought to unify her two visions.

Walker Percy of course was converted to Catholicism before he became a writer; as a result, his experience has been quite different from Tate's and Gordon's. But there are similarities. Where Tate and Gordon rejected the role of artist as literary priest and eventually turned to the Church, Percy cast aside the role of doctor as medical priest to embrace the Catholic faith. Trained as a doctor, Percy as a young man was fascinated by the beauty and order of science. Ultimately, however, he realized—mainly through his reading of European novelists and philosophers, particularly the Christian existentialists—that science failed to address the essential problems of man's existence. He reached the stunning conclusion that "the more science progressed and even as it benefited man, the less it said about what it is to be a man living in the world."[9] Like Tate and Gordon, Percy sought a stable world view and a framework of faith; like them, he found these in the Catholic Church.

Standing somewhat apart from the three writers discussed here is Katherine Anne Porter, another southern Catholic convert. Porter was converted early in life, during the first of four marriages, and then spent the rest of her days, until the final few years, repressing but (significantly) never repudiating her Catholicism. I hope to tell her story in my next projected work, which will explore the literary efforts of Porter, Eudora Welty, and Flannery O'Connor to break through the everyday world to the mysterious realms of meaning beyond.

Tate, Gordon, and Percy explore in their writing the myriad tensions and conflicts that are typically part of sensitive modern artists. As I have suggested and hope to show in the following pages, many of these conundrums and dilemmas stem from their southern upbringings. All three were acutely aware that the South of their childhoods was falling prey to the ravages of twentieth-century society, and that the old ways bore little relevance to modern culture. Shaping the imaginations of these three writers (and those of a number of other southern writers in the twentieth century) was this dichotomy of old and new. As Tate observes, this conflict lay at the heart of the twentieth-century southern Renascence: "It has made possible the curious burst of intelligence that we get at a crossing of the ways, not unlike, on an infinitesimal scale, the outburst of poetic genius at the end of the sixteenth century when commercial England had already begun to crush feudal England."[10]

For Tate, Gordon, and Percy, this "crossing of the ways" led to another "crossing"—that is, to Roman Catholicism. Though all three saw their southern identities as a way to define themselves against the modern world, at the same time they recognized that this definition was resistance, not transcendence. They turned to the Church to restore myth, meaning, and mystery to what they saw as a morally irresponsible modern world. None of the three found such a step simple or easy; rather, their conversions culminated arduous struggles to achieve perception and articulation. These struggles, together with the wide-ranging art born from them, constitute the stories about to be told.

Three Catholic Writers
of the Modern South

## CHAPTER 1

# "Gentlemen, My Secret is Damnation": Allen Tate's Search for Unity

Throughout his career as a poet and a man of letters, Allen Tate was acutely aware of the absence in contemporary society of a tradition capable of ordering and unifying existence. This awareness haunts almost all of Tate's poems, essays, and fiction. He observes in "The Profession of Letters in the South" (1935) that "the 'message' of modern art at present is that social man is living, without religion, morality, or art (without the high form that concentrates all three in an organic whole) in a mere system of money references through which neither artist nor plutocrat can perform as an entire person."[1] Feeling this fragmentation so intensely, Tate spent much of his career searching for a belief that would unify "religion, morality, and art" into "an organic whole."

As a result of this ongoing search, Tate joined the Catholic Church in 1950. He did not suddenly "find" Catholicism late in life; he was strongly attracted to it as a young man and was haunted by a deep religious sense throughout his career. His religious struggles and specifically his efforts to come to grips with Catholicism profoundly affected his career as poet and critic; indeed, his struggle to believe amidst the doubts of unbelief lies at the very center of Tate's artistic imagination. Writing in a 1950 symposium in *Partisan Review,* Tate himself admitted, "As I look back upon my own verse, written over more than twenty-five years, I see plainly that its main theme is man suffering from unbelief; and I cannot for a moment suppose that this man is some other than myself."[2]

Tate's upbringing apparently had little to do with his religious sensibility, for his childhood was steeped more in the secular traditions of Old South decorum and honor than in the creed of any church.[3] Born on 19 November 1899 in Winchester, Kentucky, Tate grew up in a small town sheltered from the uproar of the twentieth century. Life there was for the most part placid and orderly, with the code of the town's elders one of classical decorum and balance. Reflecting on his childhood years later in a commencement address delivered at the University of Minnesota, Tate described a farmer-lawyer he once knew: "He knew a little about many things—mathematics, science, the ancient classics, agronomy, the law; yet all of the little that he knew was alive in his daily life and was constantly brought to bear upon the human condition as he could know it in his place and time. Without being conscious of representing anything at all, he was an exemplar of the classical apothegm: Nothing too much. One would know he would be as considerate of the plain people of this community as of Senator James or Justice McReynolds. He was, in short, an educated man."[4]

Besides this community ideal of order and unity, the pretensions and pride of the landed gentry informed Tate's childhood. Though Tate's father was a businessman—and not a very effective one—his mother was a Virginia-born aristocrat who tenaciously maintained her family's aristocratic code. To her, the family home was Virginia, not Kentucky, and almost every summer she returned there to visit with her children in tow. According to Tate, his mother always insisted that he was born in Fairfax County, Virginia (where she herself was born); he was thirty years old, Tate said, before he discovered his true birthplace.[5]

Although Tate's upbringing was shaped heavily by the ideals of the traditional Old South, the family had a hard time living by them. Various problems undercut its stability and security. Financial worries were almost always present. Tate's father's business ventures, a string of failures, forced the family not only to struggle to make ends meet, but also to move about a great deal, following Mr. Tate as he sought new enterprises. Moreover, some mysterious scandal touched his father when Allen was about eight years old. From then on the boy's mother, together with her children, spent a great deal of time away from her husband. Essentially an aristocratic snob, she was constantly on the move in search of favorable social situations. Tate later described this experience in harsh terms: "We sometimes moved two or three times a year, moving *away* from something my mother didn't like; or perhaps withdrawing would be a better word; for my mother gradually withdrew from the world, and withdrew me also, gradually, from the time I was a small boy; so that we might as well have been living, and I been born, in a tavern at a crossroads."[6]

Religion played a minor role in the life of the Tates. Tate's mother, raised a Presbyterian, was not a strict churchgoer, although she did have a Presbyterian respect for the Sabbath—no dancing or playing cards were allowed on that day. His father, baptized an Episcopalian, later became a Robert C. Ingersoll Free Thinker and during his son's youth never attended church. Tate himself went to Presbyterian Sunday school irregularly, and there is little evidence that his church schooling influenced him much. Describing his religious upbringing, he wrote years later: "In my boyhood there was no religious influence that I felt impelled to accept or reject. In so far as we had a family religion, it was my mother's, and it was less Christian in daily practise than Chinese; for she worshiped her father and by a kind of genealogical sorites arrived at the veneration of remote, invisible forbears."[7]

Apparently, however, his brief attendance at a Catholic school had a significant religious influence on Tate. Because the family moved so often, Tate went to a number of different schools, one of which was a Catholic school his maternal grandfather had attended. His mother saw Tate's enrollment at this Catholic institution as following the best family tradition. "Her father was a lapsed, but not apostate Catholic," Tate recalls in his essay "Mere Literature and the Lost Traveller," "so I was sent to a Catholic school, not for an education either religious or secular, but because my grandfather had gone there around 1850. He went there and was perfect; if I went there I would be perfect: plausible logic, as plausible as most logical schemes when they are imposed upon human behavior. I need not say that it didn't work."[8] His experiences at this school, where he learned not only that he did not measure up to his faultless grandfather, but also that in the Church's eyes he was a fallen sinner in need of grace, emphasized the limited nature of his own character and of human existence in general. Later in this same essay, Tate says that from these experiences he acquired "a daily awareness of human imperfection and failure, the former in myself, always about to dash me into the latter; and at the same time a distrust of nature, or what the theologians call the natural order. Redemption might be possible for individuals, but the state was beyond redemption and nature was evil."[9]

Tate's early development was rounded out by his exploration in Modernist thought. During his years at Vanderbilt University, which he entered in 1918 intending to major in classical studies, he immersed himself in contemporary literature and philosophy, paying particular attention, at least early on, to the French—Baudelaire, Mallarmé, de Gourmont, LaForgue. Soon Tate was an active member of the Fugitives, the Nashville-based group of poets whose members included John Crowe Ransom, Donald Davidson, and Robert Penn Warren. He was now writing his own poetry and judging that of his friends; he saw himself, alone among the Fugitive group, as a thorough-going Modernist. Recalling Tate's remarkable awareness of the international literary scene during his university years, John Crowe Ransom wrote that Tate "had literary resources which were not the property of our region at that time. Whether in poetry or prose, it was done with a consciousness of a body of literature which was unknown to his fellow students, and to my faculty associates and myself, unless it was by the purest hearsay."[10]

By the early 1920s, then, three important traditions had surfaced in Tate's life: Old South order and community, Roman Catholicism, and Modernism. Although clearly at this point Tate's southern and Modernist allegiances were dominant, nonetheless, when his religious nature began to surface in the forthcoming years, it was the complexities of Roman Catholicism with which he found himself struggling. Over time, these three disparate traditions—the Old South, Roman Catholicism, and Modernism—most clearly shaped his thought and art. Each tradition appealed to Tate as a way to establish order and meaning in his life; throughout his career, he explored the value and significance of each tradition, working with the three forces in various combinations and playing certain aspects of one against aspects of the others. For many years their conflicting pulls tugged him this way and that, and apparently his inner turmoil was solved only through his conversion to Catholicism in 1950. But Tate's road to Catholicism was long and tortuous.

During his years as a member of the Fugitives (1922–25) Tate identified himself not so much as a southerner but as a modern artist. Both his poetry and his prose from this period reflect his Modernist allegiances. His critical insights developed quickly as an undergraduate, so that by 1922 he was already espousing and defending Modernist ideas of the role of the poet and the creation of poetry. In a 1922 essay, "Whose Ox," which appeared in *The Fugitive,* Tate summed up his views on the current state of poetry. He wrote that the prevailing and traditional outlook held that "the aesthetic problem confronting the poet is eminently practical—versification, diction, composition, in a word, mechanics being the elusive enemy to capture and subdue."[11] He added that it was also assumed that the poet's "peculiar way of viewing the world, his 'genius,' informs the poem, although neither he nor anyone else can explain the *ens realissimum* of that genius," and that "his finished product must *represent* some phase of life as ordinarily perceived, and that he must look for his effects in new combinations of images representing only the constituted material world."[12]

Though conceding that these traditional views could and still did have validity for some poets ("the old modes are not yet sapped," he wrote), Tate energetically defended what he called the "contemporary revolt," saying that its "unique virtue . . . is its break, in a positive direction, with the tyranny of representation."[13] To the charge that art (he mentions the work of Duncan Grant and Picasso) must have objective validity and must represent something, he counters that "perhaps the world as it is doesn't afford accurate correlatives of all the emotional complexes and attitudes; and so the painter, and, it may be, the poet are justified in not only re-arranging (witness entire English Tradition) but remaking, remoulding, in a subjective order, the stuff they must necessarily work with—the material world."[14]

In "Whose Ox," Tate was careful to give traditional poetry, what he was calling poetry of representation, its due. "I don't commit myself to a preference for either genre," he said, speaking of the old way versus the new subjectivism, "only recognizing the unquestionable merits of both."[15] By 1924, looking again at the poetic situation in another essay, "One Escape from the Dilemma," he unequivocally cast his lot with the moderns. Developing his idea on the necessarily subjective nature of modern verse, Tate here stressed that the subject of poetry is the poet's perception of external objects—his consciousness—rather than those objects themselves. Following the lead of the French symbolists, he said that the modern poet works with external reality to symbolize the vagaries of his consciousness. "The external world is a permanent possibility of sign-posts upon which the poet may hang his attitudes, his sensibility," Tate wrote. "Not the world, but consciousness; hence, his difficult abstractness."[16]

In this same essay, Tate made a complete break with the old style. Comparing the literary situations of nineteenth-century England and the 1920s, he wrote that the former period was "a community of faith, of aspiration (to be good even if a bit dishonest), of smuggery," and so "what needed the poet but to restate the self-evident amenities memorably, those categorical revelations common to all minds, immune to the blighting tentacle of scepticism."[17] But contemporary poets, he said, faced a drastically different situation:

> We will credit no prophets. An individualistic intellectualism is the mood of our age. There is no common-to-all-truth; poetry has no longer back of it, ready for use momently, a harmonious firmament of stage-properties and sentiments which it was the pious office of the poets to set up at the dictation of a mysterious *afflatus*—Heaven, Hell, Duty, Olympus, Immortality, as the providential array of "themes": the Modern poet of this generation has had no experience of these things, he has seen nothing even vaguely resembling them. He is grown so astute that he will be happy only in the obscure by-ways of his own perceptive processes; *a priori* utterance never escapes him. Claude Monet said: "The chief character in a group portrait is the light." So the Modern poet might tell you that his only possible themes are the manifold projections and tangents of his own perception. It is the age of the Sophist.[18]

That the modern age lacked an overarching myth by which to order itself is an idea that echoes throughout Tate's career. How the poet should respond to this dilemma was a central problem for Tate, and his perspective on it evolved through the years. Early in his career Tate did not appear to be searching for any principle of unity or central myth to reassert order amidst twentieth-century chaos. He seemed content, as his poetry shows, to emphasize the discontinuity and complexity of existence and consciousness, often violently yoking together words, ideas, and techniques without apparent meaning other than the mirroring of life's difficult ironies. Almost all of Tate's early verse is open-ended, without resolution. As Radcliffe Squires writes, "The resolution is the impossibility of resolution."[19]

Tate's deliberately jarring and difficult poetry embodies not only his Modernist views of existence, but also his rebellion against the old, stable order. He came to see himself as a warrior against what he saw as outmoded ideas and sentimentality ("Sentimentality excuses all," he wrote [7 December 1922] to Donald Davidson).[20] He wanted his art to assault those readers who, he wrote in the same letter to Davidson, liked to see reality "sentimentalized into a scheme of pretty flowers and birds" (*LCDT,* 58). "It seems to me," he wrote (8 August 1922) to Davidson, "that surprise is the touchstone of the best modern schools" (*LCDT,* 29). Tate wanted his verse to jar complacent readers; he wanted to thwart readers' expectations of easy clichés by giving them the unexpected—difficult vocabulary, jarring syntax, unresolved dilemmas.

During this period, Tate fulfilled his need for unity in his pursuit of art. He acknowledged that the confusing and complex realities of modern life made being an artist extremely difficult, both psychologically and financially. "Perhaps," he wrote in "One Escape from the Dilemma," "Oswald Spengler is right: a man is a fool to be an artist or poet in this age. But at least our poet is aware of his own age, barren for any art though it may be, for he can't write like Homer or Milton now; from the data of his experience he infers only a distracting complexity."[21] But the intellectual honesty of his artistic endeavor, as he stridently asserted in a letter to Donald Davidson (16 January 1923), provided Tate with meaning and purpose enough: "There is only one thing in life to me, and that is the continual possibility of pursuing literature as an art, and I can therefore countenance no compromise in a matter which is of the utmost vitality to me. . . . I may be impractical and too unreasonable, but I will follow this course till I honestly believe I'm wrong. If Jesus Christ should come upon earth and present me a poem I sincerely thought inferior, I would tell him *just that* to his teeth" (*LCDT,* 66).

Almost fifty years later, Tate, now a Catholic, wrote in his essay "Mere Literature and the Lost Traveller" that during these early years his was a literary religion. "A young man furnished by his literary environment could not be concerned with theological salvation," he recollected. "Was not the poetic intuition *pure*—free and uncontaminated by ritual and dogma?"[22] In the same essay, he set up an opposition between religion and literature which he said he faced as a young poet: "Like most literary men of the twentieth century I have found myself confronted with the dilemma. Religion *or* Literature. This disjunction fifty years ago was widespread, and like most of my contemporaries I went with literature, without trying to think why, because in the nineteen-twenties there was a literary religion without reflection many of us drifted into."[23]

Though there is no reason to doubt Tate's observations here on his views of the poetic vocation in the 1920s—literature was indeed a religion of sorts for him—his assertion that he had to choose between "Religion *or* Literature" seems more an observation made for his audience in the 1970s than it does an accurate description of his life during the 1920s. Apparently Tate gave little thought to religious matters during this time, except in his recognition of the breakdown of the classical-Christian heritage of Western society in the twentieth century. But even if one agrees with Andrew Lytle, who classifies Tate as a religious writer "from the very beginning" because his "subject is simply what is left of Christendom, the western knowledge of ourselves which is our identity,"[24] one must also recognize that during the early 1920s Tate was apparently not searching for religious faith; rather, he was willing to make the best of his precarious position as an artist in a chaotic world. His art, rather than religious faith, provided him then with purpose and unity.

Tate's life took a new direction when he moved to New York City in the fall of 1924. There he married Caroline Gordon, whom he had met that summer on a visit with his good friend Robert Penn Warren in Guthrie, Kentucky. For some time Tate had dreamed of making the move to New York and immersing himself in the literary culture there; in June of that year he had visited the city briefly and met, among others, Kenneth Burke, Malcolm Cowley, Edmund Wilson, Mathew Josephson, and Hart Crane. Tate was infatuated with New York and the bohemian life of the Village. Even the city's massiveness and its technology delighted him. "I'm greatly thrilled at the mere *physique* of this great city!" he wrote (8 June 1924) to Davidson. "The subway is simply marvelous. . . . The sheer wonder of it is almost atonement for its significance as a phase of triumph of the Machine" (*LCDT*, p. 120).

When Tate moved to New York that fall ("Expecting to be here rather permanently," he wrote [9 November 1924] to Davidson [*LCDT*, 127]), he reestablished the literary acquaintances he had made earlier, and along with Gordon settled in to begin a career as a professional writer. His primary activity was free-lance writing—mostly reviews—for several publications, including the *Nation* and the *New Republic*. For a while he helped edit a pulp love-story magazine, *Telling Tales*. In his spare time, he wrote verse and pursued serious independent study of the philosophy and theory of art, reading, among many others, T. E. Hulme, Herbert Read, George Santayana, and I. A. Richards.

Before long, Tate's initial rush of enthusiasm for New York began to subside. Desperately poor and now the father of a daughter (Nancy was born on 23 September 1925), Tate moved with Gordon to a farmhouse in Patterson, New York, to spend the winter of 1925–26. (Nancy was in Kentucky with Gordon's mother.) The couple saw it as a respite from the grueling pace of the city and an opportunity to get more writing done—Tate on his reviews, essays, and poetry, Gordon on her first novel. When Malcolm Cowley complained to Tate that he was wasting his time in retreating to the countryside and abandoning New York, Tate fired back: "The circle of my experience has as large a diameter as it had in New York. All I had there was a vast repetition compulsion to get drunk and sympathize with Hart Crane."[25] (Hart Crane had moved in with the Tates for the winter in Patterson.)

Tate and Gordon stayed in Patterson through the summer of 1926. That fall, now apparently bored with living in the country, they moved back to New York, determined to continue their writing careers. To help with expenses, Tate worked part-time as a janitor in the apartment building where they lived.

During these years in New York, probably beginning some time in 1925, Tate began a serious reassessment of his Modernist identity. Life in the city was wearing him down. As Radcliffe Squires points out, in the intellectual New York environment— with its "faith in 'society,' rather than 'culture,' in economics rather than spirit, in political idealism rather than life"—Tate's "whole background, his whole being, was under challenge."[26]

Cultural and artistic freedom began to look, to Tate, more like cultural and artistic anarchy, and the question where to root his identity and value system became a serious problem.

Being a "modern" among the Fugitives in Nashville had been one thing; there at least Tate had shared with his friends a common value system and view of traditional society. In New York, no such underpinning existed, and Tate found it difficult to embrace his Modernist identity wholeheartedly. Though he shared the ideals of artistic achievement and endeavor with a number of other writers, this community was itself built on alienation and exile from society. Modern artists, moreover, as Lewis P. Simpson observes—and Simpson's words speak tellingly of Tate's situation—bore a great burden, what he calls the "historicism of consciousness": "In the modern world, bereft of mythic and traditional order save as it appears in the trappings of nostalgia, the 'dark, harsh flowing of time' is channeled directly into the sensitive self instead of into the family and community."[27] Such alienation and such a burden may have led in some cases to great art, but they certainly did not make life easy. By the mid-1920s Tate knew that he would never be completely comfortable as a citizen of the modern world, though he would never disavow this citizenship. Years later he wrote that the nineteenth century ended on 5 August 1914, when Germany invaded Belgium; referring to the new world ushered in on that day, he said that he "would be both of it and opposed to it the rest of my life."[28]

Tate's poetry from the mid to the late 1920s reflects his darkening perception of modern society's cultural collapse and his own place within it. Where he had once praised the glories of the subway, he now wrote a sonnet, "The Subway" (1927),[29] in which the subway became a haunting symbol of modern man's worship of technology. The poem opens with a description of the underground train and its horrifying power:

> Dark accurate plunger down the successive knell
> Of arch on arch, where ogives burst a red
> Reverberance of hail upon the dead
> Thunder like an exploding crucible!
> Harshly articulate, musical steel shell
> Of angry worship, hurled religiously

> Upon your business of humility
> Into the iron forestries of hell.

The poem's concluding sestet shifts to the poet, who is in the city above:

> Till broken in the shift of quieter
> Dense altitudes tangential of your steel,
> I am become geometries, and glut
> Expansions like a blind astronomer
> Dazed, while the worldless heavens bulge and reel
> In the cold revery of an idiot.

Tate's initial attraction to the city was now replaced by a vision of urban hell. In this chaotic society where "angry worship" of abstraction and technology has replaced faith and has rendered the heavens "worldless"—that is, void of God—the poet is himself emptied of the mainstays of tradition. He is "broken," an "idiot" of blind abstraction: "I am become geometries."

The urgency of tone and message in "The Subway" is mirrored in a number of Tate's other poems from the same period. Time and again, Tate contrasted an earlier, more heroic and ordered time with the disarray of contemporary society. In "Retroduction to American History" (1926) (*CPT,* 11–12), he depicted a modern world that had debased the profundity of ancient myth, bringing on confusion and ugliness:

> Narcissus is vocabulary. Hermes decorates
> A cornice on the Third National Bank. Vocabulary
> Becomes confusion, decoration a blight; the Parthenon
> In Tennessee stucco, art for the sake of death.

In this world where the moral order has collapsed, "morality disciplines the other / Person; every son-of-a-bitch is Christ, at least Rousseau."

In "Causerie" (1927) (*CPT,* 13–16) he drew further parallels between the historical past and the present, between the heroes of the past and the modern narcissists locked in their egos. Early in the poem a question is posed:

> Heroes, heroes, you auguries of passion,
> Where are the heroes with sloops and telescopes
> Who got out of bed at four to vex the dawn?

These were men of action who found meaning in their lives and continually strove to expand their knowledge—"They were the men who climbed the topmost screen / Of the world." Modern man, in contrast, is worn-out and impotent:

> Now bearing a useless testimony of strife
> Gathered in a rumor of light, we know our end
> A packet of worm-seed, a garden of spent tissues.

While the true heroes searched out meaning in the world, "sworn to the portage of our confirmed sensations," modern men now bear nothing but a "useless testimony." Believing only in a naturalist conception of death, modern man seeks nothing beyond it, and wallows in a world that reduces morality to sociology:

> In an age of abstract experience, fornication
> Is self-expression, adjunct to Christian euphoria,
> And whores become delinquents; delinquents, patients;
> Patients, wards of society. Whores, by that rule,
> Are precious.

The poet ends by asking:

> Was it for this that Lucius
> Became the ass of Thessaly? For this did Kyd
> Unlock the lion of passion on the stage?
> To litter a race of politic pimps? To glut
> The Capitol with the progeny of thieves—
> Where now the antique courtesy of your myths
> Goes in to sleep under a still shadow?

Accompanying Tate's increasingly dark portrayal of the modern world was a shift in his artistic theory. He now began to question the possibility of creating great art in the twentieth century and to doubt the ultimate value of purely subjective poetry. Modern poets, he still believed, must write subjective verse to be true to the times. "I'm afraid [T. S.] Eliot is about right in saying there are no important themes for modern poets," he wrote (14 May 1926) to Davidson. "Hence we all write lyrics; we must be subjective" (*LCDT,* 166). But without a tradition and its body of accepted beliefs to order and clarify expression, Tate now believed, a series of subjective poems became merely a collection of fragmentary visions, pieces of a puzzle scattered haphazardly on a taple top. In his introduction to Hart Crane's *White Buildings,* Tate wrote that "a world set up not by inclusive assertion but by exclusive attention to the objects of sense lacks imaginative coordination; a method which refuses to exceed the dry presentation of *petites sensations* confines the creative vision to suggestions, to implicit indications, but it cannot arrive at the direct affirmation, of a complete world. A series of Imagistic poems is a series of worlds."[30] To try, like Crane, to articulate the multiplicity of experience within a merely personal vision, was an effort doomed to failure; the individual mind, Tate now thought, could not encompass and assemble the broad range of fragmented experience in today's world. Walt Whitman's attempt to capture the totality of American experience in the mind of his poetic persona, said Tate, "was possible in an America of prophecy"; but Crane's similar effort in a drastically different time became "a concentration of certain phases of Whitman's substance, the fragments of the myth."[31] Neither was it possible for the poet to impose an artificial or archaic myth onto contemporary experience and still write honestly about the current scene. This was a problem Tate saw in Donald Davidson's poetry, and he wrote him so (14 May 1926): "You can't put your epic of Tennessee into the minds of Tennesseans; the precondition of your writing it is that it must (in an equivalent of spiritual intensity) be already there" (*LCDT,* 167).

In response to his crises of identity and art, Tate began a vigorous exploration of his southern heritage. Hoping to discover a rationale in history for order and community, he pored over books of the southern past and became an expert on the Civil War, even on intricate battle strategies. Sometime during the period of these studies, he began to assume the stance of a southern gentleman, both to gird himself against what he now saw as the chaos of New York and also to assert his allegiance to his southern identity. His was a life of strict civility—or so he wanted others (and indeed himself) to believe. "I think if I'd stayed in the South," Tate later said in an interview, "I might have become anti-Southern, but I became a Southerner again by going East."[32]

Evidence of Tate's new stance surfaces both in his life and poetry. Andrew Lytle recalls visiting Tate in New York and being met "with a severe and courteous formality—it was as if the eyes reflected but did not see what was before them."[33] This "severe and courteous formality" is what one finds in Tate's poem "Mr. Pope" (1925) (*CPT*, 6), which on one level represents a formulation of the proper stance for the man of letters to assume in a chaotic world. In the poem, Pope maintains his integrity by his severe civility and decorum in his personal life and in his poetry. And so when he walks the town he makes those about him almost shudder in recognition and fear:

> When Alexander Pope strolled in the city
> Strict was the glint of pearl and gold sedans.
> Ladies leaned out more out of fear than pity
> For Pope's tight back was rather a goat's than man's.

Despite being misshapen and hunchbacked (Tate frequently described his southern ancestors and other early American pioneers as tall and straight-backed; the modern citizens he created were often short and bent), Pope creates an order unto himself. The poem ends "Around a crooked tree / A moral climbs whose name should be a wreath." That is, around Pope's crooked body circles the vine of his poetry; together the man and his verse (his "name") give cause for a wreath of celebration and esteem. As Louis Rubin emphasizes, Tate's identification with the eighteenth-century artist and gentleman is not a nostalgic retreat to the past, but "a point of view, and an instrument of strategy in his transactions with life, values, and attitudes of his own day."[34] Moreover, the poem represents Tate's reexamination of the role of the poet. As his interest in politics and the South grew, Tate began to consider the idea that the poet was not primarily the pursuer of pure consciousness but rather, like Pope, the philosophe, the powerful critic of society.

Tate's enthusiasm for southern history led him to begin work on a biography of Stonewall Jackson. In 1927, he signed a contract for the proposed book with Minton, Balch and Company, and wrote (28 April 1927) to Davidson: "Since I'm convinced that the South would have won had Jackson not been killed, I'm doing a partisan account of the Revolution. The Stars & Bars forever!" (*LCDT*, 198).

Tate's *Stonewall Jackson: The Good Soldier* (1928) conformed closely to this description—the book is a rousing narrative, full

of drama and suspense. Several aspects of it are of particular
interest. One is the character of Tate's hero, General Jackson.
Though not an aristocrat or a poet, Jackson in several significant
ways embodies Tate's persona of gentleman man of letters. He is
a man of action and self-assurance, guided by convictions of
honor and religious commitment that evolved from the society
of which he was a part and which he defended. His zeal to follow
these dictates gives him the ability to cut cleanly through both
the conventions of society that don't measure up to his code and
the chaotic tangles of war. Like Alexander Pope, Jackson is often
perceived by his society as something of an eccentric (as Tate was
beginning to see himself); by their strict adherence to their high
codes of honor and integrity, both Pope and Jackson implicitly
challenge those who don't live as they do. And Jackson's ruthlessness in war—striking fear into the hearts of his enemies—
mirrors Pope's ruthlessness in verse.

Also of interest in *Stonewall Jackson* is Tate's depiction of
northern and southern societies, since his critiques clearly embody the intellectual framework that he was putting together to
describe contemporary society. The North, to Tate, was a society
based on greedy self-interest and fearful freedom. Lacking a
historical sense, people there made judgments in the name of
abstract right, rather than on principles rooted firmly in tradition and community. Tate's scorn for John Brown, for him the
epitome of unchecked northern energy, rests on these grounds:
he saw Brown as an illiterate fanatic who committed murder to
champion the abstract cause of "freedom" and to realize his
vision of himself as God's agent. "They thought God had told
them what to do," writes Tate, speaking of abolitionists in general. "A Southern man knew better than this. He knew that God
only told people to do right: He never told them *what* was
right."[35] For Tate, the southerner's rejection of the New En-
glander's mystical "inner life" helped ground his vision in the
real and make the South the home of settled and traditional
values. In contrast to that of the North, southern society was
ordered and stable, resting on a foundation of history and realistic appraisal of practical affairs.

Despite his enthusiasm for *Stonewall Jackson* and the bits of
southern chauvinism that he enjoyed writing to Davidson ("And,
by the way, I've attacked the South for the last time," he wrote in

a letter dated 1 March 1927 [*LCDT,* 191]), Tate was also aware that revitalizing the southern past was a difficult, if not impossible, task. For all his grumblings about modernity, Tate never forgot that he was a modern artist living in the twentieth century and that his situation was quite different from Pope's. As Robert S. Dupree points out, Tate recognized that Pope lived in a time in which he could, in Dupree's words, "still pull together enough of his cultural experience to make a coherent statement of the whole of things" and that a living tradition lay at the heart of Pope's vision.[36] As a modern, however, Tate lacked such coherence; he knew that his heritage, the Old South, was dead and gone, its traditions only tenuously relevant to the current situation. Responding to Davidson's joy that he had decided to write the Jackson book, Tate replied (5 May 1927): "I doubt the good sense of my choice of subject. It unfits one for the present world" (*LCDT,* 200).

Of course Tate's most famous statement of his reservations about the reinvoking of southern history is his "Ode to the Confederate Dead" (*CPT,* 20–23), the first version of which he completed in 1927. (Quotations here are from the final 1937 version, which, except for a varying refrain added by Tate in 1930, is close to the original.) Instead of celebrating the war dead, as the title might indicate, Tate explores the impossibility of sustaining a heroic vision of the past in the modern world. "And where, O Allen Tate, are the dead?" asked the unregenerate Confederate Donald Davidson, upset that the poem was an elegy "not for the Confederate dead, but for your own dead emotion, or mine (*you* think)" (*LCDT,* 186). Tate knew where the dead were—in the graveyard; his problem was how to make their legacy vital. In the poem, therefore, the poet, seeking meaning and inspiration from history, stands outside the cemetery wall, trying to establish an identification with the dead soldiers and their heroic deeds and emotions. Try as he might, he cannot sustain his vision of past heroics; time and again sights and sounds from the graveyard and his own skeptical doubts, rooted in his modern positivism, which regards death as merely the empty end of life, deflate his vision:

> Turn your eyes to the immoderate past,
> Turn to the inscrutable infantry rising

Demons out of the earth—they will not last.
Stonewall, Stonewall, and the sunken fields of hemp,
Shiloh, Antietam, Malvern Hill, Bull Run.
Lost in that orient of the thick-and-fast
You will curse the setting sun.

> Cursing only the leaves crying
> Like an old man in a storm

You hear the shout, the crazy hemlocks point
With troubled fingers to the silence which
Smothers you, a mummy, in time.

Torn between his desire to affirm the past and his realization of the impossibility to do so, the poet finally asks:

What shall we say who have knowledge
Carried to the heart? Shall we take the act
To the grave? Shall we, more hopeful, set up the grave
In the house? The ravenous grave?

His questions are these: Should those who are aware of the past and its glories merely ignore this knowledge of the past and "take the act / To the grave?" Or should they worship the past— "the ravenous grave" in Modernist terms—and "set up the grave / In the house?" These questions go unanswered—almost. The poem concludes:

> Leave now
> The shut gate and the decomposing wall:
> The gentle serpent, green in the mulberry bush,
> Riots with his tongue through the hush—
> Sentinel of the grave who counts us all!

These lines call for the poet to leave the graveyard and continue with his life. Time, symbolized here by the silkworm in the mulberry bush, is always passing. The poet will someday join his Confederate brethren in the grave, but for now he must depart and resume his life and his search for meaning. Exactly how the poet can forge a unity of past and present is not spelled out— Tate himself at this point did not know the answer, and his struggles to reach this wisdom would continue for years.

Evidence of Tate's dissatisfaction during the mid-1920s with a purely historical vision lies not only in "Ode to the Confederate Dead" but also in his new interest in exploring a profoundly religious view of the world. Apparently for the first time, Tate began to give serious thought to what he saw as the crucial split between science and religion, and to assert the importance of a religious tradition. In a letter (3 March 1926) to Davidson, he wrote that he was preparing an essay that would "define the rights of both parties, science and religion" (*LCDT*, 158). He went on to say that at Vanderbilt he had scoffed at the contention of Herbert Sanborn (chairman of the philosophy department) that the scientific view had little to offer. But now, he said, he saw that Sanborn was right. Then he explained: "The principle is, Science as we inherit it as Mechanism from the 17th century has nothing whatever to say about reality. . . . On the other hand, the Church has no right to forestall all criticism by simply saying Science is wrong" (*LCDT*, 158). Science, he added, is classification, while religion is organization, and it is through a religious outlook that "we know ourselves to be organic and unmechanical" (*LCDT*, 158). While Tate believed that this organic view of human nature should be used as a corrective to science's mechanism, he also felt that one must not endorse the Church blindly, for "without investigating whether the existing body of religio-philosophic doctrine is capable of being an adequate critic of science, is to become a victim of worse than the infinitely multiplied entities of the schoolmen. It is simply the substitution of a wish for a fact: a wish that the Church were an integral body of doctrine, instead of finding out whether it is. To prove that science, on principle, is wrong, doesn't prove that the Church is right" (*LCDT*, 158).

Tate's projected essay (never published) was significant for several reasons. One is that it stands as further evidence of Tate's growing dismay at the prevailing mechanization about him. Even more important, it shows Tate asserting a religious view of humanity to counter the forces of mechanistic science. As seen here, the scope of Tate's thought was widening as he searched for answers to the mysteries of life. He was willing to consider not only a historical vision but also a religious one, to stem the tide of twentieth-century chaos. Tate was not endorsing here a strict religious doctrine; one shouldn't, he said, attack science merely from a belief in the rectitude of the Church, but from the philosophic base upon which the Church stands. Nevertheless, his tentative philosophic soundings of the nature of a religious vision represent a significant shift in his thought.

Religious concerns also began to appear in Tate's poetry during this period. Most revealing is his poem "Causerie" (1927) (*CPT,* 13–16), in which, after briefly describing the hero-less and profane contemporary world, the poet—certainly Tate himself—admits that he is wracked by an "innermost disturbance": "I've done no rape, arson, incest, no murder, / Yet cannot sleep." He goes on to describe his state of religious inertia; he has felt religious yearning, but waits for a miracle to make it possible for him to believe:

> For miracles are faint
> And resurrection is our weakest clause of religion,
> I have known men in my youth who foundered on
> This point of doctrine: John Ransom, boasting hardy
> Entelechies yet botched in the head, lacking grace;
> Warren thirsty in Kentucky, his hair in the rain, asleep;
> None so unbaptized as Edmund Wilson the unwearied,
> That sly parody of the devil. They lacked doctrine;
> They waited. I, who watched out the first crisis
> With them, wait:
> For the incredible image.

The poet goes on to describe a world where people no longer view their eternal souls ("Purusha"—Hindu for one's eternal self) and for whom Christ has become a "precipitate floor of silence":

> Now
> I am told that Purusha sits no more in our eyes.
> Year after year the blood of Christ will sleep
> In the holy tree, the branches sagged without bloom
> Till the plant overflowing the stale vegetation
> In May the creek swells with the anemone,
> The Lord God wastes his substance towards the ocean.
> In Christ we have lived, on the flood of Christ borne up,
> Who now is a precipitate flood of silence,
> We a drenched wreck off an imponderable shore:
> A jagged cloud is our memory of shore

Whereon we figure hills below ultimate ranges.
You cannot plot the tendency of man,
Whither it leads is not mysterious
In the various grave; but whence the impulse
To lust for the apple of apples on Christ's tree,
To desire in the eye, to penetrate your sleep,
Perhaps to catch in unexpected leaves
The light incentive of your absolute suspicion?
Over the mountains, the last barrier, you'd spill
These relics of your sires in a pool of sleep,
The sun being drained.

In this forlorn world, religious faith is for the poet an "absolute suspicion"—but no more. Like everyone else, he is a "drenched wreck off an imponderable shore," far from the holy tree of Christ and its fruit, for which he vaguely lusts.

Tate's interest in the Agrarian movement, which by 1927 was gathering steam, embodies his search for order through both history and, to a lesser extent, religion. Unlike some of the hardline Agrarians, Tate did not see Agrarianism as a commitment to reestablish the life of the Old South in the twentieth century. "I never thought of Agrarianism as a *restoration* of anything in the Old South," Tate wrote in a symposium on the Agrarians sponsored by the magazine *Shenandoah* in 1952; "I saw it as something to be created, as I think it will in the long run be created as the result of a profound change, not only in the South, but elsewhere, in the moral and religious outlook of western man. . . . What I had in mind twenty years ago, not too distinctly, I think I see more clearly now; that is the possibility of the humane life presupposes, with us, a prior order, the order of a unified Christendom."[37]

Tate wrote those words in 1952 when he was a Catholic, and I think he overstates somewhat the religious ambitions he envisioned with Agrarianism in the 1920s. Agrarianism was an essentially secular enterprise, emphasizing historical and economic order. Tate knew this, and, particularly in the early years, accepted it without much misgiving, primarily because embracing a southern idealism provided him with a way to define himself against the modern world. At the same time, he was never completely happy with Agrarianism, because a part of him yearned for a religious commitment which he felt Agrarianism lacked. His lingering disenchantment became particularly evident during his and Gordon's extended stay in Europe, which began in 1928 when Tate received a Guggenheim award to compose a long poem based on his already completed "Retroduction to American History." In Europe, Tate's thoughts on Agrarianism, and indeed his outlook in general, began to develop in surprising ways.

Away from America, first in England and later in Paris, Tate's vision of his homeland—both the South and the United States—took on a new orientation. Entering into the forefront of his thought now was a profound interest in the classical-Christian heritage of Europe and what this tradition had to do with the American experience. Tate's views came under serious reassessment. To Edmund Wilson he wrote: "We have got to think of ourselves as European in *some sense* or we shall be forever at sea with no past at all. . . . This is the only civilization that we are connected with. . . . It all depends, of course, on what we are talking about when we say civilization. . . . It is a quality, and unfortunately definition has only to do with quantities."[38]

Tate's conception of American history, as Robert Buffington has pointed out, also began to shift.[39] He now saw the history of the nation more in terms of a conflict between East and West than between North and South. The East, for Tate, represented the European heritage, the seat of classical-Christian values; the West embodied the unbridled impulse to explore and expand, to push back the frontier. The colonization of America became for Tate an example of the forces of expansionism destroying the unified Christendom that European society had established. "We've cracked the hemispheres with careless hand!" (*CPT*, 67), Tate would write several years later in his poem "The Mediterranean" (1931), reflecting this idea. Once America was settled, Tate came to think, its history became best defined by this conflict between settled order versus desire to expand.

Even the Civil War became in Tate's mind essentially a conflict between the East and West. Inklings of this idea had surfaced in *Stonewall Jackson;* but in his new Civil War biography, *Jefferson Davis: His Rise and Fall,* much of which was written in Europe and which appeared in 1929, Tate fully developed the concept. "It was another war between America and Europe,"

Tate wrote, speaking of the Civil War, "and 'America,' in the second great attempt, won."[40] "The South," he continued, "was the last stronghold of European civilization in the western hemisphere, a conservative check upon the restless expansiveness of the industrial North, and the South had to go. The South was permanently old-fashioned, backward-looking, slow, contented to live upon a modest conquest of nature, unwilling to conquer the earth's resources for the fun of the conquest; contented, in short, to take only what man needs; unwilling to juggle the needs of man in the illusory pursuit of abstract wealth" (*JD*, 301). It was not the Revolutionary War that finally cut Europe from America, Tate said, but the Civil War, and it represented a victory of the Western spirit: "The War between the States was the second and decisive struggle of the Western spirit against the European—the spirit of restless aggression against a stable spirit of ordered economy—and the Western won" (*JD*, 301). Tate went on to interpret the war as a reenactment of past European struggles between the agrarian aristocracy and the industrial state. "In a sense," he wrote, "all European history since the Reformation was concentrated in the war between the North and the South" (*JD*, 301).

Tate's interest in European tradition and his own growing, if often inchoate, religious persuasion, led him in 1929 seriously to consider joining the Roman Catholic Church. In a letter that shocked Davidson, Tate wrote (18 February 1929) from Paris: "I am more and more heading towards Catholicism. We have reached a condition of the spirit where no further compromise is possible. That is the lesson taught us by the Victorians who failed to unite naturalism and the religious spirit; we've got to do away with the one or the other; and I can never capitulate to naturalism" (*LCDT*, 223). For Tate, the Roman Catholic Church represented a secure moral and religious structure—one infinitely greater in scope than that of the Agrarian enterprise, which lacked a strong religious base. And Tate now believed that Protestantism, the only religious faith that most of the Agrarians would even consider endorsing, was little better than no religion at all. "There is no dualism," he wrote in this same letter to Davidson, "without religion, and there is no religion without a Church; nor can there be a Church without dogma. Protestantism is virtually naturalism; when morality lacks the authority of dogma, it becomes private and irresponsible, and from this it is only a step to naturalism" (*LCDT*, 224). Catholicism, in contrast, had dogma, and was also of course an integral part of the European heritage that Tate now found so appealing.

Tate did not join the Catholic Church in 1929, mainly because he came to see such a step as a repudiation of his own heritage—that is, his southern identity. Despite his attraction to the Church's universal system, Tate was at this point too much the provincial and too much the poet to join the Church. He felt that such a move would cut him from the springs of life, the sources of his creative vision, something he believed had happened to T. S. Eliot when he had become an Anglican. To Malcolm Cowley, Tate wrote, "The good in all poetry has a provincial origin, no matter how much it may be disguised. The contemporary menace to poetry lies in the complex causes which force us into an exile from which we can't return. . . . This by the way is the chief idea in Yeats's philosophy of criticism; Eliot with his New England convolutions, circles the idea but never lights upon it: he has dried up his native roots and expects to renew them with the urine of St. Thomas."[41]

Clearly Tate's decision not to join the Catholic Church was a difficult one, because the dilemma he had expressed to Davidson—that, speaking of religion and naturalism, "We've got to do away with the one or the other; and I can never capitulate to naturalism" (*LCDT*, 223)—still remained. In fact, by rejecting the Church, Tate had in fact done what he said he could not do—capitulate to naturalism. A profound and significant dualism had become firmly established in his thinking: religious faith, specifically Catholicism, represented a withdrawal from life and thus a form of abstraction; naturalism, life without faith, represented mere mortality, a failure to find any meaning in life other than scientific analysis and the responses of the senses. Tate would be haunted by this dualism for years; not until he discovered a way to resolve it would he join the Church.

Perhaps the most penetrating expression of this dualism between naturalism and religion is found in Tate's poem "The Cross" (*CPT*, 33), which he wrote in 1929 in Europe, around the time he was considering becoming a Catholic.[42] The poem opens with a statement of the poet's tentativeness in matters of faith, of his failure to embrace fully the implications of Christian commitment ("place" in these lines refers to the Cross, Christian belief):

> There is a place that some men know,
> I cannot see the whole of it
> Nor how I came there.

Then come lines describing the Resurrection and its unhinging of the natural order and humanity's naturalistic (pagan) conception of it:

> Long ago
> Flame burst out of a secret pit
> Crushing the world with such a light
> The day-sky fell to moonless black,
> The kingly sun to hateful night
> For those, once seeing, turning back:

To experience the miracle of faith means to turn away from the world and mortality:

> For love so hates mortality
> Which is the providence of life
> She will not let it blesséd be
> But curses it with mortal strife,
> Until beside the blinding rood
> Within that world-destroying pit
> —Like young wolves that have tasted blood—
> Of death, men taste no more of it.

Once accepting faith—embracing the Cross in a "world-destroying pit"—a person no longer tastes of life. But in rejecting life, one is not uplifted by a heavenly vision, as one might expect if this were simply a pious poem. Rather:

> So blind, in so severe a place
> (All life before in the black grave)
> The last alternatives they face
> Of life, without the life to save,
> Being from all salvation weaned—
> A stag charged both at heel and head:

> Who would come back is turned a fiend
> Instructed by the fiery dead.

The last alternatives are these: believe in Christ and disavow life; or reject the faith and return to a pagan naturalism. Wallace Fowlie's words on Robert Lowell apply equally well to Tate: "Lowell felt the opposites in the Supreme Parent, in God, who in the Christian tradition is our Redeemer, and who is also the great Repressor in us of desires, longings, acts, words."[43] Tate was unable at this time to resolve these opposed positions, and "The Cross" ends without resolution. Those who have felt the pull of faith remain "A stag charged both at heel and head."

Tate himself faced these "last alternatives" in 1929 when he considered joining the Catholic Church, and his choice—not to accept the faith—meant that he would have to find meaning and structure elsewhere. Not surprisingly, soon after his flirtation with Catholicism he was on his way home, not just to the United States, but to the South. Having rejected Catholicism, he was eager to embrace the Agrarian cause more heartily than he had been doing while in Europe. As he expressed in his poem "Message from Abroad" (*CPT,* 40–42), written in Paris in November 1929, he was feeling cut off from his roots. Depicting himself as a wanderer in "the cold northern track," the poet says that the spirit of his ancestors—"the red-faced man"—has drowned in the sea. Isolated from his past and now in Paris, the poet writes:

> The man with the red face, the stiff back,
> I cannot see in the rainfall
> Down Saint-Michel by the quays,
> At the corner the wind speaking
> Destiny, the four ways.

The poem ends with the poet's world shattered. He cannot hear the voices of his ancestors, and admits that he is living—if one can call it that—in "the province of the drowned":

> The universal blue
> Of heaven rots,
> Your anger is out of date—
> What did you say mornings?
> Evenings, what?

The bent eaves
On the cracked house,
The ghost of a hound. . . .
The man red-faced and tall
Will cast no shadow
From the province of the drowned.

Tate and Gordon returned to the United States in January 1930, and after a month in New York left to live on a small farm near Clarksville, Tennessee, which Tate's brother Ben had bought for them. Tate was about to enter a very productive period, becoming actively involved with the Agrarians and writing a good deal of poetry and prose. Though he fervently took up the Agrarian cause, it soon became clear that Tate's break with Catholicism was not clean. Throughout his work from the 1930s, evidence of Tate's nagging religious sentiments surfaces again and again. As much as he wanted to rest with Agrarianism and its faith in secular history, he soon discovered—perhaps had known all along—that this was simply not possible.

One of Tate's first projects in 1930 was his essay for an Agrarian symposium, published later that year as *I'll Take My Stand*. He had great difficulty completing the essay, spending close to five months putting it in order; and it turned out to be completely different from what he had planned. Early on, Tate sent to Davidson an outline of his projected piece, saying that it would be firmly written and fiery, with "fundamentalism defended, and Dayton explained historically."[44] But it is clear from the essay he ended up writing—"Remarks on the Southern Religion"—that Tate could not bring himself to follow through with his plans. Instead, he reworked his own philosophical dilemmas in the larger terms of southern culture and history, and came as close as he could, without saying it outright, to arguing the necessity of Catholicism.

Much of "Remarks on the Southern Religion" revolved around Tate's conception of the divided nature of the modern mind. He wrote that our consciousness is split into "halves that render our sanity so precarious and compel us to vacillate between a self-destroying naturalism and practicality, on the one hand, and a self-destroying mysticism, on the other."[45] For most moderns, and particularly Americans, the practical side of consciousness dominates. "This modern mind," wrote Tate, using as an illustration the idea of people looking at a horse, "sees only half of the horse—that half which may become a dynamo, or an automobile, or any other horsepowered machine. If this mind had much respect for the full-dimensioned, grass-eating horse, it would never have invented the engine which represents only half of him" (*ITMS*, 157).

Tate went on to point out that some people, like Tate himself, were not satisfied with the "religion of how things work," and possessed what he called a "religious mind," which "wants the whole horse, and . . . will be satisfied with nothing less" (*ITMS*, 157). But arriving at this unified vision is difficult, he wrote; a few pages later in the essay, he admitted that "we are not able to contemplate those qualities of the horse that are specifically religious without forgetting his merely spatial and practicable half: we cannot let the entire horse fill our minds all at once" (*ITMS*, 163). The damaging split of consciousness—each half "self-destroying" unless somehow unified with the other—remains; and this division and its consequences were what Tate had expressed in his letters to Davidson and explored in "The Cross." Pulled in two directions, modern man is a "stag charged both at heel and head" (*CPT*, 33).

As in "The Cross," Tate did not in "Remarks on the Southern Religion" resolve the split of the modern consciousness, though after defining the problem, he spent a good deal of time trying. His effort at unification centered now on probing the possibilities of reinvigorating the southern heritage. In looking at the Old South community, Tate found much to admire: its stability, its order, its solid base of history and tradition, almost European in nature and scope. As a result, southerners had an inherent knowledge of their place in society and history. This security of definition meant that "the Southern mind was simple, not top-heavy with learning it had no need of, unintellectual, and composed; it was personal and dramatic, rather than abstract and metaphysical; and it was sensuous because it lived close to a natural scene of great variety and interest" (*ITMS*, 171–72). Absent from the southern mind was the tragic split of modern consciousness. Returning to the example of viewing the horse, Tate wrote: "The Southerners were capable of using their horses, as they did one day at Brandy Station, but they could also contemplate them as absolute and inviolable objects; they were virtually incapable of abstracting from the horse the horse-power, or from history its historicity" (*ITMS,* 169).

But with all its virtues, the South was fatally flawed: it lacked what Tate called its "appropriate religion" (*ITMS,* 168)—which, though he did not say so explicitly, he clearly thought was Catholicism. "It is just possible to see the Jamestown project," Tate wrote, "as the symbol of what later happened to this country: it was a capitalistic enterprise undertaken by Europeans who were already convinced adherents of large-scale exploitation of nature, not to support a stable religious order, but to advance the interests of trade as an end in itself. They stood thus for a certain stage in the disintegration of the European religion, and their descendants stuck to their guns, which theoretically at least were Protestant, aggressive, and materialistic guns" (*ITMS,* 166–67). Though southerners went on to establish the stable society of the Old South (because, said Tate, they returned "to an older secular polity" [*ITMS,* 168]), they could not create the necessary religion (i.e., Catholicism) because of their faith in what Tate saw as terribly inadequate Protestantism. "Its religious impulse," wrote Tate, speaking of the Old South, "was inarticulate simply because it tried to encompass its destiny within the terms of Protestantism, in origin a non-agrarian and trading religion; hardly a religion at all, but a result of secular ambition" (*ITMS,* 168). Lacking a sustaining religious faith, the South was unable after its defeat in the Civil War to maintain its social structure, falling prey to what Tate called "the post-bellum temptations of the devil, who is the exploiter of nature" (*ITMS,* 173).

At the end of "Remarks on the Southern Religion," Tate posed the question towards which the essay had been moving from the beginning: "How may the Southerner take hold of his Tradition?" (*ITMS,* 171). That is, how can the modern southerner, searching for spiritual order, reinvoke a tradition that was flawed religiously and that, following Jefferson, endorsed the idea that, in Tate's words, "the ends of men are sufficiently contained in his political destiny" (*ITMS,* 173)? Tate's famous answer: "by violence" (*ITMS,* 174). He meant that the southerner must paradoxically embrace the secular tradition he inherits to forge a spiritual unity: "He must use an instrument, which is political, and so unrealistic and pretentious that he cannot believe in it, to re-establish a private, self-contained and essentially spiritual life" (*ITMS*, 175).

This violent wrenching of secular tradition in order to achieve spiritual fulfillment is of course exactly what Tate was attempting now with his involvement in Agrarianism. But as this essay shows, at some point after his return he came to see that, like the Old South, he lacked an "appropriate religion" and that southern Protestantism was a part of the problem, not the solution. He now saw that his championing of Agrarianism meant that he was putting his faith in a secular tradition while at the same time searching for and demanding a spiritual unity that lay outside the tradition he endorsed. The difficulty, even impossibility, of what he wanted was perfectly clear to Tate. The last sentence of "Remarks on the Southern Religion" is this: "I say that he [the modern southerner] must do this; but that remains to be seen" (*ITMS*, 175).

Tate's own efforts during the early to mid-1930s to seize his tradition with violence were ultimately disappointing. Despite his continued efforts on behalf of the Agrarians during this period—writing essays, making contacts, casting about for ideas on how to widen the group's influence—there is ample evidence that Tate felt frustrated with the enterprise, and particularly with his own failure to achieve the spiritual unity that he so desired. From Paris in 1932 (Gordon had won a Guggenheim Fellowship and she and Tate were spending the year abroad), Tate wrote (10 December 1932) to Davidson of his mounting doubts about Agrarianism. His major complaint was that the movement lacked the element of religious commitment that he was bringing to it: "The trouble with our agrarianism is not that we don't believe in it enough to make sacrifices; it is rather that we don't believe in it in the way that demands sacrifice. In other words not one of us has a religion that any of the others can understand. . . . *Vide* my Remarks on the Southern Religion" (*LCDT*, 280). After saying that he feared "the Agrarian movement has degenerated into pleasant poker games on Saturday night," he wrote: "I get a little bitter about all this. I came back to live in the South and I've been let down."

Tate's frustration with the Agrarians and his own predicament of searching, without success, for the spiritual in the secular explains in part his failure to complete his biography of

Robert E. Lee, which he began in 1931. After completing a major portion of the biography, Tate eventually gave up on it. Apparently the act of forging a biography of a historical figure—celebrating one of the South's heroes—no longer possessed the meaning or importance he had once seen in it. "Three of these books," he wrote (10 August 1931) to John Peale Bishop, speaking of his Civil War biographies, "in four years have done me in: the Old Confutterate wunderbusser is about petered out. (No pun intended.) The trouble is I can never resign myself to the job [the Lee book], but I keep going off into poetry."[46]

Despite his disappointments, Tate did not abandon the Agrarians, and when he returned to the United States in 1933, he once again enthusiastically took up the cause. One reason for Tate's renewed vigor was that, through Herbert Agar, a journalist with the Louisville *Courier,* he had discovered the English Distributists. Like the Agrarians, the Distributists, whose leaders were G. K. Chesterton and Hillaire Belloc, believed in breaking up huge industries and distributing the wealth and property among the people to create an economy based on small businesses and family farms. To this shared goal, the Distributists added an element that must have appealed strongly to Tate: the reemergence of the strength and authority of the Roman Catholic Church, an event which they hoped would come about after the destruction of capitalism and the creation of their state of small-property owners.

Tate was clearly excited that the English group and the Agrarians shared similar views on the economic state. In a letter (7 April 1933) to John Peale Bishop, he described the closeness of the Distributists to the Agrarians and added hopefully: "This is the first time I have felt any real enthusiasm over social ideas—I mean the kind of enthusiasm which goes beyond private conviction" (*RL,* 78). Tate's work for the Agrarians intensified when Agar returned to the United States in 1934 (he had been the *Courier*'s London correspondent). Tate began working with him on plans to expand the base of the Agrarians, to enlarge it beyond a regional movement. They felt that the Midwest and West would be fertile ground for the Agrarian cause, and they hoped to build support there. In addition, they began to lay the groundwork for the publication of a joint Agrarian-Distributist symposium.

Not surprisingly, the Agrarians did not all share Tate's enthusiasm for moving from a regional orientation or for establishing a close association with the Distributists. Bickering and disputes broke out within the group, with Davidson and Frank Owsley leading the opposition. Tate quickly lost patience with Davidson and Owsley and their supporters; he stood up for Agar and tried to edge him into a leadership role. When Davidson complained to Tate about his and Agar's plans for an Agrarian-Distributist symposium, Tate fired back (28 September 1935): "I foresaw that I would be accused of presumption, but to be perfectly frank I didn't give a damn. For this reason: we've got to put up or shut up. We can't go on writing our pleasant little laments for our own consumption. We've got to get into action or admit that we are licked. The whole agrarian movement has become a reproach" (*LCDT,* 294).

Though many of the rifts within the group were settled by the time the Agrarian-Distributist symposium *Who Owns America?* was published in 1936, the book marks the end of Tate's active involvement with the Agrarian movement. Despite his bursts of political zeal, Tate knew that his true vocation was the creation of art and that he was not a political person; he admitted in a letter to John Peale Bishop (19 October 1932) that like Robert E. Lee (as Tate interpreted him), he "was profoundly cynical of all action for the public good" (*RL,* 64). After years of work with the Agrarians, Tate was now ready to devote his energies fully to literature and teaching. "I feel that my political career is over," Tate wrote (27 June 1936) to Mark Van Doren. "In the last two years it has consisted solely in efforts to get Herbert Agar—a very high-powered person—identified with the Agrarians. I've succeeded. He is the leader. I will follow from now on at a literary distance."[47]

Tate had not, of course, abandoned literature from 1930 to 1936. In fact these years were some of his most productive for writing poetry. Interestingly, most of the poems from this period were not Agrarian in theme; rather they explored such troublesome issues as sin, guilt, and the pain of unbelief. They suggest that even while Tate was publicly casting his lot with the

Agrarians and seeking order through a secular and historical vision, he was privately unsatisfied, still wracked by problems religious in nature. These issues—rather than Agrarianism—were most important to him. As he had said of his struggles to complete his biography of Robert E. Lee, his mind would "keep going off into poetry"—that is, into the world of sin and damnation.

Recognizing the fallen state of man and nature—and the great power of evil—was for Tate crucial for the development of psychological and spiritual wholeness. In "Remarks on the Southern Religion," he wrote that a religious vision that is realistic, uniting all aspects of reality, "calls upon the traditional experience of evil which is the common lot of the race" (*ITMS*, 159). Armed with this knowledge, one is a full-dimensional person rather than an empty idealist, abstracted and blind to the world. Time and again Tate invoked this knowledge in his poetry of the early to mid-1930s. "Poetry perhaps more than any other art," Tate wrote in his essay "A Note on Elizabethan Satire" (1932), "tests with experience the illusions that the human predicament tempts us in our weakness to believe" (*EFD*, 260). And in a very real sense Tate's poetry of the 1930s tested his faith in Agrarianism.

Perhaps nowhere in that body of poetry does Tate speak more forcefully of man's need to acknowledge sin and attend to his spiritual welfare than he does in "The Last Days of Alice" (1931) (*CPT*, 38–39). The first seven stanzas describe Lewis Carroll's Alice, who sits staring endlessly into the looking glass, "Empty as the bodiless flesh of fire." She is the embodiment of modern life's self-destroying narcissism and abstraction:

> Bright Alice! always pondering to gloze
> The spoiled cruelty she had meant to say
> Gazes learnedly down her airy nose
> At nothing, nothing thinking all the day.
>
> Turned absent-minded by infinity
> She cannot move unless her double move,
> The All-Alice of the world's entity
> Smashed in the anger of her hopeless love,

> Love for herself who, as an earthly twain,
> Pouted to join her two in a sweet one.

Like abstracted modern man, Alice has no sense of God or sin; her emotions, indeed her entire self, have been drained of life:

> Alone to the weight of impassivity,
> Incest of spirit, theorem of desire,
> Without will as chalky cliffs by the sea,
> Empty as the bodiless flesh of fire.

In the last two stanzas, the poet breaks in, calling for God's wrath:

> —We too back to the world shall never pass
> Through the shattered door, a dumb shade-harried crowd
> Being all infinite, function depth and mass
> Without figure, a mathematical shroud
>
> Hurled at the air—blesséd without sin!
> O God of our flesh, return us to Your wrath,
> Let us be evil could we enter in
> Your grace, and falter on the stony path!

In place of narcissist egoism and abstract science, Tate says, modern man needs the knowledge of sin and evil—in other words, a religious awareness of the human condition. Only by accepting this knowledge can man become human again and thus capable of receiving God's grace.

This theme of the knowledge of sin and evil, together with the acknowledgement of man's inevitably flawed efforts to create social utopias, lies at the center of two of Tate's best known poems from the period, "The Mediterranean" (1932) and "Aeneas at Washington" (1933). They are important to look at here because they reveal the tension between Tate's acceptance of a historical vision and his acknowledgment of its shortcomings.

"The Mediterranean" (*CPT,* 66–67), one of Tate's finest poems, recounts the experiences of the poet during a picnic on the Mediterranean. (It was inspired by an actual outing taken by Tate and a group of friends, including Ford Madox Ford, near Cassis, a French fishing village.) The poem opens with a beautiful description of the boat making its way to a timeless cove of beauty and, because of its location on the Mediterranean, of antiquity:

> Where we went in the boat was a long bay
> A slingshot wide, walled in by towering stone—
> Peaked margin of antiquity's delay,
> And we went there out of time's monotone;
>
> Where we went in the black hull no light moved
> But a gull white-winged along the feckless wave,
> The breeze, unseen but fierce as a body loved,
> That boat drove onward like a willing slave.

When the picnickers set ashore for their meal, the poet describes them reenacting the voyage of Aeneas:

> Where we went in the small ship the seaweed
> Parted and gave to us the murmuring shore,
> And we made feast and in our secret need
> Devoured the very plates Aeneas bore:
>
> Where derelict you see through the low twilight
> The green coast that you, thunder-tossed, would win,
> Drop sail, and hastening to drink all night
> Eat dish and bowl to take that sweet land in!

Yet despite his enthusiasm for this communion with the past, the poet realizes that the experience is merely momentary and in a larger sense disturbingly ironic. What acts of prophecy can modern man, driven by "lust of power" rather than by noble aspirations, accomplish to match those of the ancients?

> Where we feasted and caroused on the sandless
> Pebbles, affecting our day of piracy,
> What prophecy of eaten plates could landless
> Wanderers fulfil by the ancient sea?
>
> We for that time might taste the famous age
> Eternal here yet hidden from our eyes
> When lust of power undid its stuffless rage;
> They, in a wineskin, bore earth's paradise.

Though recognizing that this holiday is an act of "piracy," the poet nonetheless wishes to experience a communion with the

past without these ironies. That is, he wishes to see his life structured by a faith in history that sees modern man acting on a
plane not less glorious than that of the ancients:

> Let us lie down once more by the breathing side
> Of Ocean, where our live forefathers sleep
> As if the Known Sea still were a month wide—
> Atlantis Howls but is no longer steep!
>
> What country shall we conquer, what fair land
> Unman our conquest and locate our blood?

But then the reality of history breaks through, shattering his
make-believe world with stark historical truths: "We've cracked
the hemispheres with careless hand!" the poet says, acknowledging that the westward course of empire has destroyed any order
and unity that the ancients had formerly established. His vision
of Aeneas and the Mediterranean undone, the poet turns his
thoughts from the ancient sea to his home, the American South:

> Now, from the Gates of Hercules we flood
>
> Westward, westward till the barbarous brine
> Whelms us to the tired land where tasseling corn,
> Fat beans, grapes sweeter than muscadine
> Rot on the vine: in that land were we born.

Here is the South in which, as Tate had written to Davidson, he
was disappointed: luscious and fecund, but a tired land, and far
from the Mediterranean, the center of Western civilization. The
poet's last words, "in that land were we born," seem almost to be
a despairing resignation of southern identity. It is a far cry from
Tate's chauvinism of the twenties.

"*Quem das finem, rex magne, dolorum?*" ("What limit do you set
to their griefs, great king?"), the poem's epigraph asks (*CPT*, 66).
And what are these griefs? That the historical vision linking us
to the ancients is fleeting, and finally ironic, since modern man
has undone the order of civilization; and that the modern South
is less the inheritor of civilization (as the Agrarians would have
it) than it is a tired land of overgrown farms, where people
languish and crops rot on the vine.

"Aeneas at Washington" (*CPT*, 68–69) undercuts the Agrarian dream even more drastically. Using the persona of Aeneas,

whose spirit has lived through time, and who now gives thought to his life and the movement of history up through the twentieth century, Tate voices his own wavering faith in Agrarianism and his haunting awareness of sin and guilt. Aeneas begins by describing the fall of Troy and his escape; he then thinks about his drive to establish a new empire and reflects upon his now essentially disinterested viewpoint; he ends by voicing his doubts about the end results of his efforts to rebuild civilization.

Though he does not say so explicitly, Tate is clearly retelling his own history through Aeneas's. Like Aeneas, Tate witnessed the fall of a civilization—the Old South community of his childhood—and, as Aeneas hoisted his father onto his back, so Tate carried with him the old traditions to the new world of modern life to which he journeyed. With the Agrarians, Tate took up "the vigor of prophecy"—the faith that the Agrarian South was the home of lasting values and tradition. Just as Aeneas can now see that his effort to build a lasting civilization was futile, Tate also sees the futility of the Agrarian dream:

> I saw the thirsty dove
> In the glowing fields of Troy, hemp ripening
> And tawny corn, the thickening Blue grass
> All lying rich forever in the green sun.
> I see all things apart, the towers that men
> Contrive I too contrived long, long ago.

Aeneas's reconciliation with this failure is Tate's:

> Now I demand little. The singular passion
> Abides its object and consumes desire
> In the circling shadow of its appetite.

This "singular passion," I think it is clear, is the religious awareness of sin and evil that was preoccupying Tate's thought at this time. (Religious aspiration is often associated in Tate's poetry, as in Yeats's, with a rising circular motion.) By the light of this awareness, the poet says, the desire for secular goals pales. With this knowledge of sin and the fallen condition—in the following lines symbolized by the whistle of the screech owl—the once formidable secular dreams are insignificant and forgotten:

> The city my blood had built I knew no more
> While the screech-owl whistled his new delight

Consecutively dark.

> Struck in the wet mire
> Four thousand leagues from the ninth buried city
> I thought of Troy, what we had built her for.

In "The Mediterranean" Tate revealed the ironies involved in modern man's attempt to identify with the ancient heroes, and here he does the same thing: Aeneas himself levels a criticism at civilization and what it has become. But in this poem Tate also goes a step further, suggesting that even the exploits of Aeneas—indeed all quests to establish new social orders—pale in significance under the light of a Christian vision. "I saw the thirsty dove / In the glowing fields of Troy," Aeneas says midway in the poem, and now we can understand what the poem means here: the pastoral worlds of Troy—and of Tate's Old South— were beautiful and civilized, but their "glowing fields" did not nourish the dove, the Holy Ghost, and so were spiritually empty.

If Tate was expressing in his poetry his reservations with a secular historical posture, nevertheless, as we have seen, he continued his work with the Agrarians up until 1936. And although he was voicing in his verse the necessity for religious vision, he did not yet embrace religious faith. Apparently Tate was still wracked by the unbelief that he had years earlier described in "Causerie," where he described himself waiting "For the incredible image" (*CPT*, 14). Tate did not possess the solid faith necessary for religious commitment; without it, he was in a precarious situation, as he revealed in his "Sonnets at Christmas" (1934). In the first of these paired poems (*CPT*, 103), he describes how most people celebrate Christmas ("At ease, at food and drink, others at chase,") and then describes what runs through his mind:

> Yet I, stung lassitude, with ecstasy
> Unspent argue the season's difficult case
> So: Man, dull creature of enormous head,
> What would he look at in the coiling sky?

For Tate, Christmas is not a time for celebration but a time to ponder the nature of God. If he were to turn his eyes to heaven, and away from the life about him, he asks, what would he see? The question works two ways: would he see God?—that is, does

God exist?—and, would he lose touch with the world? Tate does not answer this loaded question, but instead describes how, despite his religious doubts, he must still kneel to Christ, nourished only by the silence of his religious questionings:

> But I must kneel again unto the Dead
> While Christmas bells of paper white and red,
> Figured with boys and girls spilt from a sled,
> Ring out the silence I am nourished by.

The second sonnet (*CPT,* 103) is an even more telling statement of Tate's religious dilemma. After beginning with a declaration of his love for Christ ("Ah, Christ, I love you rings to the wild sky"), the poet recalls a childhood lie that resulted in a black boy's being whipped. He calls for these years to return and for the trumpets to blow "the ancient crackle of the Christ's deep gaze," just as the poet in "The Last Days of Alice" had called for the wrath of God to make man whole. Without the acceptance of sin, the poet knows that he must remain locked in his dilemma:

> Deafened and blind, with senses yet unfound,
> Am I, untutored to the after-wit
> Of knowledge, knowing a nightmare has no sound;
> Therefore with idle hands and head I sit
> In late December before the fire's daze
> Punished by crimes of which I would be quit.

Adding to the difficulties of his religious insecurity was the fact that Tate apparently had still not resolved his fear that belief in Christ meant disavowing the world. Hinted at in the first "Sonnets at Christmas," this concern lies at the center of "The Twelve" (1931), which describes Christ's disciples, with Jesus departed, wandering the face of the earth, vainly searching for a sign to renew their faith (*CPT,* 44). They remember Christ and his crucifixion, and his last words, which "seared the western heart / With the fire of the wind" and forever changed their relationship to the world. But with Christ gone, the disciples are "twelve living dead":

> Now the wind's empty and the twelve living dead
> Look round them for that promontory Form
> Whose mercy flashed from the sheet lightning's head;

> But the twelve lie in the sand by the dry rock
> Seeing nothing—the sand, the tree, rocks
> Without number—and turn away the face
> To the mind's briefer and more desert place.

The disciples see nothing—neither Christ nor the world about them. All that is left to these ragged searchers, having turned away from the life of the world, is their own consciousness, which, the poet says, is a "briefer and more desert place" than the lifeless world in which they wander.

That the early to mid-1930s was a productive period for Tate's poetry is in large part explained by the tension between his desire to believe and his inability—or unwillingness—to do so. He explored the problem in his verse, with power and precision. By the mid-1930s, however, Tate's poetic productivity began to taper off. It appears that the counterplay that had been forging his verse had grown so severe as to become destructive and limiting. Tate's dilemma was similar to what he saw as John Peale Bishop's, as he described it in an essay written in 1935. Tate felt that Bishop's experimentation with the Christian story to give his poems form and meaning was a dead end. Since the Gospel did not inform the modern age, the Christian myths were of no use to help solve what Tate called the modern "*impasse* of form" (*EFD*, 350). "Where shall the poet," he asked, "get a form that will permit him to make direct, comprehensive statements about modern civilization? Doubtless nowhere" (*EFD*, 354). Tate went on to say that Bishop suffered from "modern unbelieving belief" (*EFD*, 357), which, though he did not specifically say so here, was also Tate's problem. He characterized this dilemma as modern man's attempt to replace his secular philosophy with a belief in the supernatural—a belief which, try as he might, he could not bring himself to embrace. "We are so constituted as to see our experience in two ways," Tate wrote. "We are not so constituted as to see it two ways indefinitely without peril. Until we can see it in one way we shall not see it as a whole, and until we see it as a whole we shall not see it as poets" (*EFD*, 357).

Tate virtually ceased writing poetry between 1936 and 1939, in part because of the split in his vision and in part because he devoted much of his time to other projects—teaching at several universities, writing a dramatic adaptation of "The Turn of the Screw" (completed in collaboration with Anne Goodwin Winslow and entitled "The Governess"), and finishing his novel *The Fathers* (1938). Though its significance in Tate's career is frequently downplayed, *The Fathers* is both a fine novel and, on a more abstract level, a telling statement of Tate's efforts to probe and resolve his own "unbelieving belief."

*The Fathers* describes the downfall of two families whose histories become entangled: the Buchans, a southern plantation clan living in Virginia; and the Poseys, Roman Catholics residing in Georgetown. Both families succumb both to forces within their own structure and to those forced upon them from without just before and during the Civil War. In the Jamesian tradition, however, the heart of the story lies in the mind of its narrator, Lacy Buchan, who at the time of the novel's narration is an elderly man looking back at the events of his youth. Lacy is trying to construct a coherent whole out of the past and to find answers to some basic questions about life. In the process he hopes to come to a better understanding of himself.

Lacy's search for order embodies Tate's own quest for meaning and unity. With Lacy, Tate explores and evaluates the traditions central to his own life; like Lacy, Tate wishes to establish coherence and to forge a unified vision. Lacy's efforts to this end become Tate's.

The key to Lacy's search for wholeness is an understanding of the puzzling events of his childhood; to attain this understanding, he must come to grips with the nature of evil and misfortune. "Is it not something to tell," he asks early on, "when a score of people whom I knew and loved, people beyond whose lives I could imagine no other life, either out of violence in themselves or the times, or out of some misery or shame scattered into the new life of the modern age where they cannot even find themselves? Why cannot life change without tangling the lives of innocent persons? Why do innocent persons cease their innocence and become violent and evil in themselves that such great changes may take place?"[48]

To answer these questions, Lacy looks back to the time of the Civil War, when the forces of life were most in flux. As the title of the novel suggests, Lacy explores the different worlds of his "fathers"—his true father, Major Lewis Buchan, an Old South patriarch; and his surrogate father, George Posey, an unprincipled modern man who comes from a staunchly Catholic family that Lacy lives with for a time. Lacy's efforts to reach fulfillment thus encompass the probings of three traditions: Old South Stoicism, what I will call modern naturalism, and Roman Catholicism.

Major Lewis Buchan, Lacy's blood father, represents the antebellum southern social order with all its rules, decorum, and ritual. As patriarch of his home, Pleasant Hill, he lives a life founded on the traditional Stoic ideals of honor and dignity. He structures life at Pleasant Hill with attention to every detail, arranging everyone and everything in their proper places within the overall framework. His dignity and decorum demand respect, as does his moderate approach to life, which has fostered stability at the farm.

But Major Buchan and his world contain certain flaws, the most serious of which harks back to the very system of order, in many ways so admirable. Lacy observes at one point (*F,* 44) that life for the major is an "intricate game that he expected everybody else to play," with rules, written and unwritten, for all conduct. Lacy goes on to say that "everything he was and felt was in the game itself," meaning that Major Buchan has no life outside the fabric of social ritual. All goes well as long as everyone abides by the rules; but when an untamed force, such as George Posey or the Yankees, intrudes with its own set of rules, the major is powerless. When threatened, his only recourse is to retreat into himself, to find safety in the myopic world of his consciousness. When the Yankee soldiers come to burn his house, and thus destroy his world, the major hangs himself, in the only move he sees left to him.

Another liability is that Major Buchan's philosophy of deliberateness and moderation, which in many ways is very appealing, fails to take into account a crucial factor: that most of the time people do not act reasonably. "I have never been able to understand how any man can be a lawyer," Lacy comments at one point, "for the law, assuming that people act upon motives, is rational; but people never act for a reason, even a bad reason. My father was the most rational man I ever knew" (*F,* 185). Major Buchan's outlook is rooted in rational order. As a result, he often misreads people and situations, at times appearing stubbornly naive, even silly, as in several of his encounters with George Posey.

But the most glaring defect in the major's system, and certainly the one that causes the most problems, is that with its unbending emphasis on ritual and order it does not adapt to the changing world. His system does create order, but forces the major to stay firmly based in the past, oblivious to the radically altering world. As Cousin John points out to Lacy, the major still lives by the lights of eighteenth-century Virginia, believing that the government is run by intelligent gentlemen who settle problems with tact and honor. He remains blind to the approaching war, and incurs this reproach from Cousin John: "Damn it, Lacy, it's just men like your pa who are the glory of the Old Dominion, and the surest proof of her greatness, that are going to ruin us. They can't understand that reason and moderation haven't anything to do with the crisis. They won't let themselves see what's going on. Aye God, they'll see when Federal troops march through the State on the way to South Carolina" (*F*, 124).

In stark contrast to Major Buchan is Lacy's surrogate father, George Posey. Representing modern man, Posey lives eternally in the present without the guidance or stability of tradition. Unlike Major Buchan, who lives according to forms and rituals, George has no structure to objectify his feelings and experiences; as Lacy points out, George receives "the shock of the world at the end of his nerves" (*F*, 185). For George, everything becomes reduced to the level of the personal. Early in the novel he refuses to attend Mrs. Buchan's funeral because he finds death, without the meaning it attains through ritual, too overpowering. He establishes relationships to other people not according to human or familial bonds, such as those between husband and wife or brother and sister, or along lines of fidelity or loyalty, but rather according to the whims of his unbridled emotions. Not surprisingly, he often erupts in violence. Lacy comments on George's marriage: "There is no doubt that he loved Susan too much; by that I mean that he was too personal, and with his exacerbated nerves he was constantly receiving impressions out of the chasm that yawns beneath lovers; therefore he must have had a secret brutality for her when they were alone" (*F*, 185).

Living ungrounded in tradition gives George great power,

for it enables him to act in a variety of situations without scruple. Since he is not held back by any sense of decorum, he can act on impulse and passion, which often erupt into fury. Unlike Major Buchan, frozen in his defined world and lost outside it, George stands out as a man of action—and mystery, particularly to the Buchan children, who have seen no one like him. To them he exudes Faustian energy and romance. Lacy says of him at one point: "He had great energy and imagination and, as Cousin John said, he had to keep moving; but where? I always come back to the horseman riding over a precipice. It is as good a figure as any other. And that is what he gave to Semmes— mystery and imagination, the heightened vitality possessed by a man who knew no bounds" (*F,* 170). Lacy's horseman image is apt: George is forever on the move, but his course is directionless in terms of anything other than personal desire; and he is always on the brink of catastrophe.

Despite his great power and energy, George pays a price for his independence. There are times when he is haunted by his lost heritage (George was raised a Catholic) and when he acknowledges, or feels in his bones, his aloneness and purposelessness in life. He prefers to stay moving in order to divert his attention from this knowledge; hard action to satisfy his personal motives keeps him from considering larger matters and alternatives to his own desires. But he cannot avoid pain, as Lacy knows: "In a world in which all men were like him, George would not have suffered—and he did suffer—the shock of communion with a world that he could not recover; while that world existed, its piety, its order, its elaborate rigamarole—his own forfeited heritage—teased him like a nightmare in which the dreamer dreams a dream within a dream within another dream of something that he cannot name" (*F,* 180).

George's forfeited heritage is the Catholicism of his family, the Poseys. As Lacy explores the outlooks and actions of his father and of George Posey, he also evaluates the Catholicism of the Poseys. Living with the Poseys, he confronts face-to-face the bizarre qualities of this Catholic family: all of them—from Aunt Milly to Uncle Jarman—live as recluses in their dark, convent-like home. Having retreated from the hustle and bustle of life, they seem atrophied, out of touch with everything that lies outside their own individual rooms. They have cut themselves off

not only from life outside the house, but also from a common
life within; the Poseys do not congregate, for meals or otherwise.
Theirs, comments Lacy, is a "world of closed upstairs rooms, a
world where people communicated only their infirmities, in
hushed voices, a world in which the social acts became privacies"
(*F,* 182).

Lacy's insights into Catholicism deepen when he meets the
priest, Father Monahan (a potential third "father" for Lacy), at
the Poseys'. Through him, Lacy sees that Catholics live by a set of
rules within a system of order that allows for the complex problems of life to be defined and given meaning. "We've got to keep
life simple," Father Monahan says to Lacy at one point. "That is
a practical reason for saving the human soul" (*F,* 236). Though
on one level this systematic ordering appeals to Lacy—for he
himself is on a quest for knowledge to understand life—the
priest's words also speak to Lacy's reservations: the Catholic way
means simplifying the thorny complexities of experience in order to fit the pattern. As Lacy struggles to piece together the
strange chain of occurrences that led to Yellow Jim's and
Semmes's deaths, he realizes that Father Monahan would have
experienced no such problem; he "would have ordered and
named the crime and the degree, and fixed the responsibility."
And yet Lacy knows that what has happened is not that simple,
that questions would still remain and that he would not be
satisfied with Father Monahan's approach. "What could Father
Monahan have done," Lacy asks himself, asserting the limitations of Catholicism, "with George's observation after Yellow Jim
had fallen and Semmes had pitched into the whirlpool? 'I never
had any idea of killing that Nigger'" (*F,* 272).

Lacy's search for meaning culminates not in a blind acceptance of either of his "fathers" and their approaches to life.
Rather, he seems to draw insights from each, hoping to forge his
own vision of wholeness. Clearly George is the more influential;
he is a man of the world, a possessor of great strength, a sur-
vivor. At the end of the novel, Major Buchan is dead and his
home destroyed; the Posey family is still locked away in their
house. George, in contrast, is as mighty as ever. In the revised*
ending to the novel, Tate emphasizes George's durability in the
world: "As I stood by his grave in Holyrood cemetery fifty years
later I remembered how he restored his wife and small daughter

and what he did for me. What he became in himself I shall never forget. Because of this I venerate his memory more than the memory of any other man."[49]

But despite his love for George, Lacy does not accept his outlook entirely. Rather than riding off with George at the end of the novel, Lacy returns to his Confederate regiment, remaining loyal to his homeland and its ideals rather than to George and his Faustian power. Although as a youth he had struggled to develop a George-like ruthlessness, he has come to understand that he cannot live entirely without principles; too much of his father remains with him. But finally it is his attraction to and emulation for George that allows Lacy to escape the fate of his father, to survive the destruction of the Old South community. As Tate himself commented years later: "George will permit Lacy to survive in a new world in which all the old traditions, which Lacy partly represents, are dead."[50]

What of Catholicism? Does it have anything to offer to Lacy—and to Allen Tate? Apparently not yet, for in *The Fathers* Tate depicts Catholicism as a total withdrawal from life. His depiction of the frustrated writer and recluse, Uncle Jarman, who bears a striking physical resemblance to Tate ("the pallid face, the high bulging forehead under the metallic white hair, the pale blue eyes that did not focus on anything, the thin, sensual mouth, the small determined chin and the lobeless ears" [*F,* 233–34]), may represent Tate's vision of himself if he were to become Catholic. Living on the top floor of the Posey house, Jarman has so withdrawn himself from life (he is compared at one point to Poe's Roderick Usher) that he reduces its multiplicity to flat abstractions. Lacy realizes, when he goes up to Jarman's room to tell him of Aunt Jane Anne's death, that even the most basic communication with Jarman is useless. In his frustration, Lacy oberves inwardly that to Jarman "death couldn't be an old lady, his sister-in-law, downstairs; death was the sunderer, or time, or our enemy" (*F,* 235). Jarman's is a shadowy world of empty abstraction.

At the same time, however, a religious awareness of sin and evil lies at the center of Lacy's development. This knowledge, which Tate had for years coupled with his own religious—and Catholic—impulses, apparently gives Lacy a hold on life and keeps him from wallowing in narcissist self-pity, a temptation which, as is evident in "The Last Days of Alice" and elsewhere, concerned Tate frequently. At one point Lacy talks about this religious knowledge of evil—here, "the night"—and modern man's refusal to acknowledge it:

> Nobody today, fifty years after these incidents, can hear the night; nobody wishes to hear it. To hear the night, and to crave its coming, one must have deep inside one's secret being a vast metaphor controlling all the rest: a belief in the innate evil of man's nature, and the need to face that evil, of which the symbol is darkness, of which again the living image is man alone. Now that men cannot be alone, they cannot hear the dark, and they see themselves as innately good but betrayed by circumstances that render them pathetic. (*F,* 218–19)

Tate does not make it clear whether or not Lacy's knowledge of evil is Catholic in origin. Nonetheless, this emphasis on religious-based knowledge is another indication that Tate was still haunted by a religious—and Catholic—view of life, even though he had not yet entered the Church. *The Fathers* shows Tate, through Lacy, struggling to forge a unity of his southern roots and his modern identity; the novel also reveals Tate's failure to cut himself free from Catholicism, despite his deep fears of what accepting the faith would demand of him. It is a further example of his "unbelieving belief."

In his critical work from this period Tate frequently used his religious orientation to critique modern society and its citizens and to assert his desire for a vision of order and unity. Tate went on the offensive against what he called, in the preface of *Reactionary Essays on Poetry and Ideas* (1936), the "social reader," the reader who "demands that poets shall set forth the ideas that he, in his facility, has decided that the future will live by." But the greater poets, Tate adds, do not give this reader what he wants, because they "give us knowledge, not of the new programs, but of ourselves" (*EFD*, 613–14). Tate's implicit message here is that the religious problems of sin and evil cannot be explained or glossed over by social theories or social programs. Materialistic modern society, based on a doctrine of man's perfectability through education and environmental progress, demanded, Tate thought, that man sacrifice his moral nature to gnosticism. "As individuals today," Tate wrote in "Miss Emily and the Bibliographer" (1940), "we must subordinate our spiritual life and our material satisfactions to the single purpose of gaining superior material satisfactions in the future, which will be a naturalistic Utopia of mindless hygiene and Tom Swift's gadgets. There is no doubt that the most powerful attraction offered us by the totalitarian political philosophies is the promise of irresponsible perfection in the future, to be gained at the slight cost of our present consent to extinguish our moral natures in a group mind" (*EFD*, 144). In a letter to John Peale Bishop (11 January 1938) Tate wrote that he agreed with Baudelaire that someone is to blame for the ills of society; he added, "his name is Satan, or Evil. It is so simple few of our contemporaries can believe it" (*RL*, 140).

Tate's attacks on social and political solutions as answers to humanity's problems intensified as the world slid toward and then into war. While holding various positions at Princeton, the Library of Congress, and the *Sewanee Review* during the period from 1939 to 1945, he produced much poetry and criticism, through which he continued his exploration of the limited nature of a purely social vision and the need for people to have a fuller understanding of human nature. The tone of his criticism during this period is exemplified by his Preface to *Reason in Madness* (1941): "The convention of this book is the attack. It asks of people who profess knowledge: What do you know? But that is only another way of asking oneself the same question. I do not hear it asked very frequently these days" (*EFD*, 616).

Tate's attitudes towards society and man during this period are well represented in his essay "The New Provincialism" (1945). Here he defines the terms "regionalism" and "provincialism" and then uses them to critique Western society. Regionalism, according to Tate, "is that consciousness or that habit of men in a given locality which influences them to certain patterns of thought and conduct handed to them by their ancestors. Regionalism is thus limited in space but not in time." Provincialism, on the other hand, is that consciousness which cuts itself off from the past, locks itself in the present moment (which it assumes is unique), and "without benefit of the fund of traditional wisdom approaches the simplest problems of life as if nobody had ever heard of them before" (*EFD*, 539).

Premodern Western society, which Tate typifies as Europe up

until the nineteenth century, was based on a philosophy of regionalism and a belief in Christianity, which "reduced the regional heterogeneity to a manageable unity, or even sublimated it into universal forms." But modern Western society is a bare remnant of this better world: "Is not this civilization [premodern society] just about gone? Only men who are committed to perverse illusion or to public oratory believe that we have a Christian civilization today: we still have Christians in every real sense, but in neither politics nor education, by and large, do Christian motives or standards, or even references, have an effective part. We do not ask: Is this right? We ask: Will this work?" (*EFD*, 538). Industrial capitalism, Tate continues, has destroyed our regionalism and has given us in its place a sterile provincialism; as a result, "we are committed to chance solutions of 'problems' that seem unique because we have forgotten the nature of man" (*EFD*, 540). We no longer realize, Tate says, the fallen nature of man because all problems can now supposedly be solved according to our utopian schemes; but these, he continues, ignore our past and are rooted in provincial arrogance. "We guarantee to the world freedom from fear" (*EFD*, 541), Tate says here of America and modern Western society; but as he had emphasized in much of his verse from the 1930s, without a recognition and fear of evil, man cannot know either himself or God.

Meanwhile Tate's own spiritual dilemma continued, for despite his enthusiasm about Christian faith and civilization, he had not yet committed himself to the Church. He was still wracked by his religious predicament, as his series "More Sonnets at Christmas" (1942) reveals. With these four poems, Tate imagines both himself and his nation banishing Christ from consciousness, he on a private level, the United States on a public. The poems are built on a strategy of deep irony: the poet calls for Christ's banishment and for the new state of affairs which will thereby be ushered in, only in order that he can show the horror of this position—a life without meaning and a world at war.

In the first sonnet of the series (*CPT*, 104), Tate acknowledges in the opening octet the religious haunting he has experienced for years:

> Again the native hour lets down the locks
> Uncombed and black, but gray the bobbing beard;

> Ten years ago His eyes, fierce shuttlecocks,
> Pierced the close net of what I failed: I feared
> The belly-cold, the grave-clout, that betrayed
> Me dithering in the drift of cordial seas;
> Ten years are time enough to be dismayed
> By mummy Christ, head crammed between his knees.

He asserts here that ten years is long enough to be haunted by "mummy Christ," an ineffective and dried-out God. He therefore imagines in the concluding sestet disposing of Christ and the haunting he brings:

> Suppose I take an arrogant bomber, stroke
> By stroke, up to the frazzled sun to hear
> Sun-ghostlings whisper: Yes, the capital yoke—
> Remove it and there's not a ghost to fear
> This crucial day, whose decapitate joke
> Languidly winds into the inner ear.

Suppose, he says, in this time of war, I take a bomber up and listen to the murmurings of "sun-ghostlings"—that is, the words of man's reason, the sun. Reason tells him that Christ is the "capital yoke"; remove his head so that one no longer faces the "fierce shuttlecocks" of his eyes, and there is nothing left to fear—either for the poet at Christmastime or for the pilot on his mission to kill. (With the last line, the poet quietly suggests the evil of this "decapitate joke," as one thinks of Satan whispering his guiles into the ear of Eve.)

The second and third sonnets (*CPT,* 104–5) take up the "decapitate joke" and show the poet and the nation without Christ. Christmas becomes an empty and meaningless day for the poet, a day when he acts out the rites of tradition with mistletoe and Santa Claus, but with no sign of Christ:

> Get up and once again politely lying
> Invite the ladies toward the mistletoe
> With greedy eyes that stare like an old crow.
> How pleasantly the holly wreaths did hang
> And how stuffed Santa did his reindeer clang
> Above the golden oaken mantel, years ago!

Furthermore, without Christ, society willingly goes to war, its prayer one "for cold martial progress":

> Give me this day a faith not personal
> As follows: The American people fully armed
> With assurance policies, righteous and harmed,
> Battle the world of which they're not at all.

Rather than see its soldiers torn by personal guilt and fear of God, society would prefer them to fear only the mortal enemy:

> Let little boys go into violent slumber,
> Aegean squall and squalor where their fear
> Is of an enemy in remote oceans
> Unstalked by Christ: these are the better notions.

With Christ gone, the poet asserts in the final sonnet (CPT, 105–6), the only ghosts to fear—the only reminders of Christ— are "Plato's Christians in the cave." Taking up again his idea that the faithful have cut themselves off from the world, Tate describes them as sequestered from life, like the people in Plato's cave, blind to the light of the sun and the world. To rid himself of these "ghosts," he calls for them to leave the Church: "Unfix your necks, turn to the door," he says. When they do, he says, they will become part of the social system, facile flatterers of the powers that be, and therefore no longer haunting reminders of the Christian way:

> You will be Plato's kept philosopher
> Albino man bleached from the mortal clay,
> Mild-mannered, gifted in your master's ease
> While the sun squats upon the waveless seas.

"More Sonnets at Christmas" expresses both Tate's growing despair over World War II, which he feared would result in part in America's final destruction of European civilization, and his ever-present desolation of spirit. Tate's approach here is interesting: although he shows the chaos into which the world and the individual would fall if Christ were banished, he presents no clear affirmation of Christianity. This is because Tate himself still lacked commitment. He still saw the faithful as cut off from the world, and though haunted by Christ, he did not yet see Him as a vital, living force in the world. To Tate at this time, Christ really was a mummy. He was left with this dilemma: a world without Christ is terrifying; yet a world with Christ may not be worth attaining.

So profound was Tate's despair during World War II that in "Winter Mask" (1942) (*CPT,* 111–13) he asked the question "Whether there is still / To a mind frivolously dull / Anything worth living for." In this poem, the poet goes on to describe modern man's spiritual welfare in terms of a poisoned rat that "Dies of the water of life" when it finally drinks the liquid for which it thirsts. Tate here is envisioning modern man—and Allen Tate himself—as poisoned by secularism and haunted by thoughts of salvation; yet no redemption is possible until the poison is driven from man. But while sensing the truth of salvation and realizing his poisoned state, man does nothing, preferring to live poisoned and doomed. At the end the poet calls to Yeats to explain why this is so:

> I asked the master Yeats
> Whose great style could not tell
> Why it is man hates
> His own salvation,
> Prefers the way to hell,
> And finds his last safety
> In the self-made curse that bore
> Him towards damnation:
> The drowned undrowned by the sea,
> The sea worth living for.

The last line answers the poet's original question—it is the sea of life, "the flood of Christ" (as described years earlier in "Causerie"), that is worth living for; and yet man drowns there, not because of the sea but because of his "self-made curse" of preferring the life that leads to hell to the life that leads to salvation. "Winter Mask" is another expression of Tate's "unbelieving belief," and one of his gloomiest.

"Seasons of the Soul" (1944) (*CPT,* 114–22), Tate's major work from the 1940s, continues his exploration of his own and mankind's spiritual welfare. In the four parts of the poem, Tate progressively strips away man's illusory schemes for happiness. His method explains the poem's epigraph, from Canto 13 of Dante's *Inferno:*

> *Allor porsi la mano un poco avante,*
> *e colsi un ramicel de un gran pruno;*
> *e il tronco suo gridó: Perchè mi schiante?*

(Then I stretched my hand a little forward,
and plucked a branchlet from a great thorn;
and the trunk of it cried: "Why dost thou rend me?")[51]

Those in Dante's hell who are condemned to imprisonment within the thorn trees are suicides, and Tate here is suggesting that modern man is in a sense a suicide because he has turned away from God and salvation. With *Seasons of the Soul,* Tate explores man's suicidal condition, painfully revealing to modern sufferers their fallen condition and intensifying their torment. In a sense, the poem as a whole becomes an embodiment of Dante's plucking of the suicide's branch. Tate's 1944 introduction to Robert Lowell's *Land of Unlikeness* describes his own method in *Seasons* as much as Lowell's: "the Christian symbolism is intellectualized and frequently given a savage satirical direction; it points to the disappearance of the Christian experience from the modern world, and stands, perhaps, for the poet's own effort to recover it."[52] At the end Tate offers man only one suggestion for transcending the terrors of the world and the self. That option is Christian belief. And yet, not surprisingly, the poet does not wholeheartedly espouse this solution, but merely suggests its possibility, acknowledging that it is a questionable answer, one that may not even exist or be available to modern man.

In *Seasons,* Tate mentions Christian salvation only after a brutal survey of the depravity of the modern condition. In the first section of the poem, "Summer," he describes the war between the head and the heart going on in human consciousness, and also the world war then taking place. The world depicted here is thoroughly hellish, and the poet underscores this in the section's final stanza, where a centaur from Dante's hell finds the sufferings of the world more astonishing than those of the inferno. The emphasis in "Summer" is on the terrors of the present time; in the poem's second section, "Autumn," it is on the terrors of the past. Here the poet finds his search for meaning in his past a dead end. His past is imaged nightmarishly, first as the cold and stifling depths of a well and then as an empty hall from his childhood home where figures from his boyhood, including his parents, appear but fail to recognize him. At the section's end, the poet stands frozen in the empty hall; the past, rather than leading him to any insight, has closed him off from the world and seems to confuse rather than to enlighten.

The third section, "Winter," continues Tate's stripping away of man's false illusions of hope and happiness. Here the poet shows that love, which for modern man has been degraded to mere lust, offers man no salvation. Rather than God's love, modern man seeks sex, invoking Venus instead of the Lord:

> Leave the burnt earth, Venus,
> For the drying God above,
> Hanged in his windy steeple,
> No longer bears for us
> The living wound of love.

To modern man Christ is an empty figurehead, no longer bearing his wound of love for mankind. And as the struggle described in the last part of the section shows, the poet sees himself and the rest of modern mankind as damned souls who bear not Christ's "living wound of love" but "the livid wound" of animal lust.

In the poem's final section, "Spring," the poet looks towards Christian salvation, the only answer left for modern man. This is not a direct call, but merely a tentative and ambiguous suggestion of a way out of the morass. The section opens with an invocation to spring, asking it to regenerate man:

> Irritable spring, infuse
> Into the burning breast
> Your combustible juice
> That as a liquid soul
> Shall be the body's guest
> Who lights, but cannot stay
> To comfort this unease
> Which, like a dying coal,
> Hastens the cooler day
> Of the mother of silences.

But any regeneration from nature will be only temporary, with man still progressing to "the cooler day / Of the mother of silences"—that is, death. In the second stanza the poet looks be-

yond nature to the customs of the Old South as a possible source
for regeneration:

> Back in my native prime
> I saw the orient corn
> All space but no time,
> Reaching for the sun
> Of the land where I was born:
> It was a pleasant land
> Where even death could please
> Us with an ancient pun—
> All dying for the hand
> Of the mother of silences.

Though a pleasant land, where people once lived in touch with
the natural order, the Old South community offers no path towards salvation for modern man: this way of life is long gone.
Moreover, though the people there were reconciled with death
("All dying for the hand / Of the mother of silences"), they saw it
merely as the natural end of life. But the poet here is searching
for more than the meaning found in nature's cycles: he knows
man lives and dies; what he wants to understand is the life of the
soul and the nature of eternity.

The movement of the section shifts in the next two stanzas, as
the poet returns us to the present and asks, "In the time of
bloody war / Who will know the time?" He wonders if his search
for regeneration is grounded in possibility or chimera:

> Is it a new spring star
> Within the timing chill,
> Talking, or just a mime,
> That rises in the blood—
> Thin Jack-and-Jilling seas
> Without the human will?

After asking this question, the poet has a moment of enlightenment:

> Its light is at the flood,
> Mother of silences!

These important lines suggest that the illumination of the poet's quest comes from the light of Christ, whom Tate frequently images in terms of a flood. One remembers the lines from "Causerie":

> In Christ we have lived, on the flood of Christ borne up,
> Who now is a precipitate flood of silence.

"Mother of silences" takes on a new meaning. The light of Christ becomes the mother of silences in that it is the source and the goal of Tate's religious quest, the core of silence that Tate struggles to fathom.

After this illumination, the poet describes how the light of Christ's vision burns each person individually, and contrasts it with the arrogance of modern man:

> It burns us each alone
> Whose burning arrogance
> Burns up the rolling stone,
> This earth—Platonic cave
> Of vertiginous chance!

Significantly Tate here uses the image of Plato's cave to describe the condition of unregenerate man—isolated and imprisoned within the self—rather than, as he had done earlier in his career, as the image of the faithful, cut off from the world. He is now reversing the meaning of that image: modern men, rather than Christians, are cut off from life and light—in this poem, the life and light of Christ. The stanza closes with a call to Sisyphus to close the cave where the slaves—those in bondage to the self—reside:

> Come, tired Sisyphus,
> Cover the cave's egress
> Where the light reveals the slave
> Who rests when sleeps with us
> The mother of silences.

The last two lines suggest the comforting possibilities of the "mother of silences"—and here the image may mean Christian faith or more specifically the Virgin.

Having felt the pull of faith and confessed to Christ's comforting and healing potentialities, the poet invokes Saint Monica, the mother of Saint Augustine, who, at the end of the *Con-*

*fessions,* participates with her son in a silent vision of God's divine glory:

> Come, old woman, save
> Your sons who have gone down
> Into the burning cave:
> Come, mother, and lean
> At the window with your son
> And gaze through its light frame
> These fifteen centuries
> Upon the shirking scene
> Where men, blind, go lame.

At the end of the poem, the poet calls for the mother of silences—Saint Monica or perhaps the Virgin—to speak to modern man and listen to his confession:

> Then, mother of silences,
>
> Speak, that we may hear;
> Listen, while we confess
> That we conceal our fear;
> Regard us, while the eye
> Discerns by sight or guess
> Whether, as sheep foregather
> Upon their crooked knees,
> We have begun to die;
> Whether your kindness, mother,
> Is mother of silences.

These final lines are complex, but they embody the central question of Tate's religious quest. The poet calls for the mother of silences to watch over modern man as he tries to comprehend whether if believing in Christ means "We have begun to die"; that is, does accepting faith mean cutting oneself off from the world? Is faith, as Tate portrayed it in "The Cross," located in a "world-destroying pit"? The poet then ends with a double-edged question which he does not answer: Does the kindness of Saint Monica (or the Virgin) constitute the "mother of silences"? Does it beget the silence of death or the silence of the Christian mysteries, the miracles of redemption and salvation?

"Seasons of the Soul" shows Tate taking some tentative steps towards the altar; and yet, as the final unanswered question of the poem indicates, he still retained some unresolved fears of Christian commitment. While he appeared closer to Christian faith than at any time since the late 1920s (when he came close to joining the Catholic Church), Tate continued to suffer from his "unbelieving belief." Although he acknowledged in *Seasons of the Soul* that Christianity is the only way to spiritual health for modern man, Tate could make no commitment until he came to terms with "the mother of silences," a resolution still several years away.

Turmoil marked Tate's life during the years from 1945 until his conversion to Catholicism on 22 December 1950. The year 1946 saw him leave the editorship at the *Sewanee Review.* During the same year, he divorced and then several months later remarried Caroline Gordon. In 1949 he was embroiled in the bitter controversy that arose at the awarding of the Bollingen Prize to Ezra Pound for his *Pisan Cantos.* For income during these years Tate worked as an editor at Henry Holt and Company and as a lecturer at several universities.

Tate wrote very little poetry during this period. One explanation is that he was busy with other matters; another, more significant, is that once again the tension between his belief and his unbelief had become so severe that instead of provoking his poetic vision, the stress limited it. Two poems from this period, "The Eye" (1948) and "Two Conceits for the Eye to Sing, if Possible" (1950), embody Tate's crisis of being torn between what he saw as a self-destructive naturalism and an equally destructive mysticism.

In "The Eye" (*CPT,* 123–24), the poet is locked in a naturalistic universe, lamenting the eye's inability to see anything beyond the cold hard reality of the scientific world. The South of his childhood, which Tate liked to remember fondly, becomes distorted and ugly when viewed through this calculating perspective:

> I see the gray heroes and the graves
> Of my childhood in the nuclear eye—
> Horizons spent in dun caves
> Sucked down into the sinking sky.

Once again, the cave image: man locked in a naturalistic prison of self and universe. The poem ends with a statement of the poet's agony and suffering in this world of no transcendent meaning:

> I see the father and the cooling cup
> Of my childhood in the swallowing sky
> Down, down, until down is up
> And there is nothing in the eye,
>
> Shut shutter of the mineral man
> Who takes the fatherless dark to bed,
> The acid sky to the brain-pan;
> And calls the crows to peck his head.

In "Two Conceits" (*CPT,* 125–27) the poet's visionary eye has also failed him. The poem's doggerel nursery-rhyme verse suggests both the poet's desperation and his failure to transcend the ugliness of a purely material world. He stands defeated before a universe where values do not exist and religion is merely mass psychology:

> Sing a song of Bethlehem
> Star of all the Idmen
> Everybody's Jesus
> Now if never then.

In lines separated from the rest of the poem, the poet gives a brief glimpse of the Virgin Mary:

> But Mary
> Mary quite contrary
> Light as a green fairy
> Dances, dances. Mary.

Though these final lines suggest that Mary exists and is still vital, they also say that she dances somewhere out beyond the natural world and beyond the range of the poet's vision. Mary's absence makes the poet's world, as he depicts it in the rest of the poem, nightmarish and grotesque.

Tate's crisis, as suggested in these poems, recalls what he wrote years earlier in his essay on John Peale Bishop. There he said that we view experience in two ways, secular and spiritual, and that we cannot maintain this dual vision indefinitely without imperiling our well-being. "Until we can see it one way," Tate wrote, "we shall not see it as a whole, and until we see it as a whole we shall not see it as poets" (*EFD*, 357). This split in vision and consciousness also lay at the heart of his religious predicament.

On 22 December 1950, Tate joined the Roman Catholic Church, a step signaling his acceptance of a religious commitment over which he had agonized for years. His conversion came only after years of inner turmoil and questioning, and only after he had resolved the dilemmas wrought by what he saw as the split in human consciousness. Although Tate never spelled out precisely how he worked through these questions, it is clear that he was guided by three major influences—those of Jacques Maritain, Saint Augustine, and Dante.

From Jacques Maritain, whom he befriended when he and Gordon returned to live in Princeton in 1948, Tate derived many benefits. One was Maritain's example. Maritain was a Catholic in the European tradition, a rigorous intellectual who insisted that philosophy and theology must speak to man's existential dilemmas. Moreover, unlike many other Thomists, Maritain was interested in a philosophy of nature; that is, he did not bypass the world of sensual perception to probe only the realms of metaphysics. Further, Maritain put a great emphasis on a Christian's secular life; the faithful, he insisted, had a vocation both within the Church and within their society. Tate found Maritain's example invigorating: here was a man of faith *and* a man of the world, and also a man of powerful intellect whose framework of thought was at places very close to Tate's.

Particularly influential was Maritain's *The Dream of Descartes* (1944), in which he argued that the split in the consciousness of modern man derives from Descartes's quest to formulate a cosmos merely through introspective reasoning without regard to the sensible world. Descartes's efforts, in essence, separated the realm of sense from the intellect—hence the Cartesian split in consciousness. Wrote Maritain (who was quoted by Tate in his essay "The Angelic Imagination"): "Cartesian dualism breaks man up into complete substances, joined to one another no one knows how; on the one hand, the body which is only geometric extension; on the other, the soul which is only thought—an angel inhabiting a machine and directing it by means of the pineal gland."[53] Maritain saw the Cartesian split at work in the modern mind, with disastrous results since (and this too was quoted by Tate) "human intellection is living and fresh only when it is centered upon the vigilance of sense perception. The natural roots of our knowledge being cut, a general drying-up in philosophy and culture resulted, a drought for which romantic tears were later to provide only an insufficient remedy."[54]

Maritain's conception of the Cartesian split of consciousness was very similar to Tate's. Maritain thus gave Tate a fully thought-out system in which to order and confirm his own perceptions; as Radcliffe Squires notes, "Maritain stood as a confirming hero to Tate, and Maritain's book *The Dream of Descartes* (1944) gave support and vocabulary to him."[55] Tate himself wrote in a footnote to his essay "The Angelic Imagination": "My debt to Mr. Maritain is so great that I hardly know how to acknowledge it" (*EFD*, 412).

Tate's two essays on Edgar Allen Poe, "Our Cousin, Mr. Poe" (1949) and "The Angelic Imagination" (1951), show Tate openly working with Maritain's views and vocabulary. What Tate had called "self-destroying mysticism" now became Maritain's "angelism"; that is, man's attempt to reach a direct perception of God and the essences of life by circumventing the natural world. Tate saw this circumvention as Poe's flaw, and he saw it as fatal: "Since he refuses to see nature, he is doomed to see nothing. He has overleaped and cheated the condition of man. The reach of our imaginative enlargement is perhaps no longer than the ladder of analogy, at the top of which we may see all, if we still wish to *see* anything, that we have brought up with us from the bottom, where lies the sensible world. If we take nothing with us to the top but our emptied, angelic intellects, we shall see nothing when we get there" (*EFD*, 422). Avoiding the natural world was also the flaw Tate found in most modern Catholic poetry, and indeed in most modern poetry, religious and nonreligious. As he put it in his essay "The Symbolic Imagination" (1951):

> The Catholic sensibility, as we see it in modern Catholic poetry, from Thompson to Lowell, has become angelic, and it is not distinguishable (doctrinal difference aside) from poetry by Anglicans, Methodists, Presbyterians, and atheists. I take it that more than doctrine, even if that doctrine be true, is necessary for a great poetry of action. Catholic poets have lost, along with their heretical

friends, the power to start with the "common thing": they have lost the gift for concrete experience. The abstraction of the modern mind has obscured their way into the natural order. (*EFD*, 429–30)

Paving the way for Tate's conversion to Catholicism was an important realization that he reached through Maritain: that it was not, as he had once feared, a belief in Catholicism that separated one from the world, but rather man's angelism, resulting from his split consciousness. In other words, being a Catholic did not necessarily mean being cut off from the natural world.

Remaining in the here and now while at the same time exploring the mysterious realms of faith was a lesson he learned also from another mentor, Saint Augustine.[56] Both philosophically and artistically, Augustine emphasized the importance of the earthly realm, his "City of Man," in attaining the heavenly realm, the "City of God." Rather than counselling a total immersion into one of these realms at the expense of the other, Augustine urged man to seek a balance between them. The earthly realm, as emphasized by Robert S. Dupree in his fine *Allen Tate and the Augustinian Imagination,* was a means to understand the divine: "The earthly city is both foreshadowing of and antitype to the heavenly city. It is not to be rejected totally, for it is a symbol that is the means by which the heavenly city is revealed, yet it exists not in and for itself alone. When man recognizes only one city, he has mistaken the letter for the spirit."[57]

Tate also found in Augustine's writing, particularly his *Confessions,* inspiration for the future shape of his art. Two aspects particularly appealed to him: Augustine's intimate mingling of the personal and the heavenly and his emphasis on the importance of memory to perceive the divine. In his famous terza-rima poems, written soon after his conversion, Tate reevaluated his life by the light of his new faith, working with both of these concepts. As Augustine had done, Tate explored his past and the dimensions of his consciousness, not in order to flaunt his uniqueness but to suggest the divinity within us all. He wanted, in other words, to place his destiny—indeed all of mankind's—in relation to the transcendent Christian order.

Despite Augustine's significant influence, Dante was Tate's most important guide in bringing together faith and art. Tate's deep study of *The Divine Comedy,* probably more than anything else, helped him to allay his fears that Catholicism would destroy him as an artist. Using Dante's example, Tate formulated a way to resolve artistically the split between his own naturalism and angelism. His goal was to achieve what he called in the preface of a book of poems by Samuel Greenberg "that rare continuation of direct physical sight with imaginative sight . . . a double vision in which what the poem sees beyond the physical world is seen *through* that world."[58]

Tate's new ideas on poetic method rested firmly on what he saw as Dante's use of analogy. In contrast to Poe, who, Tate wrote, "circumvented the natural world and tried to put himself not in the presence of God, but in the seat of God" (*EFD*, 422), Dante approached God through analogy. "The human intellect cannot reach God as essence," Tate wrote in "The Angelic Imagination," "only God as analogy. Analogy to what? Plainly analogy to the natural world; for there is nothing in the intellect that has not previously reached it through the senses. Had Dante arrived at a vision of God by way of sense? We must answer yes, because Dante's Triune Circle is light, which the finite intelligence can see only in what has already been seen by means of it" (*EFD*, 422). Tate called this method "the symbolic imagination" and said in his essay of that name that it "conducts an action through analogy, of the human to the divine, of the natural to the supernatural, of the low to the high, of time to eternity" (*EFD*, 427). Poetry of this sort, and a mind that saw the world in this way, bridged the split in man's consciousness, uniting the natural with the supernatural. Man could be made whole.

Thus, primarily through his study of Maritain, Augustine, and Dante, Tate discovered the possibility of remaining a part of the world while at the same time asserting his faith. By keeping his vision focused on what he called "the body of this world," the everyday reality of his own time and place, "the whirling atoms, the body of a beautiful woman, or a deformed body, or the body of Christ, or even the body of this death" (*EFD*, 428), he would escape Poe's fate—spiritual suicide, with being and art abstracted into nothingness.

Soon after his conversion in 1950, Tate began working on poetry that embodied his new ideas. To Davidson he wrote (4 April 1952) that he was experimenting with a perspective in verse that he termed " 'vision' poetry, quasi-allegorical" (*LCDT,* 359). In another letter to Davidson (14 January 1953) he explained that he was trying to develop "an approach to the objective analogical method which dominated poetry up into the Renaissance—in which what looks to us today like metaphor was actually a generally accepted relation between the physical world and the invisible." (*LCDT,* 369). He added that since no generally accepted relation exists in the contemporary world, "all that I can do is to try to tone the language down and to juxtapose objects in such a way as to make them symbolic objects while remaining in the full sense physical objects" (*LCDT,* 369). Clearly following Dante's method and approach here, Tate added in this letter that he found that the formal terza rima was best suited for his purposes.

The fruits of Tate's experiments were his terza-rima poems, "The Maimed Man" (1952), "The Swimmers" (1953), and "The Buried Lake" (1953). Heavily autobiographical, these poems were planned as parts of what was to be at first a nine-part and then later a six-part poem (the project was never completed). On one level, these poems show Tate reexamining his life by the light of his newfound faith. On another, they embody Tate's conception, expressed years later in his essay "A Lost Traveller's Dream" (1972), that "the imaginative writer is the archeologist of memory, dedicated to the minute particulars of the past, definite things—*prima sacrimenti memoria.*"[59] From these particulars, Tate would reach, as Dante had, for the divine.

In the first poem of the series, "The Maimed Man" (*CPT,* 128–31), Tate recreates his early confrontation with the spirit of Christ (and more generally Catholicism). The poet invokes "Didactic Laurel," apparently a reference to intellect and reason, asking it to allow him to recall and come to terms with a boyhood experience. In the poem, the poet as a child encounters a headless man, the maimed man of the title. This headless figure is the "mummy Christ" that the poet imagined decapitating in the first sonnet of "More Sonnets at Christmas." At first the astonished boy can think of nothing to say to the figure ("Who could have told if he were live or dead" he asks), but then addresses him in lines that ring of Tate's early attraction and repulsion to Christ and his fear that accepting Christ would lead him to renounce life and enter "the fast ungreening grave":

> 'If you live here,' I said to the unbending
>    Citizen, 'it will not seem to you
>    Improper if I linger on, defending
>
> Myself from what I hate but ought to do
>    To put us in a fast ungreening grave
>    Together, lest you turn out to be true
>
> And I publicly lose face.'

The poet then speaks of his difficulty in explaining to others his relationship to this man: in terms of Tate's own life, his Catholic leanings, which his Agrarian friends, particularly Davidson, had found so hard to fathom. How could a southern Stoic defend his honor if he were known to be a slave of Christ? Writes Tate:

>                      What could save
> One's manly honor with the football coach—
> My modest hybris, were I his known slave?
>
> Our manners had no phrase to let me broach
>    To friends the secret of a friend gone lame.
>    How could I know this friend without reproach?

But now, years later, a Catholic himself, Tate recoils in shame because of his reluctance to "know this friend":

> What a question! Whence the question came
>    I am still questing in the poor boy's curse,
>    Witching for water in a waste of shame.

After exhorting himself for his actions, the poet returns to thinking of the maimed man, whom he now describes as a "scarecrow." The scarecrow is another image for the dried-up "mummy Christ" by whom Tate was haunted for so many years, suggesting also the "scariness" that this figure instilled in Tate's consciousness. The poet did not recognize the true nature of this figure until one day he experienced a moment of spiritual insight. In a process similar to Tate's description in "The Symbolic Imagination" of Dante's experiencing a vision of God through the mirror of analogy, the poet sees the scarecrow mirrored as "a black trunk without bloom" (echoing Tate's description of Christ in "Causerie": "Year after year the blood of Christ will sleep / In the holy tree, the branches sagged without bloom" [*CPT,* 14]):

> Meanwhile the scarecrow, man all coat and stem,
>> Neither dead nor living, never in this world—
>> In what worlds, or in what has essenced them,
>
> I did not know until one day I whirled
>> Towards a suggesting presence in my room
>> And saw in the waving mirror (glass swirled
>
> By old blowers) a black trunk without bloom—
>> Body that once had moved my face and feet.
>> My secret was his father, I his tomb.

Now understanding the significance of Christ, the poet recalls his struggles to find meaning and assert his faith during the years before his enlightenment. In effect, he summarizes *Seasons of the Soul:*

> And then rose in the man a small half-hell
>> Where love discorded, shade of pompous youth,
>
> Clutched shades forbearing in a family well;
>> Where the sleek senses of the simple child
>> Came back to rack spirit that could not tell
>
> Natural time: the eyes, recauled, enisled
>> In the dreamt cave by shadowy womb of beam,
>> Had played swimmer of night—the moist and mild!

The poem ends as the poet invokes the "Virgin Muse," asking it to take him up the deep stream of memory, which will carry him to the even deeper river of God's love:

> Now take him, Virgin Muse, up the deeper stream:
>> As a lost bee returning to the hive,
>> Cell after honeyed cell of sounding dream—
>
> Swimmer of noonday, lean for the perfect dive
>> To the dead Mother's face, whose subtile down
>> You had not seen take amber light alive.

"The Swimmers" (*CPT*, 132–35), the second poem of the series, continues the poet's descent into memory. As the poet confronted the spirit of Christ in "The Maimed Man," here he meets a vision of Christ, this time at a lynching he had witnessed as a boy, which becomes for the poet a reenactment of the Passion. Writing in straightforward and easy-flowing narrative verse, Tate describes this childhood scene as a posse of twelve riders passes in search of a man who they fear has been lynched. Only eleven riders return, and as the poet recalls what he remembers seeing, the story of the lynched black man becomes Christ's too:

> Into a world where sound shaded the sight
> > Dropped the dull hooves again; the horsemen came
> > Again, all but the leader: it was night

> Momently and I feared: eleven same
> > Jesus-Christers unmembered and unmade,
> > Whose corpse had died again in dirty shame.

The poet describes the sheriff as he approaches the body—the body of the black man and the body of Christ (which explains the capitalized "It" in the following lines):

> The melancholy sheriff slouched beneath
> > A giant sycamore; shaking his head
> > He plucked a sassafras twig and picked his teeth;

> 'We come too late.' He spoke to the tired dead
> > Whose ragged shirt soaked up the viscous flow
> > Of blood in which It lay discomfited.

The poem concludes with the boy watching the sheriff and a stranger who has appeared (perhaps the Devil) drag the body back to town. For the poet, the lynched man becomes another embodiment of the decapitated Christ, and his head remains before the poet's eyes:

> My breath crackled the dead air like a shotgun
> > As, sheriff and the stranger disappearing,
> > The faceless head lay still. I could not run

> Or walk, but stood. Alone in the public clearing
> > This private thing was owned by all the town,
> > Though never claimed by us within my hearing.

The easy flow of "The Swimmers" makes it different from most of Tate's other verse, yet it remains one of his most striking and powerful poems. In it Tate reevaluates his life by the light of his newly embraced faith. Moreover, the poem is his strongest attempt to follow the method of Dante and his own plan, as he had described it to Davidson, "to tone the language down and to juxtapose objects in such a way [as] to make them symbolic objects while remaining in the full sense physical objects" (*LCDT,* 369).

"The Buried Lake" (*CPT,* 136–40), the third terza-rima poem, continues the poet's probing of memory and the quest for God's love. Opening with an invocation to Saint Lucia, the "Lady of Light," one of whose virtues was the curing of blindness, the poet asks for her aid in maintaining a double vision of physical sight and imaginative insight. "And now I pray you mirror my mind, styled / To spring its waters to my memory," writes the poet. After the invocation, the poet relates a series of dreams that take him back to experiences and reveries from his youth and early manhood: a buried lake, a violin recital, a friend's reproof of his poetry, the return of a lover—all of which end in some failure on the poet's part. After the horrifying transformation of his lover's head into a skull, the poet sinks into the depths of personal hell:

> I hid the blade within the melic sheath
> > And tossed her head—but it was not her head:
> > Another's searching skull whose drying teeth
>
> Crumbled me all night long and I was dead.
> > Down, down below the wave that turned me round,
> > Head downwards where the Head of God had sped
>
> On the third day; where nature had unwound
> > And ravelled her green that she had softly laved—
> > The green reviving spray now slowly drowned
>
> Me, since the shuttling eye would not be saved.
> > In the tart undersea of slipping night
> > The dream whispered, while sight within me, caved,
>
> Deprived, poured stinging dark on cold delight,
> > And multitudinous whined invisible bees;
> > All grace being lost, and its considering rite.

Humbled by these setbacks and by the loss of his visionary eye, the poet kneels to Saint Lucia and encounters, through the mirror of her eyes, visionary light. At first the poet finds the light threatening and difficult to come to terms with; it is far easier, he says, to live as if such light does not exist:

> And yet how vexed, bitter, and hard the trance
> Of light—how I resented Lucy's play!
> Better stay dead, better not try the lance
>
> In the living bowl: living we have one way
> For all time in the twin darks where light dies
> To live: forget that you too lost the day.

But then, as he accepts what he sees, the poet's visionary eye is restored:

> Yet finding it refound it Lucy-guise
> As I, refinding where two shadows meet,
> Took from the burning umbrage mirroring eyes
>
> Like Tellico blue upon a golden sheet
> Spread out for all our stupor.

Now the poet greets Saint Lucia, and in a passage recalling Dante's gazing into Beatrice's eyes at the beginning of *Paradiso* 18, the poet receives divine vision:

> Lady coming,
> Lady not going, come Lady come: I greet
>
> You in the double of our eyes—humming
> Miles of lightning where, in a pastoral scene,
> The fretting pipe is lucent and becoming.
>
> I thought of ways to keep this image green
> (Until the leaf unfold the formal cherry)
> In an off season when the eye is lean
>
> With an inward gaze upon the wild strawberry,
> Cape jasmine, wild azalea, eglantine—
> All the sad eclogue that will soon be merry:
>
> And knew that nature could not more refine
> What it had given in a looking-glass
> And held there, after the living body's line

Has moved wherever it must move—wild grass
Inching the earth; and the quicksilver art
Throws back the invisible but lightning mass

To inhabit the room; for I have seen it part
The palpable air, the air close up above
And under you, light Lucy, light of heart—

Light choir upon my shoulder, speaking Dove
The dream is over and the dark expired.
I knew that I had known enduring love.

The poet's (and Tate's own) long search for unity, order, and faith is over: "I knew that I had known enduring love."

After "The Buried Lake," Tate published very little poetry, other than several short poems to his family and a Christmas poem. Throughout the 1950s and 1960s, he was extremely busy as a teacher and lecturer (from 1951 until 1968 he was a professor at the University of Minnesota; during these years he also frequently lectured at a number of other universities and at writers' conferences, both in the United States and abroad). Yet this plethora of public activity does not seem in itself an adequate explanation for the drop in his poetic output, for he still found time to write essays. Tate, I believe, stopped writing poetry essentially because he had resolved the tensions and problems that for so long had fired his creative genius. His conversion to Catholicism marked the resolution of his ongoing conflict between naturalism and mysticism, and terminated his search for belief; with the terza-rima poems he had made his poetic statement of faith and had reexamined his life by his new vision. Intellectually secure, Tate was no longer spurred to write verse, which perhaps explains his fondness for an epigram of Yeats to the effect that poetry results from our quarrels with ourselves, while rhetoric grows from our quarrels with others.

In the essays he continued to write during this last period of his life—the "rhetoric" arising from his quarrels with others—Tate assumed the stance of a hard-line Christian warrior. He frequently delivered blistering attacks on the secular age he saw about him, leveling his sights most often on various utopian dreams, which, he believed, led man away from Christ. "When the belief in the perfectability of man in and by means of a rationalistic society ends in slaughter," he wrote in his essay "Christ and the Unicorn" (1955), "we go to the other extreme; and, deciding that man is not merely imperfect, but actually a vicious imbecile, we frantically call in the kind of order represented by the omnicompetent state."[60] The only way to exorcise these twin demons, he said later in this essay, is to develop a Christian society; he offered no other alternatives, "for either we are a Christian civilization or we are nothing."[61]

Though his personal life during his final years did not always reflect a dogmatic adherence to Church doctrine—he divorced Caroline Gordon for a second time in 1959, went on to marry and divorce a second woman, and then to marry a third—Tate always considered himself a Catholic. Until his death in 1979, he remained secure in his faith and satisfied that his life had received order and unity from his position as a Christian in the modern world. At least in his public stance, Tate had found his calling: he was a defender of the faith.

## CHAPTER 2

# The Key to the Puzzle:
# The Literary Career of Caroline Gordon

In 1947, three years before her husband Allen Tate took the same step, Caroline Gordon joined the Roman Catholic Church. Unlike Tate, who felt a call to the Church during almost his entire career, Gordon apparently underwent a less protracted struggle. Judging from the evidence found in her fiction, she maintained an insistent pessimism until the 1940s, when her thought began to shift and she began to look for a way to set in order the confusing and disparate experiences of life. Although she and Tate must surely have discussed his religious struggles and her own views of Catholicism, there is little indication that she herself felt a commanding pull toward the Church until shortly before her conversion.

Gordon finally joined the Church after realizing the need for a vital system of belief to give structure to what she saw as the chaotic nature of twentieth-century life. The system, she had come to think, could not be merely secular in scope; rather, it had to be grounded in the secular while at the same time reaching for the divine. This outlook she also now applied to art. Not long after her conversion, she faulted the work of Hemingway for the narrow range of experience it contained, saying it explored only man's relationship to other people. Such work now seemed to her inadequate, since, she said, "the world seems to have shifted under our feet. We have seen countries ravaged and populations decimated. We can hardly believe any longer in the Divinity of Man. We are more concerned today with Man's relation to God."[1]

Though she does not say so here, Gordon's own work up until her conversion resembles Hemingway's on a broad level, in its emphasis on worldly heroes. With the exception of a few works written in the years directly preceding her acceptance into the Church, one finds in Gordon's preconversion fiction very little concern for the transcendent. After her conversion, the shape and texture of her art changed drastically, as she shifted her focus from the secular to the divine. Although she passed through other artistic and philosophical phases, none was so far-reaching as her Catholic conversion. Perhaps her most noteworthy achievement as a writer was her ability to keep her work almost uniformly fine throughout the five decades of her arduous writing career. Only late in her career, when she struggled to forge a unity of classical and Christian myth, did her work show signs of a serious falling off.

Gordon's upbringing exhibits little evidence of the religious writer she would later become.[2] Like Tate's, her childhood was steeped primarily in Old South traditions, with religious matters taking a decidedly secondary position. Born on 6 October 1895, she grew up at Merry Mont farm, on the southern border of Kentucky near Trenton. Life at the farm was traditional and established; the problems and concerns of the modern world had not yet encroached. Judging from several chapters Gordon wrote for an uncompleted autobiographical novel, her childhood was essentially happy and fulfilling. "When I think of my childhood," she writes in "Cock-Crow," one of these autobiographical chapters, "my first impression is of a rounded whole, of a world which was so self-contained, yet so fully peopled and so fully firmly rooted in time and space that today when its name is pronounced I feel a stirring of the heart which no other name can evoke."[3] In another chapter, significantly entitled "Always Summer," she writes: "When I think of those days it is always summer. June or July usually. And early morning. I know that it is early morning for the air has a delicious freshness which is savored only at that time of day. I have just waked from the deep sleep of childhood, or, rather, I have been waked from it and, lying in bed, my eyes still closed, am wondering how I came to wake."[4]

Reading these autobiographical chapters, heavy with nostalgic descriptions of the everyday life of the farm, leaves one with little doubt of Gordon's deep appreciation for the order and harmony of her childhood years. Yet there was also a dark side to life at the farm; underpinning its system of order and harmony was a recognition of human evil and of man's fate as a solitary wanderer. According to Gordon—and we must be careful here in interpretation, for she wrote these autobiographical chapters late in life when she was a Catholic, and may have tampered with her early views on religion to construct an overall fictional strategy for the proposed novel—she picked up on this disturbing knowledge early on, primarily through her own interpretation of the vague sort of Deism her family practiced.

With its belief in the separation of God from man, Deism was for many a liberating theology in that man's reason could supposedly discern in nature the wondrous results of God's almighty hand. Divine revelation was unnecessary for knowledge, and scriptural authority was suspect. But Gordon says she found God's absence from the world painful and disturbing. "I, myself," she writes in "Cock-Crow," "cannot remember a time when I was not aware that life was a desperate affair, at best, and, lying awake at night or early in the morning, I used to ponder how it came to be the way it indubitably was."[5] By day, as a public person, she subscribed to the community's views that life's deprivations resulted from the Civil War. But at night, alone in her bed, she saw things in a larger—and a darker—light; by the time she was four years old, Gordon claims, she had already decided that "the world had been created as a plaything by a group of men, who, tired of sporting with it, had gone on to other pleasures, leaving it to roll on the way it would."[6] In another autobiographical chapter, "A Narrow Heart: The Portrait of a Woman," she describes herself, again at four years old, confronting in her room the satanic force of evil, seen by the child as the shadows along the walls "that seemed to have been willed by a Presence of whose existence I had hitherto not been aware."[7] "It was a long time ago," she writes in "A Narrow Heart," "but it sometimes seems as if I had all my life been standing in that darkening room, companioned only by shadows, shadows which, as I stood there, I kept at bay by the exertion of all my childish will, for I knew even then that their very existence betokened peril and that too close communion with them meant death."[8]

Gordon's awareness of the dark shadows of life assuredly deepened when, at the age of ten, she began attending her father's school of classical studies. (She was the only girl in this school for boys.) Many years later, she acknowledged the perceptions into man's capacity for evil that she gained from her early study of the classics, saying she was thankful that she had been "forced to make the acquaintance of certain archetypes (if not all) at an early age." "If you make their acquaintance," she continued, "early enough in life, at least, you have a chance to become reconciled to the fact that the unconscious mind of every one of us harbors demons and demonesses."[9] The classics, she said, also taught her the intricacies of sentence structure and provided her with examples of perfect form, which she drew upon in her own writing.

Gordon completed her schooling at a public high school in Wilmington, Ohio, and from there she went to Bethany College in West Virginia, graduating in 1916. After teaching high school for several years, she landed a job as a reporter for the *Chattanooga News* in 1920. Though she later claimed that her years with the newspaper had no influence on her later writing career, her 1923 review essay on little magazines in the South, "U.S. Best Poets Here in Tennessee," was significant. With this essay, in which she concluded that the *Fugitive* was the most important literary magazine in the South, she gained widespread recognition within the Nashville group. John Crowe Ransom, who had corresponded with Gordon before the essay appeared, brought her to Allen Tate's attention in a letter dated 11 February 1923: "When I get copies tomorrow I'll send you one of the Saturday's Chattanooga *News* containing a Fugitive story in the magazine supplement. Written by one Miss Gordon, who has developed quite a fondness for us, and incidentally is kin to some of my kinfolks in Chattanooga."[10] During the summer of 1924, at the family farm of Robert Penn Warren, Gordon and Tate first met; shortly thereafter they went to New York together and were married.

In New York, Gordon gave serious thought to becoming a professional writer. Tate, himself thoroughly devoted to the art of letters, encouraged her and offered advice. So did other writers in the artistic circles that she and Tate frequented, particularly Ford Madox Ford, whom she served as a secretary-typist for a short time. Gordon quickly came under Madox's influence. In 1927, she wrote to her friend Sally Wood about Ford: "He's awfully nice, and I love to see him take his sentences by the tail and uncurl them—in a perfectly elegant manner. I don't believe there's anybody writing now who can do it so elegantly. At times he almost weeps over my lapses into Americanisms. 'My deah child, *do* you spell "honour" without a u?' "[11]

Ford's influence grew even more significant when Gordon and Tate went to Paris in 1928. Once again, Gordon worked for a while as his secretary. As their working relationship grew, Ford began pushing Gordon hard on her own work, urging her on and giving criticism of the fiction she showed him. "Ford took me by the scruff of the neck about three weeks before I left," Gordon wrote (21 January 1930) to Sally Wood, recalling her days in Paris, "set me down in his apartment every morning at eleven o'clock and forced me to dictate at least five thousand words, not all in one morning, of my novel [*Penhally*, then unfinished] to him. If I complained that it was hard to work with everything so hurried and Christmas presents to buy he observed 'You have no passion for your art. It is unfortunate' in such a sinister way that I would reel forth sentences in a sort of panic. Never did I see such a passion for the novel as that man has" (*SM,* 51). At this early stage in her career (Gordon's first published work was her short story, "Summer Dust," which appeared in 1929 in *Gyroscope*), Ford's encouragement was extremely important. He not only gave her insights into her craft, but also bolstered her confidence with his enthusiasm. (Gordon once said that she was ready to give up on *Penhally* until Ford started working with her on it.) Ford, moreover, took it upon himself to help get her work published and recognized.

Gordon's immersion in the literary culture of New York and Europe was for the most part a happy experience. Like Tate, she embraced the role of the modern artist and celebrated the priesthood of the imagination into which she now entered. And like Tate she quickly became a willing citizen of the modern world, relishing the excitement and the glamor of the urban scene. "Oh God, how I want to be back in Paris," she wrote (21 January 1930) to Sally Wood, shortly after her return with Tate to the States. "I complained all the way home. I think it was grief at leaving Paris that made me so sea sick" (*SM,* 50).

Yet Gordon never became thoroughly modern. Despite her realization that the aristocratic southern milieu stood far outside the mainstream of contemporary life, she never entirely repudiated her southern identity and clung fiercely to values and ideals imbibed during her childhood. On one level she felt different from the general run of writers and intellectuals at the forefront of the cultural scene, many of whom were Marxists or made out that they were. In "Cock-Crow," Gordon writes that the forbidding knowledge of human evil and depravity that she acquired during her upbringing made her cynically skeptical of the hopeful social philosophies then being so widely touted. "I had not read *Das Kapital* and could not have understood it if I had," Gordon wrote. "But I felt—in my bones if you will—not so much that Marx was wrong as that my fellow writers were wrong in accepting him, for even one step of the long way, as a guide. I did not believe that they would have subscribed to his theories if they had known what I knew."[12] She also showed little patience, at least in her letters, to those writers who, she believed, insisted (often in drunken bluster) that their every utterance was a brilliant gem of wit and intelligence. "[E. E.] Cummings, for instance," she wrote (2 and 3 December 1928) to Sally Wood, "I regard as one of the greatest bores that ever lived. He will sit for hours gearing himself up to make some brilliant stroke—when it comes out it is usually something like 'Fuckaduck'" (*SM,* 43). City life, too, as it had for Tate, eventually lost its glamor—things were just too chaotic. Even the artistic haunts of Paris became alien to her. "The Dome and the Rotonde are really quite terrible, don't you think?" she wrote (2 and 3 December 1928) to Sally Wood. "A sort of super-Greenwich village. They actually apall" (*SM,* 44).

If Gordon was not altogether happy living in modern society, neither was she content residing in the countryside. She discovered this when she and Tate returned to the South in 1930 to live and write at their farm near Clarksville, Tennessee. There certainly were many things she enjoyed about the farm—the quiet, the beauty of the land, the garden, the early-morning mists shrouding the valleys. But having lived in New York and Europe, Gordon no longer found complete fulfillment in these earthy pleasures. Moreover, many distractions arose during the time she allotted for her writing. There were many chores to be done and kinfolk to deal with (Benfolly, hers and Tate's farm, was close to the home of Gordon's maternal grandmother and her numerous brood). She had to cook for frequent visitors; to save money, she also did a good deal of sewing. "I love to sew, but you can't sew very well and have any kind of prose style," she wrote (15 June 1932) to Sally Wood, expressing her frustration at finding time to write (*SM*, 116). To Wood she also expressed her boredom and loneliness: "It will be a godsend to have somebody to talk to beside the kin," she wrote (31 July 1930) in anticipation of her friend's visit. "I am getting pretty tired of them. There is no amusement here except driving around to various creeks to go swimming. Still there is always talk. And we are making some beer today" (*SM*, 55).

Adding to Gordon's unrest was the fact that she did not share Tate's enthusiasm for embracing a southern historical identity. She saw no underlying significance in their return to the farm; Tate, as we have seen, saw it as a way to seize hold of the southern tradition, the first step in building a traditional agrarian society. Gordon could not take Tate's Agrarianism very seriously and could not help but speak of the Agrarians (who often visited the farm and whom she often referred to in her letters to Sally Wood as "the boys") in a vein of jest. When Stringfellow Barr, editor of the *Virginia Quarterly Review,* wrote an article about the merits of industrialism in the South, Gordon wrote (October 1930) to Sally Wood on the Agrarians' reaction: "The Symposiers are having a great time. . . . This [Barr's article] gives the Nashville brethren a chance to accuse him of selling out. They then proceed to recriminate each other in the pages of the Tennessean, New York Times etc. even brawling a bit on the A.P. wires" (*SM*, 60). In another letter (undated, 1931) to Wood, she wrote that her tenant "Jesse brought into our lives the other day the one true agrarian"—Jesse's ten-year-old brother, a boy who had never been to the city and who stood about on one of the farm's hills gazing dreamily at Clarksville in the distance (*SM*, 69).

With her loyalties split between two ways of life—modern and southern—neither of which she found entirely satisfactory, Gordon found herself in a precarious intellectual position. Though she never lost her nostalgic love for the traditional, orderly life of the rural South, she recognized its shortcomings and its irrelevance both to her future and to that of contemporary society. At the same time she could not embrace what she saw as the anarchy of contemporary society and the easy answers proposed by the prevailing social philosophies. Order for her came only in the creation of art, an endeavor that failed to satisfy

completely her needs for transcendent meaning. Like Allen
Tate, she suffered (returning to Lewis P. Simpson's term) from
"the historicism of consciousness"; without an overarching
framework of tradition or faith, she internalized the dilemmas
of meaning and identity that all of us face, grappling with them
alone in her consciousness rather than channeling them into the
larger communities of society or church. Not surprisingly, her
thought darkened and headed towards a profound pessimism
that saw little hope for man's achievement of permanent stability
and order. Not until the 1940s, judging from her fiction, did she
even begin to search for a transcending order. Until that time
she wrote novels and stories whose worlds were for the most part
bleak and bare, any light found therein dimmed by the shadows
of Gordon's own attitudes.

Almost all of Gordon's work up until 1940—which includes
her novels *Penhally* (1931); *Aleck Maury, Sportsman* (1934); *None
Shall Look Back* (1937); and *The Garden of Adonis* (1937), along
with a number of memorable stories, including all but one of
those about Aleck Maury—depicts heroic characters struggling
to assert order and meaning in an unstable world. At the heart
of these solitary stands against death and disintegration lie a
Stoic acceptance of man's depraved condition and a desire to
forge a code of valor and dignity. In *Penhally*, several generations
of the Llewellyn family strive to maintain family order as the
social order around them collapses; in *The Garden of Adonis*, Ben
Allard and his tenant Ote Mortimer, embodiments of agrarian
virtue, defy all odds in attempting to transform stubborn clay
into fields of abundance; and in *None Shall Look Back*, Rives and
Lucy Allard hold their marriage as a bulwark to stem the dark
flood of the Civil War. But indomitable as Gordon's heroes seem,
disaster awaits them all: the dark forces of life destroy the heroes
and—we finally see—their fragile edifices of order. *Penhally* ends
with a fratricide and the family irrevocably split; *The Garden of
Adonis* with Ote murdering Mr. Allard; *None Shall Look Back* with
Rives dead and Lucy wrapped in a mantle of bitterness and
despair.

The general picture is bleak. Yet Gordon's fiction is not
merely a series of shrill cries against life's unfairness; rather, it is
a profound exploration of heroic endeavor, which remains hon-
orable even though it is doomed. Her work achieves such depth

primarily because of Gordon's own deeply felt admiration and sympathy for her heroes. By standing their ground, by holding their heads high, these doomed figures act out the only heroism that Gordon at this point saw available to modern man—a private assertion of dignity. The bond of sympathy she felt with her heroes (derived in large part from the example of her father and from her extensive early education in the classics) allowed her to maintain a healthy tension between her dark vision of existence and her need to assert some vestige of meaning amidst life's pain and suffering. This tension vitalized her imagination and led to the creation of a number of profound novels and stories.

In a broad sense, the struggles of Gordon's heroes to achieve order resemble Gordon's own efforts to maintain stability in a chaotic world. As Willard Thorp points out, characters in these early works have lost their places in an ordered society. This predicament, in Thorp's words, "leaves men and women rootless and send them in search of some mode of living or some ritual which will compensate for the loss of position in a social order that controls one's life."[13] The situation Thorp describes is of course very similar to the one Gordon faced during the 1930s. The comparison goes further, for, like Gordon herself, her heroes possess a nostalgic love of a better life and time now past—a time which cannot be recovered. Gordon's own attempts with the writing of fiction to push back the forbidding shadows of chaos, if only momentarily, resemble her heroes' solitary stands against disorder. That Gordon saw her writing career in terms of the ancient warriors perhaps explains in part why she, unlike Tate, did not actively explore political and religious alternatives during the 1920s and 1930s: the echoes of the heroes gave her, if not transcendence, strength and courage to persevere during the dark times.

Nowhere is Gordon's sympathy with a hero's struggles for order stronger than in her masterwork, *Aleck Maury, Sportsman* (1934). In following the exploits of this active southern sportsman—Maury is based on her father—Gordon is on one level singing the praises of this grand old man. She acknowledges that his rejection of the modern world and his attraction instead to the ritual of the hunt has given him significance and purpose which most people never find. And yet, in the novel's dark undercurrent, Gordon also acknowledges the ultimate futility of Maury's exploits. She makes it clear that the forces of life will eventually catch up with Maury and destroy him.

Aleck Maury is a sportsman of the first order, an excellent fly fisherman and bird hunter. He devotes so much time and energy to sport because he sees the order and community of his childhood (he was born just after the Civil War) progressively giving way to the fast-changing times. When he leaves home as a young man, he realizes that the idyllic plantation life of his youth, fostered by strong ties of guardianship and extended family, is in the process of passing forever. "After a certain period of my life I never went back to Virginia or exchanged letters with any of my connections there," he says at one point. "Some men foster these ties all their lives. For me it has always been too painful."[14] But Maury carries with him the skills and lore of the hunt which he learned as a child, and he turns to these in trying as an adult to give his life purpose and stability.

Maury sees modern society, fast making inroads into southern life, as brutal and savage; to escape it he takes to the woods whenever he can get away from his duties as a classics teacher. By following the strict codes and rituals of the hunt, Maury achieves a private communion with the natural world. His life is full and purposeful. When he is an old man, a friend asks him to go to a health lecture to help "kill the time"; Maury bristles in rebuke: "I stood there too astounded even to answer. . . . I was annoyed to reflect that anybody could think I, Alexander Maury, could need to kill time!" (*AM*, 264). Few other of Gordon's characters achieve such dignity.

But Maury's life in communion with the natural world is ultimately doomed. As he himself discovers, his escapes to the woods can never constitute complete victories over the world about him—the ravages of time cannot be stopped, and Maury grows old, his body enfeebled. Accompanying his growth into old age is an almost terrifying awareness of death and decay. Because the rituals of the hunt provide him with no framework of belief, he is unable to see death as anything but the end; as a result, fear and despair drive him into spells of listlessness.

But Maury cannot remain morose for long; his love for the hunt pulls him back again and again to life and zest. In the joyous last scene of the novel, Maury, now a hobbling old man, is lighting out once more for the river. Like his forebear, Huck Finn, Maury makes good his escape from the snares of civilization, here his daughter and son-in-law (figures clearly based on Gordon and Allen Tate), who want him to move in with them. Though Maury knows that death will finally catch up with him, he is happy to be still on the run, to fish as many streams and rivers as possible before his time is up.

With this exuberant ending, Gordon affirms her respect and admiration for her father's life, while at the same time acknowledging its shortcomings. Though she knew that she could never completely reject modern life, as Maury had done, nonetheless she felt very deeply for a man whose life resounded with such feeling and purpose. The contrast between the passionate Maury and the rather stiff and pedantic versions of herself and Tate underscores her feelings, and suggests that Gordon knew that in many ways her life would never be as full as her father's. Adding to the intensity of Gordon's feelings is her awareness that the necessity for Maury to reject his society to attain purpose in life reflects the loss of order and community in southern—and also modern—society. Louise Cowan has observed that Maury's story illustrates that "the vital Southern love of the land and its conviction of the need for guardianship has declined in him to a self-indulgent passion for hunting and fishing; its communality has become a solitary quest for what must be a *secret* life of joy; its public figures have dwindled to private 'characters.'"[15] Maury's intense zest for life appears even more joyous against this dark background of defeat and decay.

In several short stories from this period, Gordon explores Maury's increasing enfeeblement and his fast-approaching appointment with death. They represent some of Gordon's best work; the tension between her love for her hero and her knowledge of his loss of powers and his ultimate death gives the stories depth and great power. Two of these stories are especially relevant here: "The Last Day in the Field" (1935) and "One More Time" (1935).

In "The Last Day in the Field," Maury is an old man hobbled by a bad leg and poor health. Yet in November, with the first killing frost, he takes to the woods with his young friend Joe for some bird hunting. He is still an expert shot and loves the sport as much as ever, yet as the title makes clear, this is Maury's final day of shooting. His decrepit leg will from now on bar him from the pursuit: "My leg was stiff from the hip down and every time I brought it over the pain would start in my knee, zing, and travel up and settle in the small of my back. I walked with my head down, watching the light catch on the ridges of Joe's brown corduroy trousers and then shift and catch again as he moved forward. Sometimes he would get on ahead and then there would be nothing but the black tree trunks coming up out of the dead leaves that were all over the ground."[16] The story ends as Maury takes his last shots of the day and watches the bird fall. "I saw it there for a second, its wings black against the gold light, before, wings still spread, it came whirling down, like an autumn leaf, like the leaves that were everywhere about us, all over the ground" (*CSCG*, 104). Maury knows that he too will soon be following the fallen dove and the autumn leaves.

Maury's inevitable defeat by time and death also lies at the center of "One More Time." Here, once again an old man, Maury has come to fish one of his favorite rivers, the Elk. He is staying at an inn nearby, where he runs into one of his old fishing buddies, Bob Reynolds, who is sick and can no longer fish, but nonetheless is visiting the beloved river. Reynolds is in fact a dying man, struck by cancer, though he will not admit this to his long-time friend. One of the old ladies at the inn, Aunt Zilphy, breaks the news to Maury in simple words that nonetheless capture all the horror of cancer: "Doctor says it's his liver. He ain't got but a piece of liver. Some little something been eatin' on it. Done et all of it but one little piece and when that's gone he'll be dead" (*CSCG*, 72). Himself getting on in years, Maury is shaken by Aunt Zilphy's announcement; he retreats to his room where he wonders "how it would be to know that there was something inside you that would give soon and that you could only live as long as it lasted, a year, six months, three. . . . Would you want to stay very quiet so you might live longer or would you tell yourself there was nothing the matter and try to have as good a time as you could?" (*CSCG*, pp. 72–73). Leaving this question unanswered, he puts himself to sleep by imagining an idyllic scene of fishing a quiet pool.

Maury does not appear much surprised when Reynolds drowns himself the next morning. The matter-of-fact way in which he reacts to the suicide indicates that he had expected something of the sort. For Maury knows that although Reynolds was married (his wife had accompanied him to the river), he centered his life on his sport, not his family; and that when he could no longer fish, nothing of meaning was left to him. Reynolds chose to die in the water he loved, and although he does not say so, Maury probably envisions a similar fate for himself someday. For these hunters, defeat before time is inevitable; the only question is how to face up to the final battle.

Gordon makes it clear in her other fiction from this early period that such a defeat awaits everyone. The dark forces of life are going to sweep everything away, and to try to structure reality into a meaningful whole or to transcend it with a faith in the timeless are useless endeavors. Even the potentially meaningful study of the classics, Gordon's early love and the storehouse of human archetypes, appears lost to modern man. Cousin Cave, for instance, a scholar of the ancients in *Penhally*, relishes the classical myths only as fantasy and is hopelessly out of touch with contemporary life. And Aleck Maury, although he has certainly informed his life with meaning and understanding derived from the classics, is one of a dying generation and a willing outcast of family and society.

Religious faith, too, apparently offers no transcendence. Rarely do religious concerns surface in these early works; the major exception is *The Garden of Adonis*. Here one character, Ed Mortimer, stands apart from the others in that he spends his days studying and preaching salvation. At first glance, his life appears fraught with meaning and solace. Yet it soon becomes clear that he is cut off from the vital forces of life; after his experience of being "saved," he no longer shares, as he formerly did, in the warmth and friendship of those about him. His brother Ote says of him: "He would speak to you, smiling, and then look away as if he didn't have time to listen to your answers, as if what you said couldn't make any difference to him. It was like he was studying something important all the time and didn't have time to fool with other folks."[17] For Ed, earthly life is insignificant; the theme of one of his Sunday sermons is "This world and all its pleasures. . . . Hit ain't nothin'" (*GA*, 105). But Gordon makes it abundantly clear in the novel that, to her, the world, its pleasures and its pains, is in fact everything. Like Tate during this period, Gordon sees religious absorption as a denial of life; Ed's religious intensity resembles Cousin Cave's study of the classics—both are escapes into fantasy. Meanwhile, life passes by unnoticed and unexperienced.

Gordon also makes it clear in these early works that she will take no part in the easy idealization of days gone by. Her attitude is close to Allen Tate's—at least that part of Tate which recoiled from back-to-the-farm Agrarian purists. In a poem ("To the Romantic Traditionists") written near the end of his involvement with Agrarianism, Tate underscored the limitations of idealizing the past, and he was almost certainly—on one level—addressing the poem to some of his Agrarian friends, the "Romantic Traditionists." Even more than Tate, Gordon distrusted romanticizing the past, and often in her art she too directed her skepticism at the Agrarians. Indeed, much of her early work can be read on one level as a criticism of the Agrarians—at least the hard-liners.

*Penhally*, for instance, is in a very real sense an antiplantation novel that works against the established tradition of the southern manor house where life is ordered, serene, and secure. The novel follows several generations of the Llewelyns as they try to hold the plantation together and keep it free from the encroachments of the rapacious world outside its fences. But their efforts are finally futile, primarily for two reasons. One is that nothing can stop the onslaughts of modernity; times change and the old ways die. The other is that focusing one's life on the plantation, so that all decisions are made according to their utility to the farm (including decisions about marriage, inheritance, and loyalty to the community and nation), ultimately undercuts the stability of human relationships and ends up splintering the family. The novel ends with Chance Llewelyn murdering his brother Nick and with the plantation's being sold to a northern millionaire, who plans to make it into a hunting club. Gordon's message here is that there never has been a golden age, and that to idealize the Old South and see its ways as the answer to contemporary problems—as some Agrarians were doing—is to follow the lead of earlier local-color writers who romanticized the southern plantation, ignoring all the while the difficult questions of their own day and indulging in a saccharine nostalgia.

An even more explicit criticism of the Agrarian dream appears in *The Garden of Adonis*, which is set in the contemporary South. As Gordon shows it here, the South of the 1930s is a land wracked by drought, economic depression, and exploitation. Central to the novel are two characters who strive to realize the agrarian vision: Mr. Allard, who struggles to make his farm a profitable enterprise; and Ote Mortimer, one of Mr. Allard's tenants, who works the field with love and devotion. Mr. Allard's and Ote's efforts to transform the stubborn clay into fields of abundance elevate them far above the other folks on the farm, who scratch and till merely to eke by.

Yet this is no glorification of the rewards of hard work. Terrible problems beset the two agrarian heroes, particularly lack of money and of rain, both of which lie beyond their control. Eventually these problems destroy Mr. Allard and Ote, and at the end total chaos reigns: in a fit of rage, Ote murders Mr. Allard when he cannot advance Ote the money he needs for marriage. Ote then takes off to the woods, his life now as lost as Mr. Allard's. The significance of the title now looms large. Like the ancient garden of Adonis, where plants shot up only to wither away because they lacked deep root systems, the modern South is unable to sustain a fruitful and spiritually fulfilling society. To live the Agrarian vision only initiates disaster.

No sign of an upturn in Gordon's thought appeared until her novel about eighteenth-century pioneers, *Green Centuries* (1941), and even here the overwhelmingly dark nature of life once again triumphs. Nonetheless, her descriptions of Indian life, highlighted by the contrast between the Indian and white settlements, suggest that Gordon had begun to ponder the possibility for engendering order through tradition. Though these probings were tentative and finally inconclusive, they indicate that Gordon's thought had perceptibly shifted. *Green Centuries* marked the beginning of a transition stage in Gordon's development that would become more obvious in the works that followed.

*Green Centuries* follows the exploits of two brothers, Archy and Orion Outlaw. The two have taken flight from their North Carolina home to escape the British, who are out to arrest Orion for his part in a Regulator ambush of Redcoat soldiers. They are bound for the frontier, what is now western North Carolina and eastern Tennessee. Along the way, however, the brothers are separated when Indians capture Archy and eventually initiate him into the tribe. From here on, the novel traces the now radically different lives of the two brothers and their societies, white and red.

Orion Outlaw, as his name suggests, is both a hunter and a man outside the law. He embodies the impulsiveness and restlessness that lay at the heart of the American pioneering spirit. Never content for long wherever he settles, Orion continually looks west for more fertile and open land. Such restlessness, which Gordon saw as typical of pioneers, had dire consequences for frontier settlements, leading to a weakening of family and social ties, a lack of law and order, and a deemphasis of spiritual values. While religious sects exist at the settlements, they are usually crudely organized and contradictory. When Orion's wife Jocasta, for instance, approaches the local minister for help in overcoming the guilt she feels about her child who was killed by Indians, she receives only a long-winded discourse on sin and affliction out of which she can make no sense.

Archy Outlaw, renamed the Bear-Killer, and his adopted Indian community stand in direct contrast to the impulsiveness and disorder of Orion and his society. Living with the Indians, Archy discovers unity of life and purpose within an ordered and defined society. His and the Indians' lives are established according to their places within a formalized community; absent is the fierce individualism that fragments white society. The Indian society is also based on religious beliefs and practices, again in stark contrast to the white settlements. Thomas H. Landess observes that while the whites have abandoned community ritual for a personal freedom that finally becomes destructive, the Indians live by ritual that "bonds the community together and defines the conduct of the tribe in terms of its relationship to the supernatural realm."[18]

Gordon's sympathetic portrayal of Indian society suggests that she was giving thought to the idea that a religiously oriented society, headed by a widely accepted authority, might be capable of transcending life's chaos. Yet Gordon's explorations here are tentative. The lessons we are to learn from this portrayal of the Indians are never firmly established, for the stable Indian society is merely a brief moment of light in a world of darkness. Gordon makes this perfectly clear in the novel when Orion and a group of whites destroy the last remnants of the Indian tribe, butchering scores of people, including Archy.

There is an almost imperceptible turn upwards at the very end of the novel, when Orion experiences a moment of insight into his ongoing desire to flee westward. This occurs after he returns home from the Indian massacre and finds his wife, Cassie, sick and dying. As his world crumbles about him, Orion now sees that the end results of perpetual flight are destruction and disorder. He recounts how as a boy he used to love to gaze at the constellation Orion in the night sky and imagine his namesake on mighty hunts. But now, as a man, he sees in the mythic hunter's group of stars "Orion fixed upon his burning wheel, always pursuing the bull but never making the kill. Did Orion will any longer the westward chase? No more than himself. Like the mighty hunter he had lost himself in the turning. Before him lay the empty west, behind him the loved things of which he was made. . . . Were not men raised into the westward turning stars only after they had destroyed themselves?"[19]

Orion's insight is significant; such moments of illumination for Gordon's defeated protagonists are markedly absent from her earlier novels. *Penhally* and *The Garden of Adonis*, for instance, also end in violent murder, but the protagonists gain no new insights. With Orion's new awareness, Gordon seems to suggest the possibility of renewal, that man may be able to reorder his broken life and pursue ways out of the chaos. And yet this affirmation is immediately negated, for the novel ends with Orion's stumbling out from the room where Cassie lies dead and into the darkness. He appears utterly broken, with little chance at achieving a reordering of his life by the light of his new knowledge.

The possibility for renewal was presented less ambiguously in the works that followed *Green Centuries*. With the publication of *The Women on the Porch* (1944), Gordon's work clearly entered a new stage, which had been foreshadowed by *Green Centuries* and which would last until her Catholic conversion in 1947. In the early 1940s, with the world locked in war, Gordon (like her husband Allen Tate) began to search for a system of order to transcend the dark nature of life. This quest is reflected in her one novel and several stories from this period.

In theme and focus, these new works resemble those coming before, with Gordon still exploring man's painful fate as seeker of order in a forbidding world. Once again she works with the

tensions of this quest, particularly those evolving from the realization that personal heroics are in the end futile. But there is a
crucial difference between these and the earlier works: where
the early works ended with the triumph of chaos and confusion,
the ones from the 1940s conclude with disorder being brought
into check. Out of the depths of despair, Gordon's characters
reach an understanding that there is a larger tradition, one
which transcends personal heroics and which can bring order
and unity into their lives. At this point in her career, Gordon
appeared uncertain about the nature of this tradition, and
seemed to waver between two alternatives, Christian and classical. Probably because of this uncertainty, coupled with the tentative nature of her faith in the possibility of achieving order, these
moments of reconciliation are presented with no trace of dog-
matism. We find, rather, at the end of these works, only a sense
that some kind of order and sanctity is available to man, and that
it lies waiting to be discovered out there in the whirling confusion of life.

*The Women on the Porch,* although loosely structured along the
lines of the Orpheus-Euridyce myth, suggests that this sanctity
lies in the Christian heritage. As Tate did in *Seasons of the Soul*
which was written at about the same time, Gordon here strips
away man's unsatisfactory pursuits at achieving happiness until
all that is left is the sanctity of Christian faith. Again like Tate in
*Seasons,* Gordon does not conclude with a victorious Christian
vision, but merely suggests, even more tentatively and ambiguously than Tate, that such faith is possible and viable.

Although the point of view shifts among a number of characters, thus giving us fairly full portraits of many of them, the
focus of the novel is on Catherine Chapman and her husband
Jim. The novel opens as Catherine flees New York City to her
ancestral home, Swan Quarter, a farm in Tennessee. Catherine
has discovered that Chapman, a history professor, has become
involved with one of his young female assistants. Catherine's
flight is an impulsive rejection of her husband; she also hopes to
discover how to reorder her now shattered life.

Swan Quarter, it turns out, is an appropriate place for
Catherine to reassess her life. There live her grandmother, aunt,
and niece (the "women on the porch"), all of whom in one way
or another have retreated from involvement in life. Eventually

Catherine takes her own lover, Tom Manigault (a neighbor), and decides to marry him after she obtains a divorce from Chapman. Meanwhile, Chapman realizes that his affair is empty and meaningless, and heads for Swan Quarter to seek a reconciliation with Catherine. When Catherine tells him about her affair with Tom, he is so shaken with rage that he strangles her; only Catherine's struggling fingers bring him out of his fit, and he releases his death-lock. After this confrontation, and Chapman's private reevaluation of his life later that night, the two reach a reconciliation that rejoins their lives.

Up until the very end, *The Women on the Porch* appears to be another of Gordon's novels portraying man's futile struggle against life's chaos. The action all along contributes to the bleakness: Catherine and Jim separate, Tom and his mother fight constantly, Mrs. Manigault's friend Roy Miller is caught in a homosexual liaison with a black youngster, the women at Swan Quarter live monotonous and blighted lives. These characters' efforts to renew their lives finally prove unsatisfactory, for they represent denials of life and of the responsibility to care for their loved ones. Mrs. Manigault's return to her farm is borne out of hate for and jealousy of her son Tom; Catherine's and Chapman's affairs are meaningless indulgences that threaten to destroy their marriage; Aunt Willy's devotion to her prize horse Red cuts her off from a man who loves her; Cousin Daphne, once cruelly jilted, turns for solace not to people but to her hobby of collecting mushrooms. The list could go on. Chapman's reflections upon life in New York make it clear that the environment at Swan Quarter is not solely to blame: "All over the city, people in their cubicles of stone or concrete or steel, lay as tight against one another as bees in their cells of wax, and even beyond the confines of the island the great, crowded ramparts flung themselves on and on until if one travelled far enough one might come to a building whose four walls housed one man and his wife and children."[20]

What allows the Chapmans to achieve their ultimate reconciliation, while those about them flounder in failure, is their recognition of the sanctity of their marriage. Long before they come together at the end, and even during those moments when they are acting out their betrayals of each other, both know, if not always at the conscious level, that they have gone astray. In

New York, with Catherine gone, Jim wanders the city aimlessly, haunted by lines from Dante's *Inferno:*

> In the middle of the journey of our life I came
> to myself in a dark wood where the straight way was lost.
>
> . . . . . . . . . . . . . . . . . . . . . . . . . . . . . . . . . . . . . . . . . . . . . . . . . . .
>
> I cannot rightly tell how I entered it, so full of sleep
> was I about the moment that I lost the true way . . .
>
> (*WP,* 83)

Catherine also thinks of her life in terms of a Dantean journey, though not so explicitly as Chapman. At one point she dreams of descending into a long dark tunnel, guiding a man who stands between her and another woman. The dream clearly embodies her situation with Jim and his illicit lover, and she recoils from the man's hand on her shoulder. But then comes a realization of her role as Beatrice for this man who "hovered between life and death": "She was about to shake it off when somebody on ahead called back to her that she must be vigilant, that the man's safety depended on her alone" (*WP,* 183).

Despite these warnings from within, Catherine and her husband continue to commune with the abyss and seem destined for destruction. The crisis occurs when Chapman shows up at Swan Quarter and learns of Catherine's infidelity. Utterly abandoned to his jealousy and his desire to hurt her as she has hurt him, he strangles her; her tugging fingers save her from death because they break his emotional spell, causing him to release her. Though he is not sure exactly how he knows or even if he is right, he senses that Catherine's gripping hands are reaching out to save not only her life but his. This realization, which he will ultimately confirm later, paves the way for his quest for wholeness and reconciliation.

Before Chapman can reach this state of fulfillment, however, he must first come to terms with the rootlessness of his life. This occurs later that evening when he wanders alone about Swan Quarter. At the farm's spring he encounters either the ghost of, or his own imaginary projection of (it is never made clear) the original Lewis who settled the land after the Revolutionary War. Chapman speaks to the figure, telling him not to stop and settle but to move on. Speaking from his own knowledge of how the Lewis family later splits apart, he says that the land is cursed and that his children "will have no fixed habitation, will hold no one spot dearer than another, will roam as savage as the buffalo that now flees your arquebus" (*WP*, 308). The figure says nothing, but only—so it seems to Chapman—looks back at him in mockery. Chapman eventually flees from the figure, hands before his face, fearing to look again into "the bold, shining stare of his eyes" (*WP*, 309).

What does Chapman fear seeing in those eyes? A true reflection of himself as homeless wanderer. For Chapman is the modern equivalent of Orion Outlaw from *Green Centuries;* he is a man without roots, a man, as Chapman himself admits at one point, with "no instincts, no convictions that are readily translatable into action" (*WP*, 281). On the train to Swan Quarter, he sees some soldiers, apparently headed for the distant battle lines of World War II, and he envies them: "But I wish I was one of them, for it is something, in this life, for a man to know where he is going, even if the appointment is with the minotaur" (*WP*, 286). This sense of purpose and this possession of ideals that one can act upon are what the figure of the ancestral Lewis also possesses; and Chapman's admonitions to him to move on ring empty, coming from a man whose intellectual confusions and fear of commitment have made him a mere dabbler in life. But the pioneer *will* settle the land of Swan Quarter, despite Chapman's warning, because it is good fertile land and it has been deeded to him; to do otherwise out of worry about how his descendants will perform would be to shirk his own commitment to do his best for himself and for those who depend upon him.

By the time Chapman sees Catherine the next morning, he has reached an understanding of the events of the night and now acknowledges his need for commitment. He realizes that this commitment must begin with his wife; he now knows that his love for her is of the utmost significance and that she is a figure, like Dante's Beatrice, who will guide him along the way of spiritual development. Moreover, he knows that their marriage bond is sanctified—holy and eternal and unbreakable. And so when Catherine's slipper falls from her foot, he stoops down at first to pick it up, but then to kiss her foot, offering her his forgiveness and reverence. He is ready to resume—begin, actually—his life.

With Chapman and Catherine's reconciliation, Gordon

closes *The Women on the Porch*. Though she has suggested that the way out of the modern malaise is Christian faith, she has done so without forcing the issue, and so subtly that it is possible to miss her message. The ending is indeed more ambiguous than my retelling of it, for Gordon was at this time avoiding in her art and life a definitive Christian resolution. In 1944, she was still without faith, still a seeker, still unsure about the validity of Christian belief. But as this novel shows, she was reassessing her earlier pessimism and actively considering Christianity as a way out of the darkness.

Evidence that Gordon had not yet fixed solidly on a belief in the Christian tradition is found in a short story from this period, "The Olive Garden" (1945). Here we find another rootless university professor, Edward Dabney, who like Jim Chapman eventually finds meaning and commitment. Yet Dabney's enlightenment is not Christian in scope, but classical; and Gordon seems to be suggesting here that identification with the heroes of the Western historical tradition is a path that, like Chapman's, lies open to modern man.

Dabney's illumination occurs in France, where he is visiting the village in which he and his fiancée had lived for a time years earlier, before they broke up. Much has changed for Dabney since his earlier days in Europe. Then he was enlivened with youthful love and energetic vision; now, ten years later, he is emotionally stale and intellectually fatigued. His return visit is bittersweet; it soon becomes obvious that the summer from his past stands as the most meaningful and important experience in his life—and it is long gone, lost and apparently irrecoverable. Dabney shows no signs that he carries any hope for renewal.

Near the end of the story, however, as he walks to the edge of a terrace overlooking the Mediterranean coast, Dabney has a moment of enlightenment. Looking down at the sea below, he thinks of those ancient heroes who have passed this way before him—Ulysses and the pirates from the days of Julius Caesar come directly to mind. He then thinks of Deucalion, who, he asserts, "was one hero lonelier than even Ulysses had been on his wanderings" (*CSCG*, 315). He goes on to ponder: "Deucalion, who, after the flood, walked the earth, companioned only by his wife, Pyrrha. The Delphic Oracle told them to strew the earth with the bones of their mother. Pyrrha shrank from the impiety, but Deucalion picked up stones and cast them far and wide and from those stones, just such stones as one found in this flinty soil, a new race of men had sprung up" (*CSCG*, 315).

These thoughts bring Dabney to a new level of awareness. He sees now that he—in fact everybody—is integrally linked to the classic Western tradition, and that by following the lead of the ancient heroes, he gains meaning and purpose in life. He now understands through the example of Deucalion that even after disaster and defeat, a person must resume his mission in life and renew his commitment to do the best he can. So refurbished, Dabney turns from the sea, and now all looks different: "He turned his back on the sea and walked along the moon-splotched path to the gate. He put a hand out as he went, touching a spray here, a flower there. The garden no longer seemed deserted. He did not now wish that he might meet somebody on its paths. Far below, in the rocky caves, that would always furnish refuge, that could, if they were needed, bring forth a new race of men, he could hear the heroes murmuring to each other" (*CSCG*, 315–16).

More than Tate, Gordon looked to the classical tradition as a source for furnishing modern man with meaning and order. With her profound interest in the role of the hero, she had throughout her career suggested parallels between her heroes and those of antiquity. But "The Olive Garden" marks an important shift. In earlier works, the parallels between modern man and the ancient heroes almost always pointed to a diminishment in the stature of contemporary man. Irony was inevitably present, and defeat before the forces of chaos and anarchy was imminent. In "The Olive Garden," however, the ironic vision is absent. Even though he lacks the stature of the active and energetic heroes of previous works, Edward Dabney achieves what they do not: a redemptive vision of man transcending time by taking his place in the ongoing traditions of the modern world. Tate had evoked this sort of vision in "The Mediterranean"—only to have a stark realization of the course of history come crashing through to shatter the spell. Gordon in the 1940s was more optimistic; for her the classical spirit still lived.

Together, *The Women on the Porch* and "The Olive Garden" represent the two traditions that Gordon was looking towards in the mid-1940s: Christianity and what might be called archetypal classicism. It would not be long before she would embrace the former while never completely repudiating the latter.

In 1947 Caroline Gordon joined the Catholic Church. Apparently the horrors of World War II, which prompted her to consider more seriously the flawed nature of humanity and the existence of the divine, influenced her decision. Certainly influential also were the struggles for faith that her husband Allen Tate was undergoing, though it would be three years before Tate became a Catholic. Like Tate, Gordon was also influenced by the example of Jacques Maritain, whom she met when she and Tate were at Princeton in the early 1940s. At the time of Gordon's conversion, Maritain, along with Étienne Gilson, was at the center of the Thomist revival in the United States, which was renewing interest in the Church for many intellectuals. Maritain's work and his personal example of the man of faith in the modern world influenced a number of writers and intellectuals, many of whom eventually joined the Church, Gordon among them. Later on, Maritain would also become a major influence on Gordon's literary criticism and fiction during the final stages of her life.

Finding faith, Gordon said in her essay "The Art and Mystery of Faith" (1950), meant discovering the key to life's puzzle. "In life, as well as in the writing of novels, faith is the key to the puzzle, the puzzle doesn't make any sense until you have the key," Gordon wrote. "I have been working at my particular puzzle all my life. It was only a few years ago that I got the key: faith."[21] She went on to say that discovering faith "revolutionized my life," and that "it is, to me, a little as if I had all my life been engaged in the writing of a novel and only recently had discovered that the plot is entirely different from what I thought it was!"[22] As a Catholic, Gordon now had a vital tradition and faith by which to structure her life and art.

Before her conversion, Gordon admitted in a letter to a Trappist monk, art had been her only religion. "I was nearly fifty years old," she wrote, "before I discovered that art is the handmaiden of the Church."[23] Her art now, she believed, had greater depth and was truer to reality, since her imagination was now fired with the Church's vision of the world and creation. "Mrs. Tate told me," Flannery O'Connor wrote (6 November 1955) to John Lynch, "that after she became a Catholic, she felt she could use her eyes and accept what she saw for the first time, she didn't have to make a new universe for each book but could take the one she found."[24]

But being a Catholic writer had its own challenges, not the least of which was what Gordon saw as the great gap in vision between the writer of faith and his secular reading audience. "Ours is the first age," Gordon wrote in an essay on Flannery O'Connor's *Wise Blood*, "in which a man would call himself educated and know no theology."[25] A Christian writer who ignored his audience's indifference to spiritual concerns did so at his own risk, for, as she and Tate wrote in *The House of Fiction* (1950), "Every masterpiece demands collaboration from the beholder."[26] Bridging the gap between writer and reader—that is, obtaining the reader's collaboration—was an important goal for all writers.

As a Catholic facing what she perceived as a hostile audience, Gordon gave much thought to this problem of bringing about a communion of author and reader. For the first time in her career she exerted a great deal of energy writing literary criticism, much of which defined and explored the problems that a Catholic writer faced in the modern world. One of her primary concerns now as a writer was understanding the reading public she faced, so that she could develop a fiction that would speak to her readers; consequently, in her major work of criticism, *How to Read a Novel* (1957), she explored the reading process and what readers bring away from the experience. Gordon's ideas on reading are significant for a full understanding of her postconversion fiction, for she began to shape her works in ways that she hoped not only would provide for a good story but also would force secular readers to expand their vision towards the divine.

Gordon believed that most modern readers read only for entertainment, and by this she meant that they sought through their reading merely to have their beliefs and values pleasantly reinforced. This kind of reader, she wrote in *How to Read a Novel*, "demands that his own moral code shall not be infringed upon, or his feelings lacerated by any unpleasant happenings in any books he reads"; in other words, demands "that the emotions aroused in him by the reading of any work of art shall not overflow into real life but shall be 'earthed'—and not far from his easy chair."[27] She goes on to say that this reader does not want to be improved by his reading, and she compares him to a picnicker who would rather rest in a valley than climb the surrounding mountains to enjoy the sweeping vistas. "If we spend all our time picnicking in the valley," Gordon writes, "we may come to feel that there is nothing worth seeing outside of it, may be tempted to dismiss as vain imaginings the wonders that our more energetic friends tell us they have viewed from the mountaintop and, losing touch with reality, become prisoners of our own inanition" (*HTRN*, 225).

In contrast to this safe and easy reading (in Gordon's terms, reading for amusement) is the more difficult but more rewarding enterprise, reading for enjoyment. To read for enjoyment, the reader must lay himself open to the reading experience, repressing for the time being his prejudices and opinions so that they do not overshadow the author's subject matter and point of view. Attaining this detachment and humility, Gordon says, is a very difficult accomplishment, one which few achieve. But it is only through striving for this openness and self-effacement that a reader may learn more about life and himself. "The truth of our own lives," Gordon writes, "is written in the lives—and the looks—of others. 'To see ourselves as others see us' is always a rewarding experience even if it is sometimes trying" (*HTRN*, 233). Gordon quotes Melville's phrase, "shock of recognition"— by way of Edmund Wilson—to describe the knowledge a good reader gets from a worthwhile book: this shock is a crystallization in the reader's mind of "ideas, opinions, even emotions, of which the reader himself was only half aware" (*HTRN*, 228). This moment of truth joins thinking minds from throughout the centuries in a joyous camaraderie.

Giving her readers that "shock of recognition" is what Gordon sought to do with her postconversion fiction. She knew that this would be no easy task, given the fact that, in her eyes, the modern reading public was for the most part lazy and complacent. Moreover, she saw this reading public as being primarily unmoved by religious concerns and resistant to the intrusion of any religious elements; for Gordon, now a Catholic, these spiritual matters were now at the heart of her vision. In a letter to a Trappist monk, she expressed the distance she saw between her assumptions of the subject matter of fiction and those of her readers: "It is taken for granted, by the majority of reviewers of fiction that grace—supernatural grace—is not a proper subject for fiction, when it seems to me, the interworkings, intertwinings of natural grace and supernatural grace (or the lack of it) are the only subjects for fiction, from the Greek tragedians on down."[28]

In this same letter, Gordon said that she admired the work of James Baldwin because it smashes through the delusion that God's grace has no place in fiction; her observation here also expressed what she hoped to achieve in her own fiction. To this end, she resorted in her fiction to some strategies of shock and distortion, which she hoped would shake her readers and perhaps compel them to recognize the religious message embodied in these works. Though their fiction is not recognizably similar on the surface, Gordon and Flannery O'Connor (who were friends and correspondents) in this respect shared similar approaches to assaulting the secular reader. The following observation from O'Connor's "The Fiction Writer and Her Country" is an apt statement of both O'Connor's and Gordon's approach to fiction: "When you can assume that your audience holds the same beliefs you do, you can relax a little and use more normal means of talking to it; when you have to assume that it does not, then you have to make your vision by shock—to the hard of hearing you shout and for the almost-blind you draw large and startling pictures."[29]

As O'Connor often did, Gordon frequently structured her fiction written in the decade following her conversion around a sudden reversal in the story's motion, often coming in a moment of extreme violence at the very end of the work. This jolt was Gordon's representation of divine grace manifesting itself in the world. Reversing the flow of the piece, which up until the moment of grace appeared to be moving towards a realization of man's inability to establish order in a chaotic present, the intrusion of the divine represents a bringing to order—indeed a transcendence—of all the tumult that came before. The focus of the story shifts in one fell swoop, from man's efforts to deal with disorder to the moment when a lost soul discovers God. And this shocking turnaround, wherein Gordon's characters are humbled before the Lord, also, Gordon hoped, humbles the reader, paving the way for his acceptance of Christ.

Using such a bold fictional strategy of course had its risks. To make the miracle of grace believable to an audience of unbelievers was a task of the highest order, and there were many ways to go wrong. Father John W. Simons, in his review of Gordon's *The Malefactors*, writes of difficulties facing the Catholic writer: "A conversion is admittedly a special invasion of Grace into a particular life. If the artist, in his effort to summon the mystery, gives a maximum plausibility to the motives and conditions leading up to conversion he risks an attenuation of the essentially free character of Grace. If he gives a maximum permissiveness to Grace he risks making his character seem the puppet of Grace. In this case it is the art which seems implausible, for God becomes an almost literal *deus ex machina*."[30]

Unfortunately, Gordon's moments of conversion often do appear to be a Catholic *deus ex machina,* forced and artificial. Drawn with an unduly heavy hand, the abrupt turnarounds at the end of her works tend not to compel the reader to open himself up to a similar experience but rather to make him feel cheated. Often the endings appear to be staged tricks, the action leading up to them merely a series of deft manipulations setting up the surprises. Once so complex and rich, Gordon's artistic vision seems in these later works noticeably diminished.

Adding to the thinness of her postconversion works was the absence in them of many of the tensions that had earlier fired her imagination and had added depth to her fiction. With her new-found faith, Gordon no longer struggled, as she once had, with the dilemma arising from what she saw as man's tragic condition as lost wayfarer striving to establish a dignified existence—an existence finally destroyed by life's dark forces. As a result of this profound shift in outlook, she does not give the characters in her later works the compassionate portrayal that she had given to their equally melancholy forebears. The lost souls of her postconversion works appear mean and trivial, possessing little dignity in their search for meaning—until, that is, they find the Church. That these characters, unpleasant as they are, are able to discover God's way and accept their redemption constitutes, of course, much of Gordon's point: that the Church is open to all. But often her characters appear so unattractive and empty that the reader finds it hard to care what happens to them or to believe that they would accept God's grace.

The first novel Gordon wrote after her conversion, *The Strange Children* (1951), suffers from these problems, although it remains interesting and not altogether unsuccessful. On its basic level, the novel is the story of a young girl's attempts to make sense out of the intricate entanglements between her parents and a group of friends who have come to visit at her family's Tennessee farm. With Lucy, the nine-year-old girl, as the central intelligence, the novel follows the slow and often painful growth in her understanding of the "strange children" of the title—the adults who people the farm.

Almost all of the adults of the novel are somehow warped or blighted. Lucy's parents are Aleck Maury's daughter Sarah and her husband Stephen Lewis, who had appeared earlier in *Aleck Maury, Sportsman*. They are now even more cynical than before in their cold intellectualism. This is particularly true of Stephen. His life centers on his poetry and his Civil War research—and on his enjoyment of showing off his knowledge of a wide range of subjects, usually at the expense of others. Though not quite so arrogant as her husband and more open to experience than he is, Sarah is of the same ilk, a cynical intellectual. Lucy says that her grandfather Aleck Maury finds them boring, and so does she. She can see that their lives are focused on talk rather than action, and that their words are almost always in some way critical of others.

Also living on the farm are the MacDonoughs, a poor tenant family who are fanatic religious fundamentalists. Their lives of intense religious commitment and emotional expressions of faith stand at the far extreme from the Lewises' intellectualism. Their lives focus on one thing: Jesus. Little else is important to them, as Lucy notices: "They hardly ever mentioned the radio or politics or even the Depression. They mostly just talked about God. When Mr. MacDonough or Mrs. MacDonough said 'Jesus' you felt as if He were in the next room."[31] When her parents talk about religion, in contrast, the wonders of faith shrivel to the dryness of scholarship for scholarship's sake. "Up at the house you didn't feel like you were likely to see Jesus," Lucy observes, "though her father and mother talked about him a good deal, too. *The man who fell among thieves.* It didn't seem like a real man, though, or real thieves. . . . *The grain of mustard seed.* . . . Her father said he wasn't sure that it was the same kind of mustard that Mr. MacDonough planted there on the side of the hill for greens, or not. And those people who went through the field plucking corn weren't plucking corn at all, her father said, just ears of wheat. 'In King James' time they had never heard of corn. Corn is one of the plants we got from the New World'" (*SCh*, 108–9).

Other "strange children" come to visit the farm. First to arrive is "Uncle Tubby," a poet and friend of the Lewises, who has recently struck it big in the popular market. Tubby is a dashing figure, yet he is also a snob. Furthermore, he is very devious. Then come Kevin Reardon and his wife, Isabel. Kevin is a recently converted Catholic and a millionaire; he is considering giving away his fortune to the Church to establish a contemplative order. Isabel does not share Kevin's faith and is clearly upset about her husband's financial plans and their marriage in general.

At the farm, the interaction between this odd collection of adults becomes at times filled with tension and cruelty. The central conflict involves Tubby's efforts to draw Isabel away from Kevin; he sees himself as a knight on a quest to save a damsel in distress. Kevin, meanwhile, appears to be on the brink of insanity; his commitment to the Church seems to be merely an overzealous reaction to a vision he reputedly had after an automobile accident. "I tell you that lick on his head turned him queer!" Tubby says (*SCh*, 186), and his observation seems fair.

Lucy cannot quite understand all of what is happening, but she can sense the dissonance and danger in the interplays of the adults. For her, a child in the process of growing into adulthood, the problem becomes not just one of comprehending the adults' actions but of discovering how she will structure her own life in the apparently chaotic adult world. She seems to have few alternatives. She can see the pettiness and arrogance of her parents, and says at one point that she will grow up different from them. And although she is fascinated by the zeal of Kevin and the MacDonoughs, their religious commitment seems otherworldly and mysterious. More comforting to Lucy is escaping the harsh realities of the world by coloring them according to the lights of the story *Undine* and by daydreaming of becoming a horse trainer. Neither of these pursuits, however, provides her with a satisfactory way to approach the world: the former is merely an escape into fantasy and the latter an unrealistic dream (she seems to have little riding ability), a retreat from the world of people to that of animals. Lucy's emergence into adulthood seems destined to transform her into one of the "strange children."

But then, at the end of the novel, everything is turned around when Tubby and Isabel run off together. Suddenly the true nature of events becomes clear. Asserting a dependable saneness that stands in marked contrast to the instability of the others, Kevin reveals that Isabel has been hopelessly insane for some time. He says that, despite his warnings, Tubby had refused to believe this, and preferred to see Isabel's instability as a reaction to her marriage with Kevin. Once seen as a crazy religious fanatic, Kevin now emerges as the symbol of stability and order. His Catholic faith, we are now shown, provides the way of deliverance from the world of "the strange children," and the answer to the exhortation from Psalm 144 from which the title comes: "Rid me and deliver me from the hand of strange children, whose mouth speaketh vanity." (The MacDonoughs' brand of faith, in contrast, appears at the end wild and disordered; Mr. MacDonough almost dies when he is bitten by a snake he is handling during a service.)

Lucy acknowledges her acceptance of Kevin's new role when she returns his crucifix, which she had earlier taken. Even Stephen, the most callous character in the novel, is stunned by the strange turnaround in events, and experiences a religious epiphany. At one point earlier in the novel, he had gazed at the stars and listened while Tubby had mused on the far-distant future when the moon, he said, would eventually crash into the earth; but when he looks at the stars now, Stephen envisions a Judgment Day wrought by God, not by gravity. After thinking of what Tubby had said about his (Stephen's) Scorpio zodiac sign ("The House of Death—unless a man be reborn" [*SCh*, 302]), he sees two falling stars, and thinks of the day when all the stars will fall, "when the heavens were rolled up like a scroll and the earth reeled to and fro like a drunkard and men called upon the mountains to fall upon them and hide them from the wrath to come" (*SCh*, 302–3). Then comes a vision in which the pattern of his life takes new shape:

> He passed his hand over his brow. His eyes went to the house below where a single lamp glowed murkily. There a man still lay at the point of death. He told himself that it would have been no great

matter if that man had died tonight, for all men, it appeared to him now, for the first time, die on the same day: the day on which their appointed task is finished. If that man had made his last journey tonight he would not have gone alone, but companioned by a larger presence, as the friend standing behind him had been companioned when he, too, lay at the point of death, in a strange country and in a desert. But all countries, he told himself wearily, are strange and all countries desert. He thought of another man, the friend of his youth, who only a few minutes ago had left his house without farewell. He had considered him the most gifted of all his intimates. Always when he thought of that friend a light had seemed to play about his head. He saw him now standing at the edge of a desert that he must cross: if he turned and looked back his face would be featureless, his eye sockets blank. Stephen Lewis thought of days, of years that they had spent together. He saw that those days, those years had been moving toward this moment and he wondered what moment was being prepared for him and for his wife and his child, and he groaned, so loud that the woman and the child stared at him, wondering, too. (*SCh*, 303)

With this daring vision, the point of view unexpectedly shifting from Lucy to Stephen, *The Strange Children* ends. As Kevin's emergence as the mainstay of order forces a reevaluation of the characters, Stephen's vision changes the focus of the novel: *The Strange Children*, we see now, is as much a novel about the workings of divine grace as it is a novel of adolescent initiation. By drawing us away from Lucy at the end, Gordon emphasizes that divine grace may enter into the lives not just of the young at heart and those who repent (as Lucy does when she returns Kevin's crucifix) but into anyone's, even into that of the cold and unfeeling Stephen. We can see now that the novel contains a pattern of conversions (or at least experiences that may lead to conversions; what Lucy and Stephen do with their new knowledge is not spelled out) in which a shock experience forces a reevaluation of one's life, and prepares one for accepting God's grace.

The very structure of the novel embodies the same kind of shock experience Gordon intended for the reader. By turning these things around so drastically at the end, forcing a complete reassessment of the characters and the novel's focus, Gordon hoped to shake up the complacent modern readers whom she viewed as her audience. She wanted to shock their sensibilities so that, like Stephen at the novel's end, they would readjust their vision of the world in light of the divine. Gordon's assault on the reader brings to mind Flannery O'Connor's remarks to a fellow writer: "You can suggest something obvious is going to happen but you cannot have it happen in a story. You can't clobber any reader while he is looking. You divert his attention, then you clobber him, and he never knows what hit him."[32]

Unfortunately, the bold strategy Gordon used in *The Strange Children* to communicate with a secular audience is not entirely successful. The turnaround at the end is too forced; the reader is made to feel that what came before was not a faithful portrayal of life, but merely part of an intricate game plan leading up to the trick ending. Moreover, the shift to Stephen's point of view, after the point of view has rested with Lucy for the entire novel, is distracting. Although this technical maneuver is crucial to Gordon's message, it asks too much of the reader, and only adds to his suspicions that the author's main goal at the end is to manipulate him with outrageous tricks. One leaves *The Strange Children* disappointed, and unconvinced that the novel's characters have in fact transcended their problems through the grace of God.

Gordon's next novel, *The Malefactors* (1956), also relies heavily on shock effects and unexpected reversals, and like *The Strange Children* it is not entirely successful because Gordon fails to use these techniques convincingly. In *The Malefactors*, it appears almost that Gordon believes she can reveal the necessity of Catholic faith merely by presenting its presence at the end as a way to solve all the problems raised throughout the novel. Though ushered in with a drastic turnaround in plot that Gordon hopes will open the reader to its significance, this Catholic *deus ex machina* device nonetheless appears to be too pat and easy a resolution, particularly for readers of the modern age not open to such persuasion.

*The Malefactors* is primarily the story of Tom Claiborne, a middle-aged poet who embarks on a quest of sorts to reinvigorate his life with meaning and purpose. In the novel's early chapters, it soon becomes clear that Tom has lost his inspiration for both life and poetry; he spends a good deal of his time in his study, supposedly writing, but usually just lying around in a stupor. He feels locked in an unsatisfactory routine, and his mental fatigue makes him suffer almost physical pain, as if his bones itched. In the opening scene, a party organized by his wife, he obediently makes the rounds with all the guests, but it is obvious that he finds most of these friends, as well as his wife, unendurably dull.

At times, Tom dreams of living a different life, but these yearnings remain vague and tentative and seem completely unrealistic. Twice, early in the novel, he gives thought to alternative lives for himself, but he quickly rejects both schemes without serious consideration. One alternative is merely to retreat from life and live alone as a hermit. When a friend tells him of a hermit she knows, he remembers a time when he visited a farm where a hermit lived in a dilapidated stable. Tom was fascinated by the makeshift home, and he acknowledged to himself that "this is the way I'd like to have it. This is the way we'd all like to have it if we could only find it."[33] Years later this attraction still haunts him, though he realizes that he could never live in such a way. Another alternative is to ground his life in religious faith. Though he does not actively seek out religious conviction, a part of him is receptive to the order and purpose that an active faith would bring. When he sees a friend praying before a statue of St. Ciannic, he thinks: *"I would give anything to pray!"* (*Mal*, 88). Tom's egotism and cynicism, however, effectively smother any urge in him for a life of faith and for spiritual salvation, and he never makes any real move towards the Church.

Tom's religious skepticism certainly seems warranted, judging from the thoughts and actions of those people of faith with whom Tom comes in contact. Religion, and specifically Catholicism, appears to be merely a naive and faddish solution to life's complex problems. The example of Tom's friend Catherine Pollard, once an unhappy and dissipated woman and now, at the time of the novel, a Catholic lay worker, underscores this impression of religious faith. Early in the novel, she admits that she joined the Church after Tom had told her to give up her writing and do "anything! Get drunk. Join the Church" (*Mal*, 80–81). She says she knew Tom was speaking metaphorically, "but that was the first time it had ever occurred to me that *I* could join the Church" (*Mal*, 80–81). After a bout of drinking, and with a terrible hangover, she began instruction for the Church.

Catherine's conversion seems less an act of faith than an impulsive retreat from her failures.

Once in the Church, Catherine adopts what seems to be a naive and facile idealism. She works for a project called the "Green Revolution," which operates a communal farm for the downtrodden and a soup kitchen in New York City where nuns peddle religion, along with free meals, to people who would just as soon eat in quiet. Catherine may have gained some direction and purpose by joining the Church, but her life—and the Church's as well—seems insignificant, almost frivolous, and out of touch with reality.

The answer to Tom's emptiness and boredom apparently comes with the arrival of Cynthia Vail, a young woman who has just left her husband and aspires to be a poet. He initiates an affair with her, thereby shattering his marriage and his old way of life. At first Tom seems to recover his old energies, both to love and to create, and he seems a new man when he moves to New York with Cynthia to become the editor of a new literary journal.

But this new life soon begins to sour. His relationship with Cynthia deteriorates, as it becomes obvious that her primary motive for the affair is a desire for the literary advancement that Tom can bring her. His editorship proves to be as empty and indeed as tedious as his love life. And even more distressing, he realizes that he still cannot write poetry. The most surprising and disturbing factor is that he finds himself missing his wife, Vera, in a vague and undefined way.

As the structures of Tom's new life crumble, he realizes that he is in an even more precarious position than he had been in when he was living with Vera. Now he is essentially alone in the city, without any meaningful vocation or relationship, and without the security of his former life. His hope for a better life evaporates; and he cannot seek a reconciliation with Vera because she refuses to see or talk with him. He is not even sure he wants to. When Vera tries to commit suicide as a result of his desertion, Tom sinks even deeper into despair. Terrible nightmares haunt his consciousness; awake and asleep he lives in torment.

In the midst of his deteriorating life, Tom once again comes face-to-face with the alternative of the Church and once again rejects it. This confrontation occurs when Sister Immaculata, a nun who is preparing a biography of Horne Watts, a homosexual poet and victim of suicide who had been a friend of Tom's (Watts bears an obvious resemblance to Hart Crane), asks him to come to the Green Revolution soup kitchen for an interview for her research. There Tom meets Joseph Tardieu, the founder of the Green Revolution who is now a tottering old man apparently bordering on insanity resulting from a stroke. Using the arrogant prerogative of the mad, Tardieu tells Tom to go and read St. Augustine for guidance. Not surprisingly, Tom does not take Tardieu seriously; along with the Church he represents, Tardieu appears ridiculous and out of touch with life.

Tom's interview with Sister Immaculata only deepens this impression. Her interpretation of the debauched and depraved life of Watts seems wild and irresponsible. She believes that all the dead poet's perversions—his homosexuality, his drunkenness, his blood lust, his suicide—were his own tortured ways of seeking the mysteries of God and salvation. Drawing a parallel between Watts's long poem *Pontifex,* with its central symbol of a bridge (evidently, as in Crane's *The Bridge,* the Brooklyn Bridge) and St. Catherine of Siena's *Divino Dialogo,* she develops the idea that Watts's fascination with the bridge stemmed from his vision of it as the "Humanity of the Word." "It's the Humanity of the Word is the bridge between earth and heaven," she tells Tom. "And it has three steps: the feet that were nailed to the cross, the side that was pierced to reveal the ineffable love of the heart, and the mouth in which gall and vinegar were turned to sweetness. Horne ran to and fro among creatures like a madman, but he ran along the bridge too, else how could he have brought back the stones of virtue that he planted in his garden" (*Mal,* 241–42).

Sister Immaculata's interpretation seems to Tom bizarre and unconvincing. His own explanation for Watts's fascination with the bridge is a good deal more prosaic and plausible: there were homosexual hangouts in the neighborhood around the bridge where he could pick up disembarking sailors. Sister Immaculata's theory, which he sees coming from "the cracked brain of an old nun" (*Mal,* 241), only underscores for Tom the unreality of the Church.

After his visit with Sister Immaculata, Tom breaks with Cynthia and sinks deeper into his nightmare existence. He talks with his cousin George Crenshaw, a psychiatrist, and decides to visit Vera, who is now working at a Green Revolution farm. He is hoping for a reconciliation, but an inner voice taunts him, saying he is a man beset by a pernicious and egotistical pride. *"There isn't anything to go back to—"* the voice says, *"except that circle that long ago you described and then of your own free will stepped inside, keeping it inviolate by flailing down any living thing that sprung up in it, so that there should be left in it nothing but yourself and the air that goes in and out of your rotting lungs."* "Would a woman," the voice continues, *"want to step again inside that circle, breathe again that impoverished air?"* (*Mal,* 298). Despite these taunts, Tom seeks out Vera. There is nowhere else for him to turn, as everything else has failed.

Tom's visit with Vera is disastrous. He finds her tending both a mute child and the increasingly senile Joseph Tardieu. Tom sees Vera's care of these two invalids as degrading and humiliating; when she says that she plans to adopt the child and look after Tardieu, he cruelly berates her. He then tells her that he is leaving for good: "You're rid of me! You can do any damn thing you want to do. Spend the rest of your life working in an orphan asylum . . . or an insane asylum if that suits you better. . . . Have a religious conversion!" (*Mal* 306). Vera cries out that she thinks she may already have had a conversion, and Tom rushes blindly away.

As Tom returns to the city, there is little reason to expect an upward turn in events. Everything is in ruins, and his life is utterly devastated. But now an unexpected and unlikely event occurs, which brings him to a point where he can accept God's grace. When he returns to his apartment, he dreams of being led through a cave by Horne Watts; Watts stops and points to a kneeling woman who turns and looks at Tom. Tom recognizes her as Catherine Pollard. When Tom awakes he goes to the soup kitchen's chapel to lay flowers at the altar and to find Catherine, who he is sure has a message for him. There Catherine tells him that she has been praying for him and Watts, and she counsels him to return to Vera, who, she explains, was baptized a Catholic as a child (Tom did not know this). "A wife is subject to her husband, as the Church is subject to Christ," she says (*Mal,* 311).

Tom now understands that the sanctity of religious faith and Christian marriage must lie at the center of his life, and that faith in Christ is humanity's bulwark against chaos. Acknowledging his conversion with a kiss for Catherine, he sets off on his journey back to the work farm and Vera.

Here the novel ends, with Gordon pointing to Catholicism as the way to transcend the modern malaise. By reversing so suddenly the direction of the novel, she means to jar readers and force them to recognize the importance of the spiritual issues she introduces at the end. She has delayed making a clear statement of her Catholic sympathies to catch her readers unaware; she hopes by this bold maneuver to get their attention and to underscore her message of faith. Moreover, by the time Gordon poses Catholicism as the answer to Tom's plight and more generally to that of modern man, she has already worked through in the novel a number of other possible ways to bring order, all of which fail. Her message is that one chooses Catholicism or chaos; there are no other alternatives. With eyes burned clean by divine grace, Tom comes to this realization and makes his choice: Gordon's readers are implicitly challenged to share in Tom's vision and follow his lead.

As in *The Strange Children*, Gordon's strategy does not work smoothly. Tom's conversion at the end is purposely abrupt and startling, but unconvincing; it seems unlikely that Tom would find and embrace the Church primarily because of a dream, for this action works against every tendency he has shown throughout the novel and could easily be viewed as another impulsive decision doomed like the others to failure. Once again, the reader is likely to feel that the ending is a manipulation merely for the expression of the author's theological message. The conclusion may succeed in terms of theology but not in terms of fiction. In most good religious literature, the larger spiritual issues arise straight from the action itself; only when this integrity is achieved can the story then suggest a convincing meaning beyond the literal in a way that the reader must acknowledge, even without full agreement with the work's spiritual vision. This is not the case with *The Malefactors*.

Gordon was a good deal more successful in merging her religious message with her fiction in a story from this period, "The Presence" (1947). In this story, Gordon returns again to

Aleck Maury, who is now too enfeebled for any type of sport. He spends his days at the boarding house of two friends, Jim and Jenny Mowbray, living the adventures of the hunt vicariously through Jim's exploits. As he frequently did in the earlier works about him, here too Maury ponders his approaching death. Maury's fears of the problems of old age intensify when Jenny discovers that Jim wants to desert her for one of the young female boarders; if Jenny carries through with her threats to divorce Jim and sell the boarding house and move away, Maury's everyday stability will be destroyed. Pondering the whole disturbing situation, he retreats to his room, where he has a moment of religious enlightenment. He thinks of a time in his childhood when he had sat in the room of his dying Aunt Vic, a Roman Catholic who had raised Maury after his mother had died. As Maury was reciting the Angelic Salutation (Aunt Vic had taught him Catholic liturgy), his aunt had witnessed a vision which the boy could not see, and then had died. Thinking of this long-past experience, Maury is once again driven to his knees to pray to the Virgin: "Holy Mary, Mother of God, pray for us sinners, now and at the *hour* . . . of our death" (*CSCG*, 120).

Several things make this story a good deal more powerful than *The Strange Children* and *The Malefactors.* One is that Gordon does not deal as contemptuously with Maury as she did with the protagonists in the two novels. In those longer works, Gordon emphasized the trivial and indeed evil nature of man's efforts to achieve a private order; not heroism but vanity and destructive pride lie at the heart of these attempts. In the novels, her characters, such as Stephen Lewis and Tom Claiborne, are for the most part unlikable and uninspiring, and the reader finds it hard to maintain much interest in them. In "The Presence," however, Gordon writes about her beloved Aleck Maury, image of her father and man of passion and zest. Maury is certainly faulted in the story (he focuses his concern for Jenny and Jim, for instance, not on the problems now facing his friends, but on his losing a place to stay); nonetheless, he still possesses a dignity and stature that Stephen Lewis and Tom Claiborne lack. Indeed, there is so much feeling in this story for Maury that one almost feels that Gordon wrote it because she *wanted* him to become a Catholic and achieve salvation. Such intensity of feeling adds a depth missing from *The Strange Children* and *The Malefactors.*

The ending of "The Presence," which, like those of the two novels, is built on a stunning reversal, is also much more successful, partly because Gordon does not overplay her hand. Certainly Maury's appeal to the Virgin is shocking, coming from him, but given the circumstances—a man near death, whose world has suddenly begun crumbling about him—his reaching out for religious faith is certainly believable. With this conclusion, Gordon successfully underscores the limitations of Maury's life while at the same time showing how a crisis may open up an individual to the divine. "It is at a time like this," says Miss Gilbert to Maury, explaining why she chose to read litanies to comfort the distraught Jenny, "when the hard core of the personality is shattered, that the real self has a chance to emerge" (*CSCG*, 119). Maury himself experiences such an emergence at the end of the story, and Gordon implicitly challenges the reader to do the same.

After the publication of *The Malefactors* in 1956, Gordon's fiction went off in a new direction, away from being explicitly Catholic. She now began to base her work on classical myths and archetypal patterns of experience, with a particular emphasis on those of the hero. Perhaps after her initial discovery of the Church, which brought with it an enthusiasm for its order and resolution, she realized that there was a part of her which remained unsatisfied: that part which had a strong sympathy for man's courage against the dark forces of life. She had carried these feelings with her since her upbringing and for decades, before her conversion to Catholicism, had placed them at the forefront of her vision of life and art. In a sense what she now tried to do was to reinvigorate her work with this awareness of man's heroic battles against the forces of evil. She sought, in other words, to merge the classical hero with the Christian, thereby unifying the two important traditions of her life.

What might be called Gordon's manifesto for her new fiction came in an essay she wrote for the *Sewanee Review* in 1953, "Some Readings and Misreadings." Here she develops a definition of Christian art that is based not on its literal subject matter, but on its archetypal patterns. She opens the essay with two passages from Jacques Maritain's *Art and Scholasticism*, passages central to her new line of thinking:

By Christian art I do not mean *ecclesiastical* art, an art specified by an object, an end and definite rules. By Christian art I mean art bearing on the face of it the character of Christianity. Christian art in this sense is not a particular genus of the species art; we do not talk of Christian art as we do of pictorial art or poetic, Gothic or Byzantine art. A young man does not say to himself: "I am going in for Christian art" as he might say "I am going in for agriculture." There is no school for teaching Christian art. The definition of Christian art is to be found in its subject and its spirit; we talk of Christian art or the art of a Christian as we talk of the art of the bee or the art of man. It is Christianity redeemed.

. . . wherever art, Egyptian, Greek, or Chinese, has attained a certain degree of grandeur and purity, it is already Christian. . . . Christian in hope, because every spiritual splendour is a promise and a symbol of the divine harmonies of the Gospel.[34]

Gordon goes on, citing Maritain as her authority, to develop the idea that "a novelist's conscious mind may be influenced by what is going on around him, he may announce himself a pragmatist, a skeptic, an atheist while his creative faculties seem to move in and subscribe to a totally different order."[35] This leads her to conclude that the imaginations of many fiction writers of the nineteenth and twentieth centuries followed patterns of Christian symbolism rather than those of contemporary thought. Many of their works, she says, are based on "the Christian Scheme of Redemption," what she calls a "primal plot." This she defines later as an archetype "so deeply rooted in us all that . . . we may apprehend it without realizing what we are doing."[36]

Most striking here is Gordon's idea, drawn from Maritain, that a work need not be explicitly Christian to be called Christian. The pivotal focus in a work of fiction has become for her not its surface (though obviously she does not ignore this) but the archetypes that lie deep beneath. "A fiction—a novel, a short story, a play—comes into being," she wrote later in an essay entitled "On Learning to Write," "when one of these timeless patterns reveals itself in time in a conflict in which human beings are involved."[37] The great artists are those who intuit these archetypal patterns and allow them to inform their work.

Gordon's interest in archetypal knowledge signaled her renewed interest in the classics. She saw the classics as storehouses of archetypal patterns, and, as such, embodiments of the knowledge found in the unconscious mind of all of us. To study the classics, for Gordon, was to realize that we all possess inside us demons we must confront and do battle with, as did the ancient heroes. By descending into the dark abyss of the unconscious mind to wrestle with the powers of darkness, man assumes the role of classic hero and gains knowledge of the inner realities of life. And this knowledge, she believed, led ultimately to a Christian vision, since, as she pointed out in a letter to a Trappist monk, "there is only one author, the Holy Ghost and only one book, a book made up of His revelations—even if we get hold of only one page at a time."[38] The classical hero, in other words, ultimately develops into the Christian hero.

Gordon's desire to merge the classical and Christian heroes was foreshadowed in *The Malefactors*. There the psychiatrist George Crenfew, who helps Tom in his decision to return to Vera, says that his knowledge of life lies in his study of the ancient heroes. "I'm not so deep," he tells Tom. "It's like I told you. I'm just a fellow keeps on thinking about the heroes" (*Mal*, 278). George then reminds Tom of his own earlier study of the classics, and Tom takes the hint. Just before he drives out to the work farm to seek out Vera, he thinks of several ancient heroes (Perseus, Theseus, Herakles) and attempts, even if he does not draw any successful conclusions, to understand his situation through theirs.

Despite this focus on the classical hero, *The Malefactors* remains a novel formed primarily by Gordon's Catholic vision. Her new approach to fiction, with its central union of archetypal and Christian vision, did not fully emerge until her story "One Against Thebes" (1961, originally entitled "The Dragon's Teeth"), which is a rewritten version of her first published story, "Summer Dust" (1929). Both versions are about a young girl confronting the disillusioning knowledge that comes with growing up, but there are some important differences, which reveal Gordon's new interests. The original story follows the basic plot pattern of her early work, with a character, here Sally Maury, confronting the chaotic nature of life with no satisfactory way in which to order it. When Sally has the upsetting experiences of overhearing a tenant call her parents ugly names and her brother and a friend talk about sexual adventure, she retreats into the comforting world of fairy tale. But her fairy-tale vision is finally an inadequate guide for growing up, because it is a retreat from life and provides no realistic interpretation of it. The story ends with her mind drifting from the hot summer into a pleasant dream world, where a fairy godmother promises to lead her, the little princess, away on a cloud to a distant crystal palace.

"One Against Thebes" also ends with the young girl (she is not named here) having a similar fairy-tale vision, but with a crucial difference. In this later story, the girl prefaces the vision with the observation that she will never see her fairy tale book again because she has given it away; referring to the vision, she says it is a mere remembrance of words. Unlike Sally Maury in "Summer Dust," who retreats to the fairy-tale world for safety, the young girl in "One Against Thebes" has outgrown fairy tales and in her vision gives them only one last backward glance. The story suggests that this girl (unlike Sally Maury) will go on to order her life around her knowledge of archetypal experience, just as her father, a classics scholar, does. She reveals her already strong awareness of archetypal knowledge when she watches a boy make snakelike marks with his feet in the dusty road:

> She stepped to one side of the road to avoid the serpentine trail that Son's feet had left in the dust. . . . Her father said Heracles and her grandmother said Hercules but they were the same person. . . . Aunt Maria didn't know that serpents were the same as snakes. . . . Sometimes they were called monsters instead of serpents and sometimes they were called dragons and were big enough to cover a whole acre and when they threw their heads back fire came out instead of breath—enough to burn up the whole countryside. But no matter how large they were or where they lived they always had tails like snakes. And their heads were snaky, too. Sometimes there would be seven or nine serpent heads on one body. Like the Lernean Hydra. That was the first monster that Heracles killed. (*CSCG*, 133)

With this knowledge, the girl does not retreat from life, but attempts to plumb its depths; and in so doing (we can infer from what Gordon says elsewhere) she will eventually discover that at the wellspring of life flows the spirit of the Holy Ghost.

With "One Against Thebes" Gordon sought to bring together her classical and Christian visions, though the Christianity is barely visible, residing not on the story's surface but in what Gordon saw as its "primal plot." Her writing here regains some of the depth and power of her early work, primarily because with it Gordon once again explores the trials and exploits of the hero. By the end of "One Against Thebes" the young heroine of the story is to Gordon just that—a true heroine, a battler against the evil forces of life. As the title suggests, her efforts resemble those of the ancient heroes who battled the evil forces at Thebes; and her use of archetypes to understand and explore life is the "way" referred to in the lines from *Oedipus at Colonus* (as translated by Robert Fitzgerald) that serve as the story's epigraph: "That way you shall forever hold this city, / Safe from the men of Thebes, the dragon's sons" (*CSCG*, 121).

Much of Gordon's work from this last period of her fiction, primarily a number of stories, focuses on the trials of heroes whose actions reverberate with archetypal patterns. A number of stories are autobiographical, mostly set in Gordon's childhood, and depict her waging a battle against darkness and evil. Two other stories are about Meriwether Lewis and John Cauvin (John Calvin); they, too, establish the exploits of these men in terms of the heroic archetype. Most of these works are sketchy and uneven, written as if by a tentative hand.

Gordon at one time suggested that she was eventually going to bring all of these stories together as a novel, which was to be called *A Narrow Heart: The Portrait of a Woman,* later to be called *Behold My Trembling Heart.* This novel, she said, was to be half of a double novel, an ambitious project she described in a 1971 letter to Donald Stanford:

> The upper pattern purports to be my own autobiography but is actually the history of the lives of certain members of my family who have been associated, to some extent, with public figures (Dr. John Hunter, Thomas Jefferson, Meriwether Lewis, Sir Walter Scott, et al.). The lower pattern winds serpent-wise through the upper pattern of action and deals with the archetypal world which the present day Jungians and the archaic Greek inform us lies at the very bottom of every human consciousness.[39]

While vague about the mechanics of uniting these two novels, she made clear her intention to reveal the archetypal reverberations which all actions of life carry, with a particular emphasis on heroic endeavor against misfortune.

There appear to be several reasons why Gordon decided that a double novel, a plan that seems anything but graceful, might prove to be effective. In her essay "On Learning to Write," Gordon decried the ignorance of classical tales on the part of the general reading public. Evidently she came to believe that if she wanted to suggest to modern readers the heroic archetypes that reverberate in historical and contemporary life, as embodied in the planned companion novel, she would first have to give them the classical tale—"the lower pattern"—straight out. Gordon wanted not only to provide the archetypal backdrop, but also to revive an interest in the classical myths. She saw her planned novel of archetypal experience as an effort to call forth the classical world, to bring this universe out from the dusty confines of classical dictionaries and make it ring with life for contemporary readers. But the most significant reason for her double novel was that its very form, an archetypal tale and its later representations, embodied her belief that all fiction derives from "primal plots" and that the process of artistic creation might best be seen as the plumbing of the depths of human life in order to reveal its timeless patterns.

In 1972, Gordon published "the lower pattern" of her proposed project, *The Glory of Hera,* a novel that recounts the tale of Heracles, with a primary focus on his twelve labors and his eventual deification. This strange and lively novel, with the Olympian gods serving not only as active characters but also as intelligences by whom the novel is told, establishes Heracles as the primary archetypal hero and, with his deification, suggests that he was a precursor to Christ. The novel also laid the foundation of archetypal experience within which the action of the planned companion novel would be embodied.

Caroline Gordon died in 1981 without completing her double-novel project. Had she finished the second novel, I imagine it would have focused primarily on her own life, ending with a conversion experience that would have endowed it and *The Glory of Hera* with a meaningful symmetry (her tale of Heracles concludes with his deification). Together the two novels would have signified the progression from classical to Christian vision and served as a just representation of her final artistic vision merging classicism and Catholicism, the two traditions so significant in Gordon's life and art.

## CHAPTER 3

# Man the Wayfarer, Man the Stoic: The Art of Walker Percy

More than Allen Tate and Caroline Gordon, Walker Percy has been profoundly influenced by the European existentialists, whose works he has studied seriously for close to four decades. Not surprisingly, there is a strong tendency among critics to place him squarely in this tradition while downplaying other influences. While the Europeans have played a major role in Percy's life and art—and still do, there is nonetheless good reason to approach Percy also by way of his southern upbringing and Catholic faith. Percy certainly holds much in common with the southern Catholic converts looked at previously, as well as with Flannery O'Connor. Indeed, the intellectual dilemma that pointed Percy to the Church—how to live after the collapse of the Old South's Stoic tradition—bears a strong resemblance to that which pointed Allen Tate and Caroline Gordon in the same direction. Moreover, Percy's novels, though uniquely his own, exhibit tendencies seen in the fiction of Caroline Gordon and Flannery O'Connor. And, although Percy does not talk much in his essays and interviews about Tate, Gordon, and O'Connor, he corresponded with all three, and certainly sees himself as writer and believer, sharing with them a similar stance and similar concerns.

Walker Percy was born on 28 May 1916 in Birmingham, Alabama.[1] The major influence during Percy's formative years came not from his parents, but from his second cousin, William Alexander Percy ("Uncle Will" to Walker and his brothers). In 1930, a year after Percy's father, LeRoy Percy, committed suicide, Will became father to young Walker when he invited LeRoy's widow and three sons to live with him in Greenville, Mississippi. To Walker, this new guardian was a mysterious and "fabled" relative, "the one," Percy writes in his introduction to a recent edition of Will Percy's autobiography *(Lanterns on the Levee),* "you liked to speculate about. His father was a United States senator and he had been a decorated infantry officer in World War I. Besides that, he was a poet. The fact that he was also a lawyer and a planter didn't cut much ice—after all, the South was full of lawyer-planters. But how many people did you know who were war heroes and wrote books of poetry? One had heard of Rupert Brooke and Joyce Kilmer, but they were dead."[2] Though he lived in Uncle Will's home for twelve years, Walker's impression of William Percy has remained throughout his life "no less fabled than my earliest imaginings. The image of him that takes form in my mind still owes more to Rupert Brooke and those photographs of young English officers killed in Flanders than to a flesh-and-blood cousin from Greenville, Mississippi."[3]

Living in Uncle Will's home opened up for Walker Percy and his brothers a world of culture not many are lucky enough to experience. The boys heard classical music played on a huge Capehart, and listened to their uncle read poetry, particularly Shakespeare and Keats, Uncle Will's two favorite writers. Such activities had their effect; when asked later if Will influenced his own decision to become a writer, Percy replied: "Most certainly he did because he had an extraordinary quality which only a few really good teachers, as you know, have, and that's the quality of making you see a poem or a painting the way he sees it. . . . He could turn you on."[4] Besides the example of Uncle Will himself to draw on, Walker must have been influenced by the steady stream of distinguished visitors to his guardian's home— including William Faulkner, Harry Stack Sullivan, Carl Sandburg, Stephen Vincent Benet, Stark Young, and Langston Hughes.

Learning and the arts were not all that Walker Percy encountered in his Uncle Will's household. He also bore witness to Will's decidedly Stoic view of life. To live with Uncle Will, Percy later wrote, "was to encounter a complete, articulated view of the world as tragic as it was noble."[5] Raised a Catholic, Will Percy had, as a college student at Sewanee, lost his faith. "How it came about did not seem sudden or dramatic or anything but sad," he wrote in his autobiography, *Lanterns on the Levee* (1941). "As I started to the confessional I knew there was no use going, no priest could absolve me, no church could direct my life or my judgment, what most believed I could not believe."[6] More congenial to him was the essentially pessimistic Stoic view of life. "Our dread and torment," he commented in his autobiography, "in this life we lead are its apartness, its eternal isolation. We try to rid us of ourselves by love, by prayers, by vice, by the Lethe of activity, and we never wholly succeed" (*LL*, 321). He summed up man's duty in a world that is "poor in spirit and common as hell" (*LL*, 62) with words from his father: "I guess a man's job is to make the world a better place to live in, so far as he is able— always remembering the results will be infinitesimal—and to attend to his own soul" (*LL*, 75).

William Percy came to exemplify for Walker Percy this Stoic philosophy, which the latter described as "a paternalism, a *noblesse oblige,* and a rather dark view which is based on stoicism, Greco-Roman stoicism, in which a man doesn't expect much in the world and does the best he can and tries to make one place a little better and knows in the end . . . knows that he'll probably be defeated in the end."[7] Though Percy says he was never merely Uncle Will's disciple, he admits that his guardian was the guiding force in his early development. "What he was to me was a fixed point in a confusing world," Percy writes in his introduction to *Lanterns on the Levee.* "This is not to say I always took him for my true north and set my course accordingly. I did not. . . . But even when I did not follow him, it was usually in *relation* to him, whether with him or against him, that I defined myself and my own direction."[8] Though he has turned toward the same Church away from which his guardian moved, Percy has never ceased to admire Uncle Will's Stoicism; time and again in his fiction, he invokes the Stoic philosophy to help define his own Catholic faith and his vision of modern life.

After he graduated from Greenville High School, Percy attended the University of North Carolina at Chapel Hill. There he immersed himself in science, majoring in chemistry and taking courses in physics and biology. "It was the elegance and order," Percy later wrote, "and, yes, beauty of science which attracted me. It is not merely the truth of science that makes it beautiful, but its simplicity. That is to say, its constant movement is in the direction of ordering the endless variety and the seeming haphazardness of ordinary life by discovering underlying principles which as science progresses become ever fewer and more rigorously and exactly formulated—at least in the physical sciences."[9]

Upon completion of his undergraduate degree, Percy continued his scientific studies at Columbia University's College of Physicians and Surgeons. He enjoyed his studies there, marveling at what his teachers called "the mechanism of disease," a view that saw disease not as a disruption of order but as the patient's logical response to infection. "This response *was* the disease as the physician sees it!" Percy wrote, admitting that this idea—hardly new—struck him as "an idea of the most revolutionary simplicity and beauty."[10]

But Percy's studies were abruptly interrupted in 1942 when he contracted pulmonary tuberculosis while working as a pathologist at Bellevue Hospital. He describes this event in one of his essays as a "cataclysm, brought to pass appropriately enough by one of these elegant agents of disease, the same scarlet tubercle bacillus I used to see lying crisscrossed like Chinese characters in the sputum and lymphoid tissue of the patients at Bellevue. Now I was one of them."[11]

Confined to a sanitarium at Lake Saranac (in upper New York State) for two years, and then, after a brief remission, to one in Connecticut for another year, Percy did a great deal of thinking and reading. That the world was in the midst of a devastating war greatly affected him: "I was in bed so much, alone so much, that I had nothing to do but read and think. I began to question everything I had once believed. I began to ask why Europe, why the world had come to such a sorry state."[12] His reading took him to the European novelists, especially Thomas Mann, Dostoevski, Kafka, and Tolstoy, and then later to continental philosophers, particularly Kierkegaard, Heidegger, Jaspers, and Marcel. The focus of his thought shifted. He did not repudiate his allegiance to science; rather, he broadened the scope of his inquiry so that, in his own words, "what began to interest me was not so much a different question as a larger question, not the physiological and pathological processes within man's body but the problem of man himself, the nature and destiny of man; specifically and more immediately, the predicament of man in a modern technological society."[13] Eventually, as he explains in "From Facts to Fiction," Percy reached the startling conclusion "that the more science progressed and even as it benefited man, the less it said about what it is like to be a man living in the world." "Every advance in science," he goes on to say, "seemed to take it farther from the concrete here-and-now in which we live. . . . After twelve years of a scientific education, I felt somewhat like the Danish philosopher Soren Kierkegaard when he finished reading Hegel. Hegel, said Kierkegaard, explained everything under the sun, except one small detail: what it means to be a man living in the world who must die."[14]

Eventually Percy left the second sanitarium, decided to give up his career in medicine, and returned to Greenville. The war was over, and he was one of many returning home to start anew. But he was unsure of what he wanted to do with his life. "I guess I wanted to settle down, too—" he remembers, "but at the time I didn't know that was what I wanted. I'd been alone in the woods so long, I was blinking at the strong sun, and all the people."[15] With his old high-school classmate Shelby Foote, he moved to New Mexico and settled in Santa Fe. There he roamed about the deserts, the Indian reservations, and the Grand Canyon, and continued his reading of European novelists and philosophers.

After about a year in Santa Fe, Percy decided to return to Greenville and there, still undecided about his future, he continued his private study. Near the end of 1946, he married Mary Bernice Townsend, a medical technician he had met years earlier, and he and his wife moved to a country home near Sewanee, Tennessee. Six months later, both he and Mary joined the Catholic Church.

Percy has written very little about his decision to become a Catholic. According to his close friend Robert Coles, Percy experienced a very intense religious crisis during 1946 and 1947, which led him eventually to the Church. Coles says that Percy experienced no dramatic moment of conversion; rather, in Coles's words, "a deeply introspective and somewhat withdrawn man gradually began to make commitments, and affiliation to a particular faith was one of them."[16]

Certainly Percy must have found the Catholic view of man compatible with the existential dilemma he saw facing modern man. In an interview, he characterized the Catholic view as being "that man is neither an organism controlled by his environment, nor a creature controlled by the forces of history as the Marxists would say, nor is he a detached, wholly objective, angelic being who views the world in a godlike way and makes pronouncements only to himself or to an elite group of people. No, he's somewhere between the angels and the beasts. He's a strange creature whom both Thomas Aquinas and Marcel called *homo viator,* man the wayfarer, man the wanderer."[17] Certainly, too, Percy must have been attracted to the great historical authority of the Catholic Church, the original bride of Christ, the Church of Peter and John and the Apostle Paul. His only substantive published statement about his choice to enter the Church does not at first glance appear to bear this out, but closer examination reveals that it does. "If I had to single out one piece of writing which was more responsible than anything else for my becoming a Catholic," Percy has said, "it would be that essay of Kierkegaard's ["Of the Difference between a Genius and an Apostle"]."[18] Percy was fascinated by the dichotomy Kierkegaard drew between what he called the genius and the apostle. A genius, says Kierkegaard, is a man who discovers truth; he uses the example of a scientist who works in the realm of the immanent; he can discover truth anywhere, anytime, anyplace. The apostle, however, bears news, his realm is the transcendent, and he speaks with divine authority. Those who hear the apostles are faced with a choice, as Kierkegaard describes, using the example of an apostle's message: "These words were spoken by Him to whom, according to His own statement, is given all power in heaven and on earth. You who hear me must consider within yourselves whether you will bow before this authority or not, accept and believe the words or not."[19] Walker Percy heard the message of the modern apostles, whom he saw as present-day Catholic priests, and he believed.

Percy's decision to join the Catholic Church also I think reflects a need, like that felt by Allen Tate and Caroline Gordon, for a stable world view. Before his conversion, Percy lacked a clear-cut orientation towards life. Several traditions exerted pulls within him. One was Uncle Will's Stoicism, embodying the ancient ideals of honor and integrity and also allegiance to one's community. Another perspective was the scientific view, absorbed when Percy was an undergraduate and medical student, which explained life by means of a system of biological and physical theories. And finally there was the European existentialism he had discovered during his bouts with tuberculosis, which defined man as a wayfarer and elaborated on his lost condition. While his existentialist readings undoubtedly influenced Percy's thought most heavily, it seems clear that during the period before his conversion his life lacked direction. As Percy remembers it, his decision to come home from Santa Fe vividly illustrates his disordered state: "Don't ask me why [I decided to come back]. I didn't know why I was out there, and when I decided eventually to go back I didn't know why I was going back, either. I just decided I'd been away too long, after a year or so, from the grass and the trees and the bayous in Mississippi and Louisiana."[20]

During these years after leaving the sanitarium, Walker Percy was, in short, searching for a purpose to his life, and he found no simple solutions. His decision to return to Greenville after his trip west seems particularly significant, revealing a desire to live somewhat according to the lines established by William Percy. Percy's ambiguous yearnings for home embody a distinctly southern desire to be a part of a community, to establish a role in society, and, like William Percy, to be as good a man as possible. In 1930 Allen Tate embarked on a similar return to the South in an effort to seize hold of its traditions. But, having become one of the modern literary elite, Tate was soon disappointed with life on the farm, despite his involvement with Agrarianism. Walker Percy's homecoming also proved unfulfilling—as Percy himself probably knew it would. Now a member of the modern world, not only as scientist but as existentialist thinker, Percy realized that he could not simply take up where Uncle Will had left off. Although he felt the pull of his guardian's idealism, he also knew from experience that this *noblesse oblige* bore little relevance to life in the 1940s.

Later in his career, Percy wrote two essays, "Stoicism in the South" (1956) and "The Failure and the Hope" (1968), which describe the cultural dilemma that he saw modern southerners facing. In these essays he establishes early on that the South's general orientation has traditionally been more Greek than Christian, and that its virtues were those of the old Stoa. "How immediately we recognize," Percy writes in "Stoicism in the South," "the best of the South in the words of the Emperor: 'Every moment think steadily, as a Roman and a man, to do what thou hast in hand with perfect and simple dignity, and a feeling of affection, and freedom, and justice.' And how curiously foreign to the South sound the Decalogue, the Beatitudes, the doctrine of the Mystical Body. The South's virtues were the broadsword virtues of the clan, as were her vices too—the hubris of *noblesse* gone arrogant."[21] Percy goes on to say that a Christian presence existed in the Old South, but that it was merely, as he calls it, a "cultural Christendom" (as opposed, one gathers, to a "theological Christendom"). He describes the situation in terms of a "Christian edifice": "The Southern gentleman did live in a Christian edifice, but he lived there in the strange fashion Chesterton spoke of, that of a man who will neither go inside nor put it entirely behind him but stands forever grumbling on the porch."[22]

The Stoic tradition, says Percy in "The Failure and the Hope," met its political end around 1890 but persisted as a social force until recent times. Today, however, Stoicism is at a low ebb: "Nearly everyone in the South has known someone like Atticus Finch in *To Kill a Mockingbird* with his quite Attic sense of decency (and his correspondingly low regard for Christianity) and his courage before the lynch mob. It is, however, this very Stoic tradition which has finally collapsed as a significant influence in the Southern community."[23] And with the collapse of Stoicism also came the demise of its attendant cultural Christianity: "What is the case is that the Christian porch is no longer habitable, that pleasant site of cultural Christendom neither quite inside the Church nor altogether in the street from which one had the best of both, church on Sundays and at Baptism and marriage and death, and the rest of the time lived in the sunny old Stoa of natural grace and good manners. It doesn't work now."[24] What does work, says Percy, is a return to a tradition even more timeworn and unlikely: the Catholic Church.

Percy's discussion of the dilemma facing the South is a restatement, in larger terms, of the dilemma that he himself faced before he was converted. Aware of the collapse of the Stoic tradition and also believing that liberal humanism could never fulfill man's spiritual needs (a belief arrived at partly through his readings in existentialism), Percy found himself confronting a cultural and spiritual vacuum.

In a sense Percy's dilemma resembled that of the poet's in

Allen Tate's "Ode to the Confederate Dead": how does a modern southerner live, when he has emotional ties to the ideals of the past but cannot sustain them beause he is also fully aware of his modernity? For Percy, as for Tate himself, the answer lay with the acceptance of Roman Catholicism. Catholicism gave Percy not only a view of man's fate consistent with existentialist thinking (man as wayfarer), but also an ordered view of life and a system of morality in which he could believe. Well aware of the collapse of the Stoic tradition in the South and of the need to establish a new order, Percy believed that for the South as a whole, as well as for himself alone, the answer to the problem of how to live was the same: accept a way of life based solidly in Christian theology, which in Percy's own case meant becoming a Roman Catholic.

Shortly after joining the Church, Percy and his wife moved to New Orleans. Percy did not have a job, but he now felt he had an occupation as professional philosopher. No longer an aimless wanderer, he gave himself over to the contemplative life of reading and thinking. After three years in New Orleans, the Percys moved to Covington, a small Louisiana town outside New Orleans. Covington has proved to be much to Percy's liking. As he said in an article in *Esquire,* living in this relatively isolated community (though, he complains, it is not so isolated anymore) allowed him to remain in his beloved home country "in such a way as not to succumb to the ghosts of the old South or the happy hustlers of the new Sunbelt South."[25] "It is necessary," Percy went on to say in this *Esquire* article, "to escape the place of one's origins, and the ghosts of one's ancestors but not too far. You wouldn't want to move to Tucumcari."[26]

Except for two essays which appeared in the *Carolina Magazine* while he was an undergraduate, Percy did not attempt to publish anything until 1954. After his first essay, "Symbol as Need," appeared in *Thought,* there followed a substantial flow of essays through the 1950s. Some, such as "Symbol as Hermeneutic in Existentialism: A Possible Bridge to Empiricism," were extremely esoteric, addressed to professional philosophers and linguists; others, such as "Stoicism in the South," were more wide ranging and were written for the general public.

Also during the 1950s Percy began to try his hand at writing novels. His first attempt, a manuscript entitled *The Charterhouse,* centered on the idea that the country club had superseded the medieval church as a center of spiritual life. When Allen Tate read the manuscript he wrote back: "This is dreadful—you've simply got to put some action in it!"[27] Caroline Gordon's response to the novel was thirty pages of typed single-spaced commentary. After several rejections by publishers, Percy gave up on this first novel and began another, this time about a pathologist who performed autopsies on tubercular patients. He never even sent this manuscript off to a publisher.

There appear to be several significant reasons why Percy began experimenting with fiction. One obvious motive, as Percy himself admits, was that he could reach more people by embodying his observations of the world in fiction. The audience for essays on metaphysics is small, but there are plenty of novel readers. Another impetus was that the philosophical problems he was studying seemed appropriate for a novel. He elaborated on this compatibility between ideas and genre in an interview, saying that he was interested in existentialism, which "means a concrete view of man, man in a situation, man in a predicament, man's anxiety, and so on. And I believed that this view of man could be handled very well in a novel, and I was interested in phenomenology, which is very strongly existentialist: the idea of describing accurately how a man feels in a given situation. And that's certainly novelistic."[28] But perhaps most important was the tremendous value of fiction, in Percy's eyes, in discovering and communicating knowledge. Percy saw as a mistake the popular notion that science was fact and knowledge, while art was merely play and emotion; to him both science and art were important ways of exploring reality. To dismiss art as mere emotion was to overlook its invaluable cognitive function. "I think that serious novel writing, that serious art," Percy said in an interview, "is just as important, and just as cognitive [as science]; it concerns areas of knowing, of discovering and knowing, just as much as any science. In fact, in art, particularly in the modern novel, you are dealing with areas of life which cannot be reached in any other way."[29]

Percy's first two attempts at fiction apparently were doomed by his failure to merge successfully the philosophical concerns that were so important to him with the concrete nature of fiction. He was too much the philosopher and not enough the storyteller. He needed to ground his fiction more in the central dilemma of his own life: how does modern man live? By probing this problem Walker Percy could become a novelist. His philosophical concerns could be expressed while the real and vibrant tensions from his own life kept the novel down to earth.

This mining of his own dilemma made *The Moviegoer*, and later *The Last Gentleman*, work as novels where Percy's two earlier attempts failed. In one of his essays, "From Facts to Fiction," he describes the breakthrough he made when planning *The Moviegoer*. He says that he decided to discard the conventional notions of plot and character and instead "begin with a *man* who finds himself in a *world*, a very concrete man who is located in a very concrete place and time. Such a man might be represented as *coming to himself* in somewhat the same sense as Robinson Crusoe came to himself on that island after his shipwreck, with the same wonder and curiosity."[30] In *The Moviegoer* we do indeed find a very concrete southern man, one who experiences the same torments with which Walker Percy himself struggled.

*The Moviegoer* follows one week in the life of John Bickerson (Binx) Bolling, a twenty-nine-year-old stockbroker who lives in Gentilly, a suburb of New Orleans. Binx is the scion of an old distinguished southern family, which for generations has lived according to the Stoic ideals of the aristocratic South. Binx's great-aunt Emily, who brought him up, is the embodiment of this tradition, and she pushes him constantly to buck up and live by the family's ideals. "A man must live by his lights," she tells Binx at one point, "and do what little he can and do it as best he can. In this world goodness is destined to be defeated. But a man must go down fighting. That is the victory. To do anything less is to be less than a man."[31]

But Binx finds little meaning in his aunt's Stoicism; to him it seems an empty form that fails to account for one's deepest feelings. Early in the novel, for instance, Binx recalls what Aunt Emily told him when he was eight years old, after his brother's death: "Scotty is dead. Now it's all up to you. It's going to be difficult for you but I know you're going to act like a soldier" (*Mg*, 4). Binx's response to this advice: "This was true. I could easily act like a soldier. Was that all I had to do?" (*Mg*, 4).

Binx's distrust of the family tradition appears to be just a more radical version of his father's aloofness from the code.

Though in his actions he appeared to be a worthy upholder of family tradition, his father apparently did not really believe in the system he represented. In a photograph of his father along-side his two brothers, good southern gentlemen, Binx notices something in his father's expression that sets him apart: "His eyes are alight with an expression I can't identify; it is not far from what his elders might have called smart-alecky. He is some-thing of a dude, with his round head and tricky tab collar. . . . Again I search the eyes, each eye a stipple or two in a blurred oval. Beyond a doubt they are ironical" (*Mg*, 25).

What is meaningful to Binx is not his family's Stoicism but what he calls his "search." Early in the novel he describes the nature of his quest, saying that it is "what anyone would under-take if he were not sunk in the everydayness of his own life. This morning, for example, I felt as if I had come to myself on a strange island. And what does such a castaway do? Why, he pokes around the neighborhood and he doesn't miss a trick" (*Mg*, 13). He became aware of the possibility of the search, he tells us, when he lay wounded on a Korean battlefield and watched a dung beetle dig around the leaves. "As I watched," Binx says, "there awoke in me an immense curiosity. I was onto something. I vowed that if I ever got out of this fix, I would pursue the search. Naturally, as soon as I recovered and got home, I forgot all about it" (*Mg*, 11).

But in fact Binx never completely abandoned his quest. For a while, he tells us later, he engaged in a "vertical" search; that is, he sought to understand the workings of the universe, without letting his own personal problems and feelings intrude. His greatest success came, he says, when he read a book called *The Chemistry of Life*, which purported to explain life and the world. But something was missing: "The only difficulty was that though the universe had been disposed of, I myself was left over. There I lay in my own hotel room with my search over yet still obliged to draw one breath and then the next" (*Mg*, 70). After this fail-ure, he embarked on what he now sees as the more important quest, the "horizontal" search, which is essentially an attempt to place himself in the universe. Establishing his niche is of the utmost importance to Binx; one of his greatest fears is the possi-bility of suddenly slipping out of space and time, of finding himself "No one and Nowhere" (*Mg*, 99).

Despite the value he sees in the quest, Binx continues to flounder around in Gentilly, making little progress in discovering anything. There are several reasons for his failure. One is that he has not made a clear-cut plan for his quest, nor is he even sure precisely what he is looking for. To his dismay, he realizes that he does not even know what he needs to discover in order to bring fulfillment and meaning into his life. Another problem is that Binx cannot decide whether everyone else knows what he is searching for, and has already found it, or whether they have not even realized the possibility of a search. "Am I, in my search," he wonders, "a hundred miles ahead of my fellow Americans, or a hundred miles behind them?" (*Mg,* 14). Moreover, Binx has never been able to discard completely the notion that his search, by the standards of Aunt Emily and the clan, is silly and meaningless. At one point, for instance, after his aunt has given him a lecture about his duty in life, he tries to explain to her what he is after. But he stops in the middle of his spiel, for he feels that next to her convictions, "my idea of a search seems absurd" (*Mg,* 54).

Perhaps Binx's biggest distraction from the search is the fact that it is much easier and more enjoyable not to worry about any quest and instead just to live the role of the "model citizen." A good deal of the time, Binx relishes this social identity:

> I am a model tenant and a model citizen and take pleasure in doing all that is expected of me. My wallet is full of identity cards, library cards, credit cards. Last year I purchased a flat olive-drab strong box, very smooth and heavily built with double walls for fire protection, in which I placed my birth certificate, college diploma, honorable discharge, G.I. insurance, a few stock certificates, and my inheritance: a deed to ten acres of a defunct duck club down in St. Bernard Parish, the only relic of my father's many enthusiasms. It is a pleasure to carry out the duties of a citizen and to receive in return a receipt or a neat styrene card with one's name on it certifying, so to speak, one's right to exist. What satisfaction I take in appearing the first day to get my auto tag and brake sticker! I subscribe to *Consumer Reports* and as a consequence I own a first-class television set, an all but silent air conditioner and a very long lasting deodorant. (*Mg,* 6–7)

But as much as he enjoys the banal propriety of this existence, Binx can never thoroughly forget his search. He knows that the anxiety fostered by his awareness of the search is not true despair: "To become aware of the possibility of the search is to be onto something. Not to be onto something is to be in despair" (*Mg*, 13).

All in all, Binx is a confused man, torn by the several traditions that pull within him—his family's traditional Stoicism, his role as the model modern citizen, and his existential awareness of the need for a search. Binx's question reflects Walker Percy's: how does a southerner, raised by Old South ideals whose validity he cannot totally deny, live in the twentieth century? This is the problem lying at the heart of the novel, and Binx wanders the suburban desert of Gentilly seeking an answer. For the most part, he merely see-saws between the different tensions in his life—at times engaged in his search, at times living as a true suburban man, at times considering the offerings of the "good life" as proffered by his aunt and her kin.

Late in the novel, however, Binx's life finally appears to take some direction. After his seemingly disastrous trip to Chicago, Aunt Emily gives him a good dressing down for his aimlessness. She accuses him of failing to accept his heritage and his inbred nobility, which she describes as "a certain quality of spirit, a gaiety, a sense of duty, a nobility worn lightly, a sweetness, a gentleness with women—the only good things the South ever had and the only things that really matter in this life" (*Mg*, 224). His aunt's words stun Binx: "My search has been abandoned; it is no match for my aunt, her rightness and her despair, her despairing of me and her despairing of herself" (*Mg*, 228). Eventually, just as his aunt wishes, he decides to enroll in medical school, and he marries one of his cousins, Kate, an unstable young woman to whom he has always felt close. And, as we see in the "Epilogue," which describes the situation a year after the other events in the novel, Binx seems well adjusted and happy. It seems clear that the shock effect of his aunt's lecture has finally brought him around, and that Binx has cast his allegiance with the Stoicism of his father's ancestors and has thereby found peace and meaning.

It is certainly possible to read the ending of the novel as Binx's response to society's higher callings—to believe that he has become a husband, a doctor, and a "good man." But there is also ample evidence in the "Epilogue" to suggest that Binx is not yet entirely the man of honor that his aunt envisioned. Most important to this interpretation is the fact that Binx has become a believing Catholic. At the end of the last chapter before the "Epilogue," he and Kate sit in a car outside a Catholic church watching others go in. But by the time of the "Epilogue," Binx himself has evidently stepped inside the Church. He tells us that he has come to realize that he is a member of his mother's family (Roman Catholic) and not his father's (the Stoics). Evidence of Binx's faith manifests itself when, at the scene of his brother Lonnie's death, he accepts Lonnie's gruesome suffering, certain, as he tells his younger brothers and sisters, that when the Lord raises Lonnie to heaven, he will arise healthy and whole.

Becoming a Catholic apparently gives Binx's life direction and meaning. The wholeness that he gains through the Church allows him to solve the problematic situation of being torn by the conflicts of various traditions. For he now sees that the meaning and authority of Catholicism overshadow the other traditions. Binx realizes that the fate of man is to be a wayfarer, a pilgrim in search of God, and that his worldly occupation—be it stock-broker, doctor, or whatever else—does not affect his wayward-ness. His own search, he knows now, will be ongoing and ever present; it will have nothing to do with social matters but will instead be private and spiritual. Knowing this, he can freely devote himself to helping others—by becoming a doctor to please his aunt, by marrying Kate and helping her towards san-ity, by bringing joy and understanding to his brothers and sis-ters—without worrying, selfishly, about whether such things will distract him from his search.

The knowledge that Binx possesses at the end of *The Moviegoer* is, I would guess, similar to that which Percy attained during his religious crisis in the 1940s. Percy decided, I think, that with Catholicism at the center of his life, he did not have to choose between his southern heritage, his scientific learning, and his existential search. His Catholicism was *the* way; he could pursue these other traditions as he wished, for what really mat-tered was his faith in Christ. As a Christian man, he was also free to be southern gentleman, modern consumer, and existentialist prober.

In his second novel, *The Last Gentleman*, Percy again probed the problem of how a modern southerner, with his searingly contradictory attitudes towards life, can live in the twentieth century. The novel centers on another search for meaning, here undertaken by Will Barrett, a young southerner now living in New York City. This quest for self-definition takes Barrett on a long journey throughout the South, including a visit to his home in the Delta, and finally to Santa Fe and the deserts of the Southwest.

As Percy has said of him, Barrett "is a curious young man beset by curious symptoms."[32] When the novel opens, Barrett, a Princeton dropout, is working as a humidification engineer at Macy's department store. He lacks a clear orientation as to his place in the world and is possibly even very sick, beset by what he terms "fugue" states and spells of amnesia. These attacks, which can be very severe, make his life seem a series of gaps; he sometimes goes weeks without knowing who or where he is. He also seems to have gotten life backwards, feeling "bad when other people felt good and good when they felt bad."[33] Facing a disaster, such as a raging hurricane, is an exhilarating experience for Barrett; what depresses him is "the prospect of living through an ordinary Wednesday morning" (*LG*, 23).

Adding to Barrett's problems is his feeling that his life is without definition and direction. Instead of having a firm grip on events and a clear goal for his future, he lives "in a state of pure possibility, not knowing what sort of man he was or what he must do, and supposing therefore that he must be all men and do everything" (*LG*, 4). As a boy he had dreamed of growing up and finding a calling in life; he "had lived his life in a state of the liveliest expectation, thinking to himself: what a fine thing it will be to become a man and to know what to do—like an Apache youth who at the right time goes out into the plains alone, dreams dreams, sees visions, returns and knows he is a man" (*LG*, 11). But Barrett never does learn what to do, and now, a young adult, "he still didn't know how to live" (*LG*, 11).

Barrett's problems of self-definition seem to stem in part from his ancestry. Like Binx Bolling, he is from an old and distinguished southern family, but one which through the years has found it progressively harder to live up to the Stoic tradition of the aristocratic South:

> Over the years his family had turned ironical and lost its gift for action. It was an honorable and violent family, but gradually the

violence had been deflected and turned inward. The great grandfather knew what was what and said so and acted accordingly and
did not care what anyone thought. He even wore a pistol in a holster
like a Western hero and once met the Grand Wizard of the Ku Klux
Klan in a barbershop and invited him then and there to shoot it out
in the street. The next generation, the grandfather, seemed to know
what was what but he was not really so sure. He was brave but he
gave much thought to the business of being brave. He too would
have shot it out with the Grand Wizard if only he could have made
certain it was the thing to do. The father was a brave man too and
he said he didn't care what others thought, but he did care. More
than anything else, he wished to act with honor and to be thought
well of by other men. So living for him was a strain. He became
ironical. For him it was not a small thing to walk down the street on
an ordinary September morning. In the end he was killed by his
own irony and sadness and by the strain of living out an ordinary
day in a perfect dance of honor. (*LG*, 9–10)

A scion of this line, Barrett lacks any certainty about how to act
and so has become "a watcher and a listener and a wanderer"
(*LG*, 10).

As we learn when he returns to his home, Barrett was raised
by his father according to the aristocratic code of the Old South.
Lawyer Barrett, like Aunt Emily in *The Moviegoer*, was the para-
gon of this tradition. To him life's meaning resided in the up-
holding of the time-honored traditions of personal honor and
integrity in a world of pain and sorrow. Barrett remembers the
pleasure his father took in talking about man's insignificance in
the awesome universe and in reciting "Dover Beach," particularly the lines

> for the world which seems
> To lie before us like a land of dreams,
> So various, so beautiful, so new
> Hath really neither joy, nor love, nor light,
> Nor certitude, nor peace, nor help for pain—
>
> (*LG*, 309–10)

Appealing as his father's life was, with its emphasis on honor
and integrity, its shortcomings became painfully obvious to Will
Barrett while he was still a boy. This awakening occurs, with
crushing violence and horror, when his father commits suicide
after a confrontation with the town riffraff. Even though the

troublemakers back down from Lawyer Barrett's challenge, he announces that he is defeated. His way of life, he tells Will, has fallen before the barbarians: "Once they were the fornicators and the bribers and the takers of bribes and we were not and that was why they hated us. Now we are like them, so why should they stay? They know that they don't have to kill me" (*LG*, 330). Declaring, "They may have won, but I don't have to choose that," he goes up into his attic and blows his head off with a shotgun.

The motives for his father's suicide are not fully understood by the boy, but later, as an adult returning home from New York, Barrett reaches an understanding of the deed. As Louis Rubin observes, Barrett comes to realize that his father's Stoicism was merely a romantic escape from the world, and that it had at its foundation a false proposition. Rubin also notes: "Such a view necessarily presupposed a former time in which men were better and wiser, more disinterested and virtuous than humans could ever be, as well as a society that had been more nearly free from all temptations to covetousness, avarice, lust, and cruelty than had ever existed on earth."[34]

Will's basic dilemma shapes up very much like that of Binx Bolling: how does a southern man who carries the knowledge of the old Stoic tradition, while also seeing its insufficiencies, live in the modern world, which seems so empty and lacking in values? Though in some ways Barrett is very different from Binx—he is, as Percy himself has said, a good deal sicker and much more of a seeker—they are both after the same thing: a way to live in the world. Neither character finds an easy answer.

On his quest Barrett encounters people whose different outlooks and life-styles represent possible roads out of his dilemma. Three such figures stand out—Kitty, Sutter, and Val—but none of them seems to offer an entirely satisfactory solution.

Kitty Vaught, with whom Barrett is immediately smitten, is a flighty and essentially empty-headed southern belle in modern dress. To Barrett she represents normality, and consequently his feelings toward her are highly ambivalent. At times, he feels he might achieve with her the happiness and serenity associated with family life and the security that comes with conforming to society's norms. Dreams of getting married, settling down, raising a family, and holding a respectable job (her father offers him a job as personnel manager at his Chevrolet dealership) float through his mind. Although he knows that his life has been anything but normal, and although he continually backslides to his vagueness and eccentricities, the thought of Kitty often makes him want to set his life straight: "No more crazy up-sidedownness, he resolved. Good was better than bad. Good environments are better than bad environments. Back to the South, finish his education, make use of his connections, be a business or professional man, marry him a wife and live him a life" (*LG*, 88). But there are also times when some part of Barrett is painfully aware of the ultimate emptiness that lies at the heart of Kitty's suburban life-style.

One reason why Barrett cannot immediately embrace a life with Kitty is his fascination with her brother, Dr. Sutter Vaught, who represents another possible stance towards the world. A physician whose career and personal life are in shambles, Sutter has a profound sense of the alienation permeating modern society. Barrett instinctively feels that Sutter possesses this knowledge, and sees in him a fellow seeker. Instead of recoiling from Sutter's wildness, as most people do, Barrett continually hunts him out, pressing him for insights into his own problems. But Sutter is coy with Barrett and will not provide him with any straight answers. He does, however, leave Barrett his journal to read.

Most of the observations in Sutter's journal center on the idea that in the modern age—what he calls the age of science—people have become abstracted. By this he means that while people may, through scientific theory, understand the workings of the universe, they fail to understand themselves. Sutter believes that most people have cut themselves off from immediate reality by abstracting themselves out of it, and that only through sex can they reenter the realm of immanence. "Lewdness = sole concrete metaphysic of laymen in age of science = sacrament of the dispossessed," Sutter writes in his scientific shorthand. "Things, persons, relations emptied out, not by theory but by lay reading of theory. There remains only relation of skin to skin and hand under dress" (*LG*, 279–80).

Sutter levels much of his harshest criticism at American society. He sees America as a hotbed of hypocrisy, a place where people give lip service to decency and generosity while engaging in all types of lewdness. Americans, says Sutter, masquerade as humans (believing in such ideals as the goodness of man, freedom, and dignity) while living "like dogs greeting each other nose to tail and tail to nose" (*LG*, 281). Raging against this distinctly American hypocrisy, Sutter declares that he is the only sincere American because he alone is overtly lewd. "I accept," he declares, "the current genital condition of all human relations and try to go beyond it. I may sniff like a dog but then I try to be human rather than masquerade as human and sniff like a dog."

Barrett finds these ideas harsh and disturbing. "My God, what is all this stuff," he thinks, after reading one section of the journal (*LG*, 293). Despite this reaction, Barrett continues to feel sure that Sutter is onto something that can help him shape his own life. This feeling, along with his inherited Stoic knowledge that the modern world breeds commonness and paltriness, makes Barrett keep pestering Sutter for answers, and also keeps him from settling down with Kitty.

Kitty's and Sutter's sister, Val Vaught, a Roman Catholic nun, represents the third way of approaching life. In his journal, Sutter sums up her view of the human condition as being "that man is a wayfarer (i.e., not transcending being nor immanent being but wayfarer) who therefore stands in the way of hearing a piece of news which is of the utmost importance to him (i.e., his salvation) and which he had better attend to" (*LG*, 353). For several reasons, Barrett has little sympathy for Val's beliefs. One is that he sees religion as being important merely for its psychological insights, not its theology. Early in the novel we learn that "he had read widely among modern psychologists and he knew that we have much to learn from the psychological insights of the World's Great Religions" (*LG*, 12). Moreover, his family has traditionally steered clear of Catholics. He remembers with pleasure how his father once slammed down the telephone receiver when a priest called asking him to reinstate an indigent servant. Barrett even goes so far as to say that "it is in stern protest against Catholic monkey business that we feel ourselves most ourselves" (*LG*, 212).

But even if Barrett were not prejudiced against Val from the start, there is apparently little reason for him to take her seriously. He finds most disturbing her impulsiveness and her apparent lack of serious commitment. Her decision to become a nun, for instance, was not a premeditated act representing great love of God or charity towards mankind, but rather a spur-of-the-moment decision, which occurred during a fit of depression. She tells Barrett that one day when she was in school at Columbia University, a nun approached her and offered her a way to be whole. "She said how would you like to be alive," Val recounts to Barrett. "I said I'd like that. She said all right, come with me. That was it" (*LG*, 300). Six weeks later she made her first vows. Even the bishop found it hard to understand her decision and required her to get a doctor's statement that her family was free from any cases of insanity.

Val now works in a mission in Alabama, described as "a raw settlement of surplus army buildings, Quonset huts, and one geodesic dome, stretching out into the piney woods, each building fed by a silver butane sphere" (*LG*, 296). She teaches poor black children, and to Barrett her life seems a useless endeavor. As Sutter points out in an entry to Val in his journal, "Ten years from now it won't even mean anything to them: either they'll be Muslims and hate your guts or they'll be middle-class and buggered like everybody else" (*LG*, 308). She also spends a lot of time begging contributions for the colony; one of her successes is persuading the local leader of the Ku Klux Klan to donate a 7-Up machine.

Val's vocation seems as frivolous as her faith. When Barrett visits the mission, she talks to him about her spiritual problems: "That's what I don't understand, you know: that I believe the whole business: God, the Jews, Christ, the Church, grace and the forgiveness of sins—and that I'm meaner than ever. Christ is my lord and I love him but I'm a good hater and you know what he said about that. I still hope my enemies fry in hell. What to do about that? Will God forgive me?" (*LG*, 301). Not only is her flawed piety evident here but also her erratic judgment: it is not every day that one finds a Roman Catholic nun asking an agnostic mental patient for spiritual guidance. Predictably, Barrett dismisses Val and the approach to life that she represents.

Near the end of the novel, as Barrett arrives in Santa Fe, he has narrowed his choices: he will either return to Kitty or continue to follow Sutter, searching for some truth and value outside modern society. While in Santa Fe, he decides, apparently once and for all, that he will return to Birmingham, marry Kitty, and work in her father's Chevrolet dealership. He believes that a solid marriage will put an end to his waywardness, that "tender feelings of love would take the place of this great butting billy-goat surge" (*LG*, 375) that disrupts his serenity. After settling his plans with Kitty on the phone, he still presses Sutter for some answers, but his probings now seem merely an attempt to tie up loose ends before returning to the South.

His having read in Sutter's journal that Sutter sees no ulti-mate alternative for himself but suicide may have aided Barrett in his decision to head back home. Sutter says that he has been living what he calls a life of lewdness because, he thinks, life poses only two alternatives: either accept Christ or don't, and if you don't, all that is left is lewdness. Wracked by unbelief, Sutter has opted for a life without Christ. Addressing much of his journal to his sister Val, Sutter writes:

> I do not deny, Val, that a revival of your sacramental system is an alternative to lewdness (the only other alternative is the forgetting of the old sacrament), for lewdness itself is a kind of sacrament (devilish, if you like). The difference is that my sacrament is opera-tional and yours is not. (*LG*, 281)

> The only difference between me and you is that you think that purity and life can only come from eating the body and drinking the blood of Christ. I don't know where it comes from. (*LG*, 282)

> You opted for the Scandalous Thing, the Wrinkle in Time, the Jew-Christ-Church business, God's alleged intervention in history. You acted on it, left all and went away to sojourn among strangers. I can understand this even though I could never accept the propositions (1) that my salvation comes from the Jews, (2) that my salvation depends upon hearing news rather than figuring it out, (3) that I must spend eternity with Southern Baptists. (*LG*, 307)

But then something very important happens—Jamie's death-bed acceptance of Catholicism—which not only shakes up his older brother Sutter's thinking but also greatly affects Barrett, causing him to reassess his decision to marry Kitty. Both Sutter and Barrett are present in the hospital room when Father Boomer administers the sacrament to Jamie. Barrett, although he interprets Jamie's weak voice to the priest, is unaware of the spiritual significance of what is taking place. Jamie looks to him for guidance, asking Barrett if what the priest says is true. Barrett can give him no answer. But Sutter can sense that something important is happening: as the priest talks with Jamie, "Sutter hung fire, his chin on his knuckles, his eyes half-closed and gleaming like a Buddha's" (*LG*, 404). As Jamie slips quickly towards death, Sutter takes charge of the situation, holding Jamie up and urging the priest to finish the baptism before the boy's heart stops. Though there is no blinding moment of epiphany, and indeed no clear statement that Sutter even accepts the significance of the baptism, I think we are to understand that God's grace has touched his lost soul. The seed has been planted.

Deliberately ambiguous here, Percy nonetheless suggests, I believe, that Sutter has seen the way out of the dichotomous dilemma that seemed to lead only to suicide. He now senses that Val's choice may after all be "operational." He sets out into the desert—the classic setting for wrestling with existential problems—to think some more. Although Barrett has missed all this, he is nonetheless aware that a change has come over Sutter. "What happened back there?" Barrett asks him after they have left Jamie's room (*LG*, 407). Sutter replies that Barrett was there, he saw what happened. "I know," Barrett responds, "but what did you think? I could tell you were thinking something." Characteristically, Sutter does not answer his question and instead gets in his car to drive off. But Barrett won't let him drive off alone. Though perhaps he simply fears Sutter will commit suicide ("Wait," he calls out, as he did in his memory/dream, when he saw his father climbing to the attic to shoot himself), he also senses, as he had all along, that Sutter still holds the key to the answers. This time he is right; Sutter, I think we are meant to see, is finally on the right track.

The ending to *The Last Gentleman* is highly ambiguous, but the message embodied there is similar to that in the conclusion of *The Moviegoer.* In order for Will Barrett, a modern southerner pulled by both the southern past and the modern world, to survive in society, he must attain a larger sense of order and meaning than what society offers; that order and meaning, according to Percy, can come only from a theological view of existence, specifically Catholicism. If Barrett is ever going to achieve control of his life, as Binx Bolling does (and also as Val does, we now realize), he must first, like Binx and Val—and Walker Percy—step into the Church.

Percy's first two novels are successful explorations of the conflicts that he found so central to his own life. To understand fully, however, the final shape Percy gave to these novels, one needs to look at Percy's conceptions of the novelist and of the relationship that the writer holds with his audience. For, like Caroline Gordon, Percy knew well the many pitfalls that lay in wait for a Catholic writer attempting to communicate with anyone but the faithful, and he shaped his novels accordingly.

In his essay "From Facts to Fiction," Percy says that when he thinks of a writer sitting down to work, what comes to mind is the picture "of a scientist who has come to the dead end of a traditional hypothesis which no longer accounts for the data at hand."[35] "It is my belief," he continues, "that anyone writing serious fiction today is somewhat like the physicists around 1900 after the Michelson-Morley experiment and quantum data had overthrown Newtonian physics. That is to say, in modern literature it is man himself who is called into question and who must be defended, and it is the very nature of man which must be rediscovered and re-expressed in fresh language of a new poetry and fiction and theatre."[36]

Percy's point here is that a person can no longer take for granted the old platitudes about life and human nature. He sees the conventional orientation of the modern age as being a disparate combination of science and humanism. In his essay "The Message in the Bottle," he defines this general orientation ("a kind of low common denominator of belief held more or less unconsciously by most denizens of the century"[37]), with two propositions:

> (1) Man can be understood as an organism in an environment, a sociological unit, an encultured creature, a psychological dynamism endowed genetically like other organisms with needs and drives, who through evolution has developed strategies for learning and surviving by means of certain adaptive transactions with the environment.
>
> (2) Man is also understood to be somehow endowed with certain other unique properties which he does not share with other organisms—with certain inalienable rights, reason, freedom, and an in-

trinsic dignity—and as a consequence the highest value to which a democratic society can be committed is the respect of the sacredness and worth of the individual. (*MB*, 20)

The prevailing modern attitude, believes Percy, asserts that the human race can look forward to living happily ever after by adapting man's environment to fit his physical needs, by following the ethical principles of Christianity, and by building efficient educational systems. Absent from this modern perspective are those depressing old ideas about the Fall, and man's essential state of alienation resulting from his separation from God.

But something has gone wrong. Eden, says Percy, has become the twentieth century; what should have happened has not, and, as a result, the modern view is no longer tenable. Percy's line of thinking becomes clear when we look at the questions that open his essay "The Delta Factor":

Why does man feel so sad in the twentieth century?

Why does man feel so bad in the very age when, more than in any other age, he has succeeded in satisfying his needs and making over the world for his own use?

Why has man entered on an orgy of war, murder, torture, and self-destruction unparalleled in history and in the very century when he had hoped to see the dawn of universal peace and brotherhood?

Why do people often feel bad in good environments and good in bad environments? (*MB*, 3)

The theories of the scientists and the humanists, which leave no room to account for widespread symptoms of profound weakness and discontent, cannot answer these questions.

So, says Percy, the modern age has come to an end, because people can no longer understand themselves by the light of the age's professed beliefs. With this demise of modern thinking, Percy adds, "its anthropology [Percy uses the word here in its root sense, the study of man] was still professed for a while and the denizens of the age still believed that they believed it, but they felt otherwise and they could not understand their feelings. They were like men who live by reason during the day and at night dream bad dreams" (*MB*, 25). This is the milieu in which the contemporary novelist finds himself and this, says Percy, is why the novelist is like the "scientist who has come to the dead end of a traditional hypothesis which no longer accounts for the data at hand," and why his task is the rediscovery and reexpression in new language of "the very nature of man."[38]

In his essay "The State of the Novel: Dying Art or New Science?" (1977), Percy examines the role of the novelist in the late twentieth century. Here he asserts that the stance of the writer during this period is diagnostic. That is, in this age "when people don't know who they are or where they are going," the novelist can, through the cognitive process of art, explore the problems of alienation and despair for which the theories of the age cannot account. If successful, the novelist can even tell "the reader how things are, how we are, in a way that the reader can confirm with as much certitude as a scientist taking a pointer-reading."[39]

But, Percy adds, the writer's task is by no means simple or clear-cut; he faces some baffling problems in communicating with his audience. Percy makes his point by comparing the situation Charles Dickens faced to that facing the modern novelist. Dickens, says Percy, attacked the evils of industrial England from a stance affirmed by the shared assumptions of the writer and audience; the values underlying society's systems of belief were not called into question, but instead were used to expose those aspects of nineteenth-century English life which fell short of the accepted values. Percy explains that the challenge is quite different for the contemporary writer:

> But now it seems that whatever has gone wrong strikes to the heart and core of meaning itself, the very ways people see and understand themselves. What is called into question in novels *now* is the very enterprise of human life itself. Instead of writing about this or that social evil from a posture of consensus from which we agree to deplore social evils, it is now the consensus itself and the posture which are called into question. This state of affairs creates problems for the novelist. For in order to create a literature, whether of celebration or dissent, a certain shared universe of discourse is required. It is now these very shared assumptions which are called into question.[40]

The contemporary novelist, Percy says later in the essay, "is less like the Tolstoy or Fielding or Jane Austen who set forth and celebrated a still intact society, than he is like a somewhat bemused psychiatrist gazing at a patient who in one sense lives in the best of all possible worlds and yet is suffering from a depression and anxiety which he doesn't understand."[41]

For contemporary writers writing from a Christian perspective, like Walker Percy, the situation is especially precarious. The Christian novelist's dilemma, writes Percy in his essay "Notes for a Novel about the End of the World," is that "though he professes a belief which he holds saves himself and the world and nourishes his art besides, it is also true that Christendom seems in some sense to have failed. Its vocabulary is worn out. This twin failure raises problems for a man who is a Christian and whose trade is with words" (*MB*, 116). This writer finds himself addressing readers who, by and large, find his vision of life outmoded and his vocabulary meaningless. "The old words of grace," Percy continues, "are worn smooth as poker chips and a certain devaluation has occurred, like a poker chip after it is cashed in" (*MB*, 116).

Judging from his interpretation of the modern world, Percy saw himself, while he was writing the first two novels, potentially facing two broad audiences. One was that group of people who are aware that the modern theories of science of humanism have failed to provide them with an adequate explanation of the human condition. These people are in the throes of modern discontent, daily enduring bewildering pain and fear without having the means to understand or transcend it. The second audience Percy saw was that group of people who do not worry about questions of meaning and existence—people who, in Percy's words from "The Delta Factor," "are quite content to live out their lives as the organisms and consumer units their scientists understand them to be" (*MB*, 19). These are the people in the grips of genuine despair; Percy writes in his essay "The Message in the Bottle," that true despair is not the knowledge that one's life is out of joint, but the pretense that all is well: "The worst of all despairs is to imagine one is at home when one is really homeless" (*MB*, 144).

Obviously, there is a big difference between these two classes of readers, with each group having different expectations and ideals. What I want to suggest is that, besides exploring his own dilemmas, Walker Percy was using *The Moviegoer* and *The Last Gentleman* to diagnose the dilemmas facing those readers conscious of their alienation from their own deeper selves and from

the center of life. Significantly, the fate of the modern southerner closely resembles what Percy saw as the fate of these
alienated readers: both groups are cut off from the traditions by
which they had been raised, since both traditions (Stoicism for
the southerner, scientific humanism for the modern man) fail to
account for what is happening in the modern world.

What I think Percy hopes to achieve for these alienated
readers is discussed in another context in Percy's essay "The
Man on the Train." Here he describes a narrative strategy, which
he calls an "aesthetic reversal of alienation" (*MB*, 83) and which I
believe he had in mind when he wrote his first two novels. He
illustrates his concept by describing what happens when an
alienated commuter riding a train reads a book about another
alienated commuter: "the reading commuter rejoices in the
speakability of his alienation and in the new triple alliance of
himself, the alienated character, and the author. His mood is
affirmatory and glad: Yes! that is how it is!—which is an aesthetic
reversal of alienation" (*MB*, 83). Later in this essay Percy adds:
"The modern literature of alienation is in reality the triumphant
reversal of alienation through its re-presenting. It is . . . an
aesthetic victory of comradeliness, a recognition of plight in
common. Its motto is not 'I despair and do not know that I
despair' but 'At least we know that we are lost to ourselves'—
which is very great knowledge indeed" (*MB*, 93). Besides allowing the reader to join in an alliance with the character and the
author, the novels also implicitly point out the way for those who
are alienated and do not know why, as both stories end with
alienated heroes reaching religious perceptions, however tentative and ambiguous, of their own positions in the world.

Unlike Caroline Gordon, who in her postconversion novels
sought to give her readers a concluding shock (by reversing the
flow of the novels and by openly affirming a Catholic vision of
life—a vision that had been undercut up until that point), Percy
kept the endings of his first two novels ambiguous and open to
question. He did not want to sound like an evangelist. "I think I
am conscious of the danger," Percy said in an interview, "of the
novelist trying to draw a moral. What Kierkegaard called 'edify-
ing' would be a fatal step for a novelist."[42] Percy did not want to
put himself in the same class with Mort Prince, whose porno-
graphic novel, *Love*, described in *The Last Gentleman*, ends with a

bluntly religious moral: "'And so I humbly ask of life,' said the hero to his last partner with whose assistance he had managed to coincide with his best expectations, 'that it grant us the only salvation, that of one human being discovering himself through another and through the miracle of love'" (*LG,* 138). "The themes," Percy has said, referring specifically to religious themes, "have to be implicit rather than explicit."[43] Instead of demanding in these first two novels that the reader see Catholicism as the way out of modern malaise, Percy has merely suggested, in a quiet voice, that this is an option to consider.

Sometime after finishing *The Last Gentleman,* Percy's conception of his role as a novelist began to shift. In the Winter 1967–68 issue of *Katallagete* he published an essay entitled "Notes for a Novel about the End of the World," in which he voiced his changing perspective. He speaks in this essay in a new strident voice and with a greater sense of urgency; he talks not about the novelist's role as diagnostician, but about the novelist's role as prophet:

> Since true prophets, i.e., men called by God to communicate something urgent to other men, are currently in short supply, the novelist may perform a quasi-prophetic function. Like the prophet his news is generally bad. . . . It is fitting that he should shock and therefore warn his readers by speaking of last things—if not the Last Day of the Gospels, then of a possible coming destruction, of a laying waste of cities, of vineyards reverting to the wilderness. Like the prophet, he may find himself in radical disagreement with his fellow countrymen. (*MB,* 104)

In a later essay, "The State of the Novel: Dying Art or New Science?" Percy says that the modern writer "may in his own perverse way be a modern version of the Old-Testament prophet who, like Hosea, may have a bad home life, yet who nevertheless and despite himself finds himself stuck with the unpleasant assignment of pointing out to his fellow citizens that something is wrong, that they are on the wrong track."[44]

In coming to see the novelist's role as being similar to a prophet's, Percy became more the religious writer and less the autobiographical—and southern—novelist. He now began to use the novel, to a large extent, as an open assault on modernity rather than as an exploration of his own inner conflicts. No

longer did he attempt to achieve an aesthetic reversal of alienation for the consciously alienated reader (whom he calls in
"Notes for a Novel" "the stranded objectivized consciousness, a
ghost of a man who wanders the earth like Ishmael" [*MB*, 115]).
Instead, in his third and fourth novels, Percy hoped to shock the
complacent reader ("the consumer long since anesthetized and
lost to himself in the rounds of consumership") into an
awareness of his alienated condition. His method became the
attack, and his target the reader's modern sensibilities.

In a 1974 interview Percy admitted that he enjoyed being on
the attack, and he cited the influence of Kierkegaard: "Kierkegaard's whole polemical attitude is very valuable to me. The
idea of being on the attack is very congenial to me because unless
I can build up some steam, generate some polemical steam, I
have difficulty writing. There has to be something under attack."[45] Perhaps even more influential than Kierkegaard's example, however, was that of Flannery O'Connor, who also assaulted
secular modern readers, oftentimes with a vengeance. Percy
owes much to O'Connor, and he mentions her (along with James
Joyce) at the end of "Notes for a Novel" when he answers his
own question of how the Christian novelist should write, "having
cast his lot with a discredited Christendom and having inherited
a defunct vocabulary":

> He does the only thing he can do. Like Joyce's Stephen Dedalus,
> he calls on every ounce of cunning, craft, and guile he can muster
> from the darker regions of his soul. The fictional use of violence,
> shock, comedy, insult, the bizarre, are the everyday tools of his
> trade. How could it be otherwise? How can one possibly write of
> baptism as an event of immense significance when baptism is al-
> ready accepted but accepted by and large as a minor tribal rite
> somewhat secondary in importance to taking the kids to see Santa at
> the department store? Flannery O'Connor conveyed baptism
> through its exaggeration, in one novel as a violent death by drown-
> ing. In answer to a question about why she created such bizarre
> characters, she replied that for the near-blind you have to draw very
> large, simple caricatures. (*MB*, 118)

"So too may it be useful," adds Percy after the above words, "to
write a novel about the end of the world"—which of course he
did, a novel entitled *Love in the Ruins: The Adventures of a Bad
Catholic at a Time near the End of the World* (1971).

By writing a novel set in the future, Percy in effect armed himself with heavy ammunition to attack the ills he saw in present-day society. "It's a good way to do satire," Percy said in an interview, referring to the writing of a futuristic novel. "It gives you a chance to speak to the present society from a futuristic point of view. Then you can exaggerate present trends so that they become noticeable and more subject to satire."[46] And his satire in *Love in the Ruins* is relentless and wide ranging; as Percy himself said, "There's a little something in the book to offend everybody: liberal, conservative, white, black, hawk, dove, Catholic, Protestant, Jew, the english [*sic*], the Irish, the Swedes, Ohioans, Alabamans, to mention only a few."[47]

Percy wanted to shock people from their complacency by walking over their most treasured maxims and attitudes towards life. He has said of *Love in the Ruins* that he did not want merely to rock the boat, he wanted to swamp it: "I wanted to explore how the boat could go under while we are still using words like 'the dignity of the individual' and 'the quality of life.' "[48] By putting the reader through such an ordeal, Percy hoped that the reader could break free of his world of "everydayness," and realize that, like all human beings since the Fall, he is a castaway, a sojourner passing through life to an eternal home.

Showing a person "coming to himself"—that is, realizing his own true nature—is an important element in Percy's novels and essays. In the novels, characters often emerge from ordeals with new insights into their condition; in the essays, one of Percy's favorite anecdotes is the story of the commuter who suffers a heart attack and regains consciousness with a new vision of life. Such an experience is precisely what Percy hoped to give his compacent readers in *Love in the Ruins* and *Lancelot.* Jolted by these novels into a knowledge of man's alienation from God, the reader might now be in a better position to accept what Percy in his essay "The Message in the Bottle" calls "news from across the seas" (*MB,* 147)—that is, the word of God brought by a priest or apostle, or through the sacrament of Christ's body and blood. For, as Percy continues in this same essay, this news "is not news to a fallen man who is a castaway but believes himself to be at home in the world, for he does not recognize his own predicament. It is only news to a castaway who knows himself to be a castaway" (*MB,* 148). Percy does not pretend to be God's messenger, except in the sense that any person can be a vehicle of God's grace to another person. He does hope, however, to put the reader in a position to listen when the messenger comes.

*Love in the Ruins* clearly illustrates Percy's new approach. The novel is set in the not-too-distant future when American civilization as we know it (referred to in the novel as the "Auto Age") has collapsed. We follow the adventures of Dr. Thomas More, a middle-aged physician and scientist, as he tries to keep his three women happy, avoid a pursuing sniper, and save the world with a device he has invented, which he calls a "lapsometer." The lapsometer measures the electrical activity of the different areas of the brain. As More admits, this machine is hardly revolutionary, but his hopes for it certainly are: "But here was the problem: given such a machine, given such readings, could the readings then be correlated with the manifold woes of the Western world, its terrors and rages and murderous impulses? And if so, could the latter be treated by treating the former?"[49] Later More calls the lapsometer a "stethescope of the spirit" (*LR*, 62) and envisions for it nothing less than the possibility of restoring to wholeness the rent soul of modern man.

Much of the first part of the novel consists of Dr. More's description of America and its problems. In this era of the future, people no longer repair things; abandoned cars litter the highways, buildings stand deserted, creeping vines appear everywhere. American society is torn by dissension and polarization: "Americans have turned against each other; race against race, right against left, believer against heathen, San Francisco against Los Angeles, Chicago against Cicero. Vines sprout in sections of New York where not even Negroes will live. Wolves have been seen in downtown Cleveland, like Rome during the Black Plague" (*LR*, 17). Polarized against itself, America is a nation in ruins.

More's descriptions of America and its problems are a significant aspect of Percy's overall narrative strategy in this novel; not only do they establish for the reader the condition of the times, but they also serve to discomfort him. Right from the start Percy wants to knock the reader off guard, to make him aware of the insanity that passes for normalcy in modern life. Heavy exaggeration marks these early pages, with wrenching extremes characterizing all aspects of life, in order to drive

Percy's point home. "Perhaps it is only through the conjuring of catastrophe," Percy writes in "Notes for a Novel," clearly describing his strategy in *Love in the Ruins,* "the destruction of all Exxon signs, and the sprouting of vines in the church pews, that the novelist can make vicarious use of catastrophe in order that he and his reader may come to themselves" (*MB,* 118).

After this description of the disintegration of modern life, Percy then goes on to introduce a number of popular utopian schemes—based on theories of mysticism, primitivism, revolution, and sex—that might be seen as ways to establish a new order. But all of the various utopian visions ultimately fail. Percy's message to the reader is that man *cannot* create a New Eden; and the novel is in a sense an admonition to all those who think they can. "A novelist likes to think that he can issue warnings and influence the course of history,"[50] Percy said at a National Book Award ceremony shortly before *Love in the Ruins* came out, and it is obvious that he was referring to his own intention with this novel.

To this end Percy fiercely attacks a number of popular utopian schemes. Exotic mystical religion, to which More's wife turns after the death of their daughter, is presented as an escapist crutch used to avoid the realities of life and death. Percy exposes the shortcomings of the "back-to-nature" option through Dr. More's visit to a group of young people who have dropped out to follow what one of them calls "a life of perfect freedom and peace" (*LR,* 50) in the swamps; their failure to maintain both themselves (they must continually sneak back to town for supplies) and their happiness (sensual gratification gratifies only for so long) underscore the unreality of such a life.

Percy reserves some of his harshest criticism for a third utopian vision, one based on the idea that a perfect life is one free from sexual tension. He levels his sights at the scientific investigators of the Love Clinic, who believe that if they could discover the formula for the perfect orgasm, the problems of the world would cease: no more hang-ups, no more frustrations. Almost as caustic is his attack on the belief that only by violent revolution and the destruction of society can a new age of peace be ushered in. This vision, held by the black revolutionaries out to overrun Paradise Estates, is, Percy reveals, based not on brotherhood but on greed: when oil is discovered on their land, the blacks forget their call to revolution and instead buy out the whites so that they can enjoy the luxuries they had affected to despise.

As one by one these utopian dreams prove worthless, the impending crisis projected by the novel becomes more imminent. The Roman Catholic Church, that old standby of order and tradition, appears off and on throughout the novel, but it, too, has fallen victim to the polarization that has rent secular society, and apparently can serve as no antidote to the prevailing madness. Early in the novel (*LR*, 5–6) More describes the Church as being now split into three segments: "(1) the American Catholic Church whose new Rome is Cicero, Illinois; (2) the Dutch schismatics who believe in relevance but not God; (3) the Roman Catholic remnant, a tiny scattered flock with no place to go." Not theological issues, but the belief that priests should be allowed to marry, is the overriding issue of the Dutch schismatics, while the creed of the American Catholics epitomizes the absurdity of society: "The American Catholic Church, which emphasizes property rights and the integrity of neighborhoods, retained the Latin mass and plays *The Star-Spangled Banner* at the elevation." The Roman Catholics, retainers of the faith, are "scattered and demoralized." Rather than offering hope, the Church only underscores society's downfall.

The only solution to society's ills held out as a real possibility throughout the novel is Dr. More's lapsometer, which, by implication, represents scientific investigation. According to More, in a train of thought similar to Sutter's in *The Last Gentleman,* the problems tearing civilization apart stem from the split of modern man's psyche into two opposing parts: one promoting abstract activity and the other initiating physical adjustment to the environment. An overemphasis of the former results in what More calls "angelism" ("a person has so abstracted himself from himself and from the world around him, seeing things as theories and himself as a shadow, that he cannot, so to speak, reenter the lovely ordinary world" [*LR*, 341]), while too heavy a tilt to the latter results in "bestialism," which usually manifests itself in an overwhelming sexual appetite. As More observes, the two conditions often occur together: "It is not uncommon nowadays to see patients suffering from angelism-bestialism. A man, for instance, can feel at one and the same time extremely abstracted and inordinately lustful toward lovely young women who may be perfect strangers" (*LR*, 27).

But More hopes to cure these conditions with the lapsometer, what he calls "the first caliper of the soul and the first hope of bridging the dread chasm that has rent the soul of Western man ever since the famous philosopher Descartes ripped the body loose from mind and turned the very soul into a ghost that haunts its own house" (*LR*, 191). So far he has been able to use the lapsometer only for diagnosis; to attain his goal of welding the torn self whole, he needs to discover how to use the lapsometer for treatment as well. More's breakthrough comes when Art Immelman, clearly a Mephistopheles figure, arrives on the scene with a "differential stereotactic emission ionizer" (*LR*, 211). This device is just what Dr. More has been looking for, as it turns the lapsometer into an active tool. The world, it seems, can be saved after all, and Dr. More will get his Nobel Prize.

But events do not work out as planned. Art Immelman passes lapsometers out right and left, and leaves the rest to human nature. People use the machines to stimulate their already dominant characteristics, to attack their enemies, and to seduce their acquaintances. Orgies and riots result. The world appears to be on the brink of disaster. Art Immelman is omnipresent, helping people to get into the act. Dr. More, sensing Immelman's great power, closes his eyes and says a prayer to his namesake: "*Sir Thomas More, kinsman, saint, best dearest merriest of Englishmen, pray for us and drive this son of a bitch hence*" (*LR*, 376). Immelman whirls away and disappears. The next-to-the-last chapter ends here, right in the midst of the crisis.

In the final chapter, set five years after the previous events, the situation has quieted down and the world seems essentially unchanged, except that the once revolutionary, now oil-rich Bantus have moved into Paradise Estates. Dr. More's life has also settled down. Rather than chasing after three women, More has married his former secretary, Ellen Oglethorpe, and they now live in a bare but comfortable old slave cabin raising their two children. More lives a quiet life. He has come to realize that the lapsometer is no panacea for man's problems, and he no longer pursues the Nobel Prize. He still experiments with his invention, but now sees it not as an instrument to bring about a utopia, but merely as a tool which may one day reveal to man his true condition of "sovereign wanderer, lordly exile, worker and waiter and watcher" (*LR*, 383). Another change, of great significance, is that Dr. More has returned to his old faith, Roman Catholicism. For the first time in years he feels ashamed of his sins; he confesses, attends mass, and receives communion.

Percy's message here at the end—after revealing the short-comings of many utopian schemes—is not that man must live without hope for himself or for the future, but that he should live according to his fate as fallen creature. According to Percy, man is a wayfarer, whose alienation is an inevitable result of his separation from God, inherited from Adam—*not* a psychological disorder. Rather than daydreaming about a utopia, man should follow Father Smith's advice to More: "Meanwhile, forgive me but there are other things we must think about: like doing our jobs, you being a better doctor, I being a better priest, showing a bit of ordinary kindness to people, particularly our own families—unkindness to those close to us is such a pitiful thing—doing what we can for our poor unhappy country—things which, please forgive me, sometimes seem more important than dwelling on a few middle-aged daydreams" (*LR*, 399). The priest's admonition humbles More, and Percy hopes that it will have the same effect on the reader. The novel's final message is that the way to health is to accept man's fallen condition and his fate as wayfarer.

With *Love in the Ruins* Percy exposes not only what he sees as the most pressing problems of modern existence, but also the finally ineffective utopian solutions so commonly proposed to answer them. Like Allen Tate and Caroline Gordon, Percy boldly attacks any scheme for man's betterment that fails to take into account man's fallen condition and his propensity for evil. Only after revealing the myopia of man's utopian vision does he quietly suggest, with Father Smith's words, the Catholic alterna-tive. Perhaps now, having seen the failures of the other solutions, the reader will listen to Father Smith and follow Dr. More's example. There is nothing heavy-handed in Percy's description of More's return to the Church, and indeed much of this final chapter is concerned not with More's religious struggles but with his happy life with his wife Ellen, their children, and his job. The novel ends on a note of quiet domestic optimism and content-ment: "To bed we go for a long winter's nap, twined about each other as the ivy twineth, not under a bush or in a car or on the floor or any such humbug as marked the past peculiar years of Christendom, but at home in bed where all good folk belong" (*LR*, 403).

*Love in the Ruins* succeeds as a satirical futuristic novel resting on a theological vision. Through its distorted and exaggerated action, Percy communicates his theological concerns. But in the process of molding a work designed to shock and disorient, Percy must necessarily flatten out his artistic vision; he must downplay the complexities of man's identity and fate in the modern world—particularly the tension between Stoicism and Christianity—in order to adopt a less complex satirical vision integrally tied to his didactic intent. For this reason, *Love in the Ruins* lacks the depth and intensity of Percy's previous novels, though on the level of satire it is very effective.

With his fourth novel, *Lancelot* (1977), Percy sought to combine his two strategies for reaching modern readers: he rooted his novel in the crucial action of the consciously alienated man's search for meaning and identity (as in *The Moviegoer* and *The Last Gentleman*), while at the same time boldly assaulting the complacent reader with abusive language and satire (as in *Love in the Ruins*). As a result, *Lancelot* is Percy's most intense and most upsetting novel. While unmistakably his—as in all Percy novels there is the hilarious songlike dialogue, the beautiful-absurd places and women, the quasi-scientific precision of color and gesture and voice—*Lancelot* focuses, in a manner different from that of the other novels, on the violence and hatred of a man gone mad, a man who time and again lashes out at the civilization which the reader calls home.

Percy's new focus is not wholly evident during the opening pages of the novel, as Lancelot ("Lance") Andrewes Lamar tells his story to Percival, his boyhood friend turned Roman Catholic priest. There is a good deal of lighthearted humor, and Lancelot himself appears to be another of Percy's disoriented but not unattractive heroes. As the novel progresses, however, Lance's views of the world soon begin to lose their comic vitality, and it becomes clear that he is quite different from the essentially gentle protagonists of Percy's other novels. Lance's observations soon become the distorted ravings of a man who has let his Stoic ideals of honor and courtesy run wild. Over and over again he blasts offensively worded indictments against today's society, focusing most scathingly on what he sees as the insidious forces of permissiveness, sexual and otherwise. Women, whose liberation movement infuriates Lance because his idol, the Southern belle, falls before it, bear the brunt of his most caustic attacks: "A generation stoned and pussy free and devalued, pricks after pussy, pricks after pricks, pussy after pussy. But most of all pussy after pricks. Christ what a country! A nation of 100 million voracious cunts."[51]

With Lancelot's tirades, which grotesquely exaggerate modern life, Percy hopes not only to reveal the limits of Stoicism, but also to electrify the callous sensibilities of complacent readers. Undoubtedly Percy realized that the novel's violent insults and shocks would fill many readers with disgust. But he also hoped that for many others the discomforting extremes would have a purgative effect, that these readers would be propelled out of their locked-in confines of everydayness. Once these readers begin to feel a little disoriented, the novel speaks tellingly to them; for *Lancelot* examines the problem of searching for options in today's madhouse society, when one has realized its absurdity and one's fate of being a stranger in its midst.

Lance's story begins disarmingly enough. Like the complacent readers at whom Percy aims the novel, he lives a quiet and unassuming life; he is a husband and father, and caretaker of his ancestral home, which has become a tourist attraction. Mired in what he calls a life of "unacknowledged idleness," he passes his days in a stale routine, "drinking and watching TV, working at play, playing at work" (*L*, 65). But when he discovers that he cannot possibly be the actual father of his daughter, Lance finds himself in a new realm of freedom and action. As he steps free from the worn path of his old life, he enters a new realm: "There was a sense of astonishment, of discovery, of a new world opening up, but the new world was totally unknown. Where does one go from here?" (*L*, 42). Lance's problem of not knowing how to act or where to go is shared by the suddenly uncomplacent reader of the novel, and Lance's actions therefore take on a grand importance, for they represent one way to pass through this uncharted realm.

Lance's first move is to declare that, like his medieval namesake, Lancelot du Lak, he will set out on a quest. But unlike the original Lancelot who sought the Holy Grail, Lance will be a "Knight of the Unholy Grail," searching for "one 'sin,' one pure act of malevolence" (*L*, 138). "'Evil,'" Lance continues, "is surely the clue to this age, the only quest appropriate to the age. For everything and everyone's either wonderful or sick and nothing is evil." If he could find just one true sin, he thinks, unmitigated and unexcused by today's limp amorality, then the old Judeo-Christian way of life would begin to make sense. He says that he might even return to the Church if his quest proves successful, since "if there is such a thing as sin, evil, a living malignant force, there must be a God!" (*L*, 52).

Lance's first move, then, is an instinctive search for God, although his pursuit of this goal is twisted and bizarre. To discover sin, he plans to make a film of his wife's adultery. Later he says that he has not found sin and that his quest is a failure—this despite the fact that he actually walked in on his wife having sex with her lover, committed adultery himself, and coldly calculated and executed a triple murder. To his disappointment, his act of murder brought no sense of evil or guilt. "All it came down to," he says, "was steel molecules entering skin molecules, artery molecules, blood cells" (*L*, 254). He concludes that there is no evil in the world: the Unholy Grail, together with the Holy one, is a sham.

After Lance becomes convinced that his quest has revealed nothing, he declares that he is rejecting both the present age and the Catholic faith, and is going to start a new society, which he calls at one point "the new Reformation" (*L*, 177). He says that he could live in modern society as it is only if he could believe in God; but he cannot believe. Catholicism itself, Lance declares to the priest Percival, has been diluted by modern permissiveness: "I might have tolerated you and your Catholic Church, and even joined it, if you had remained true to yourself. Now you're part of the age. You've the same fleas as the dogs you've lain down with" (*L*, 157). The old ways have nothing to offer him; Lance will start afresh, initiating a new order in that old womblike seat of southern glory and defeat, the Shenandoah Valley.

Lance's vision of a new society is clearly an embodiment of the Stoic tradition of the Old South. Life there will be based on the codes of courtesy and chivalry by which Lance believes noble men of the past acted. People will be self-reliant and will live simple, wholesome lives: "One will work and take care of one's own, live and let live, and behave with a decent respect toward others" (*L*,158). One will find in this new life "a tight-lipped courtesy between men. And chivalry toward women. . . . Women will once again be strong and modest. Children will be merry because they will know what they are to do" (*L*, 158–59). Christian love is not part of the plan; the only virtues here will be those of the old broadsword.

In some ways Lance's vision seems like *the* answer; compared to the chaos of modern civilization, a retreat to the woods to initiate a simpler life (such an American dream!) carries a strong appeal. Lance's vision seems also, on one level, close to the Agrarian dream that Allen Tate found so attractive for a while. Tate eventually turned away from Agrarianism, criticizing it for its lack of a religious base. Percy carries the criticism of such dreams even further. As he makes clear in the novel, the new order Lance plans is rooted not in honor and integrity but in anger and hate. His vision also fails to come to grips with the problems of modern alienation and despair; he skirts these issues with the simple assertion that all one has to do to clear the air is to start over again. This is an unrealistic dream, Percy makes clear, and certainly no method of curing man's and society's broken condition.

One way to understand the futility of Lance's dream is to compare it with the life Thomas More establishes at the end of *Love in the Ruins*. At first glance, Lance's vision of a new way seems to coincide with More's new life: More has retreated with his new wife and family to an old brick slave cabin, where they live a quiet life and enjoy the simple pleasures of good boots and hot morning grits. But upon closer examination some crucial differences appear. Thomas More's rejection of modern emptiness and his achievement of inner peace include his acceptance, however reluctant, of Christian faith. More is not a new Adam, as Lance hopes to be, starting afresh without the taint of sin. Significantly, at the end of the book More feels ashamed of his sins and attends confession for the first time in eleven years. In contrast, the life Lancelot is planning will be one of secular chivalry, founded not on charity but on rage. When Percival hints at this shortcoming in Lance's plans, Lance's reply goes right to the terrorist anger that lies at the heart of his vision:

"What did you whisper? Love? That I am full of hatred, anger? Don't talk to me of love until we shovel out the shit" (*L*, 179). Again in contrast with Thomas More, Lance believes that he can cut himself off from the past, and asserts that he is not responsible for the actions of his old life. But this is only a pipe dream: having refused the comfort of confession and absolution, Lance is bound forever to the numbness and emptiness that his sins have wrought in him. "I feel so cold, Percival," he says when he finishes his tale (*L*, 253), and running off to the Shenandoah Valley will not cure this chill.

In contrast to Lance's dream of a new order stands Percival's Catholicism. Throughout most of the novel Percival maintains his patient silence, calling to mind Percy's statement, in "Notes for a Novel about the End of the World," that "the old words of grace are worn smooth as poker chips" (*MB*, 116). But he and his Catholicism clearly represent Percy's alternative to Lance's Stoic vision. Near the end of the book, a crucial exchange takes place between Lance and Percival, with Lance speaking first:

> It's [modern civilization] all over, isn't it? I can see it in your eyes. We agree after all.
> *Yes.*
> Yes, but? But what? There must be a new beginning, right?
> *Yes—*
> But? You don't like the new beginning I propose?
> You are silent. So you are going to go to your little church in Alabama and that's it.
> *Yes.*
> So what's the new beginning in that? Isn't that just more of the same?
> You are silent.
> Very well. But you know this! One of us is wrong. It will be your way or it will be my way.
> *Yes.*
> All we can agree on is that it will not be their way. Out there.
> *Yes.*
> There is no other way than yours or mine, true?
> *Yes.* (*L*, 256–57)

This conversation asserts that only two real alternatives to modern life exist: Lance's Stoicism or Percival's Catholicism. The choice must be made. As Lance says, "One of us is wrong. It will be your way or it will be my way."

Like Lance, the reader must also decide which way is right. Percy's strategy here is simple: to force the reader to choose between Lancelot and Percival. But he offers this choice only after he has revealed the hatred and horror that forms the foundation of Lancelot's vision. Unlike the conclusions of his previous novels, where Percy asks us to come around to the protagonist's perspective, here he compels us to reject Lance's vision and to find an alternative—in this case the *only* alternative, the Church, which Percival represents. Otherwise, we must take sides with Lancelot, an extremist burning with rage and described at one point as appearing like "Lucifer blown out of hell, great wings spread against the starlight" (*L*, 246).

That Lancelot's vision ultimately comes up short next to Percival's should come as no surprise when we remember that Percy strikes corresponding chords between the action of the novel and the medieval legend of the Quest for the Holy Grail. While Robert Coles has provided us with an excellent discussion of the relationship between Tennyson's *Idylls of the King* and *Lancelot*,[52] an even more instructive comparison comes when one reads Percy's novel in the light of another version of the Lancelot tale, the twelfth-century French romance *Queste del Saint Graal*. The Round Table society in this medieval tale is near collapse, beset from within by the sins of the various unchaste knights and unchaste ladies. To heal the kingdom, King Arthur sends his knights on the holiest quest possible, the search for the chalice used by Christ at the Last Supper. Most of them fail, however, including the noble Lancelot, because their secular chivalry is useless in bringing them this highest, holiest privilege. Lancelot almost succeeds, through his courage and great heart, but he is denied the final victory because his highest allegiance is not to Christ, but to the chivalric ideals of love and honor. His best love is saved not for the Lord, but for Guinevere. Percival, on the other hand, is a true knight of Christ and succeeds in his quest.

Both *Queste del Saint Graal* and Percy's *Lancelot* ultimately explore the same crucial questions: can one initiate a new life, free from the decadence of society, by practicing a purely secular chivalric code of honor and simplicity? Or must one grapple with the significance of Christ's love and death and resurrection? Both works end by affirming the need to follow Christ.

"Very well, I've finished," Lancelot says at the end of the novel. "Is there anything you wish to tell me before I leave?" *"Yes,"* answers Percival *(L, 257)*. This affirmative reply is the novel's last word. Lance's story and his wild theorizing are finished. Percival, as God's spokesman, can now help Lance pick up the pieces of his destroyed life by pointing out to him the true path; Percy hopes that the jolted reader, also, will someday listen to the voice of God's messenger in his own life. Percy means us to see that if Percival reaches Lancelot with Christ's message, then Lancelot Andrewes Lamar (the French name "Lamar" means "dweller by the pool," recalling the medieval Lancelot's title "Lancelot du Lak") will reject the heritage of the chivalric knights as typified by his medieval namesake. Instead, he will follow the path embodied in the life of his other namesake: Lancelot Andrewes, the Anglican divine. Rather than raging against the world as he does in the novel, Lancelot will humbly and quietly confess his sins and plead for God's mercy, as Lancelot Andrewes does in his private *Devotions:*

> Remove the dark and muddy flood
> of foul and wicked thoughts.
> O Lord,
> I have destroyed myself:
> whatever I have done amiss,
> pardon mercifully.[53]

*Lancelot* is a powerful and compelling novel in which Percy traces once again, in much more violent terms than before, the dilemma he sees modern southerners facing: how to live in the modern world after the collapse of the Stoic tradition. The novel is perhaps flawed by its violence, arguably turning the reader away from, instead of towards, the spiritual issues embodied in the action. Percy here faces the same type of problem that plagued Flannery O'Connor (to whose work *Lancelot* owes a great deal): that is, how far could the writer, using O'Connor's words, "distort without destroying"?[54] How far, in other words, could Percy distort the novel's action for the purpose of spiritual edification without making it self-destruct on its basic level of story?

If some readers see *Lancelot* as being too violent, others will see *The Second Coming* (1980), Percy's fifth novel, as not being violent enough, not sufficiently compelling to embody the serious theological questions it addresses. With *The Second Coming* Percy abandons, at least for the time being, his stance of novelist as prophet, and returns—his own second coming—to the less strident and more subtle stance of the novelist as diagnostician, the stance he had taken in *The Moviegoer* and *The Last Gentleman.* Once again, Percy seeks to establish an "aesthetic reversal of alienation" between himself, his characters, and those readers who find themselves living without meaning or order in the twentieth century.

*The Second Coming* is also Will Barrett's second coming. The novel picks up Will's life about twenty years after his exploits in *The Last Gentleman,* in which we last saw him taking off into the desert with Sutter Vaught. Barrett, we now learn, apparently gave up his perilous search for meaning and decided to live a more nearly normal life. He moved north, became a successful Wall Street lawyer, married a stunningly rich woman, and now, at the time of *The Second Coming,* is spending an early retirement in Linwood, North Carolina, a small town in the mountains. Most of the time he takes life easy; he plays lots of golf. His deceased wife, Marion, has left Barrett a fortune of fifty million dollars. Many people would say that Barrett has it made.

But has he? Although he is immensely wealthy and no longer suffers from the fugue states and fits of amnesia that beset him during *The Last Gentleman,* Barrett now faces other problems. One of these is the disturbing fact that, although he has achieved what he set out to do, he still has a feeling that his life has slipped by. This realization first became apparent during Marion's illness and death. "How can it be?" Will remembers asking himself while talking with his wife on her deathbed. "How can it happen that one day you are young, you marry, and then another day you come to yourself and your life has passed like a dream?"[55] "Not once in his entire life had he allowed himself to come to rest in the quiet center of himself," Will comments elsewhere, "but had forever cast himself forward from some dark past he could not remember to a future which did not exist. Not once had he been present for his life. So his life had passed like a dream" (*SC,* 123–24).

Another symptom is even more disturbing. In a process one doctor calls an "association response," a trivial image such as hawk flying across the sky can cause Barrett to block out present reality as his mind slips into the past to relive events associated with that image. These fits of intense memory are so overwhelming that Barrett sometimes blacks out, becoming in a sense a time traveler, lost to the present world.

One particularly persistent intrusion from his past is a hunting trip that Barrett took with his father when he was twelve. On this trip his father wounded both himself and his son, hitting the boy apparently when a quail rose up in front of him and then somehow also shooting himself. Over and over again, Barrett relives the scene, sorting out the details like a detective on a murder case, trying to create a pattern by which to explain this disturbing scene. Particularly puzzling to him is the fact that his father loaded, shot, and reloaded his shotgun; moreover, he wonders, how could his father, expert marksman and skilled outdoorsman, have wounded himself by accident?

Finally Barrett reaches an inescapable conlusion: Lawyer Barrett had tried to kill both himself and Will, and, for some finally unexplained reason, had missed the mark on all three shots (he had fired both barrels at his son). "Well, whatever the reason," Will says to himself, in words addressed to his father, "you corrected it the next time, didn't you?" (*SC*, 148). He refers here to his father's later suicide (described in *The Last Gentleman*), when he eliminated the possibility of error by putting the shotgun into his mouth.

Will understands the motives for both his father's suicide and his attempted murder-suicide during the hunting trip: through these acts, his father was rejecting the modern world. His father's Stoic philosophy, which called for a life based on honor and integrity, was so drastically undercut by the onslaughts of the modern world that existence had become for him a death-in-life. "You loved only death," Will addresses the ghost of his father, "because for you what passed for life was really a death-in-life, which has no name and so is worse than death" (*SC*, 133). Anger, says Will, was the bedrock of his father's Stoicism; Lawyer Barrett acted out the ultimate rejection, declaring, "I will not put up with a life which is not life or death" (*SC*, 131).

After his father's death, Will tried to free himself from the grip of his influence, and particularly from the gloom embodied in his suicide. His move north and his immersion into "an ordinary mild mercantile money-making life" was an effort to move as far as possible from the world represented by his father. "And I was never so glad of anything," he tells his father in his thoughts, "as I was to get away from your doom and your death-dealing and your great honor and great hunts and great hates (Jesus, you could not even walk down the street on Monday morning without either wanting to kill somebody or swear a blood oath of allegiance with somebody else), yes, your great allegiance swearing and your old stories of great deeds which not even you had done but had just heard about, and under it all the death-dealing which nearly killed me and did you" (*SC*, 72). He says that he even tried—and failed—to believe in the Christian God, merely in order to differ from his unbelieving father.

Finally, however, Will is forced to reassess his life by his father's standards. He is compelled to do this by those haunting memories of the hunting expedition and by the nagging sense that his life has been an empty dream ("Now Marion is dead and I can't believe I spent all those years in New York in Trusts and Estates and taking dogs down elevators and out to the park to take a crap" [*SC*,73]). Will is tormented by his father's words to him during that fateful hunt: *"You're one of us, I'm afraid"* (*SC*, 55). Now, years later, in a moment of almost uncontrollable rage at a lazy servant, he finally accepts the fact that he is of the same ilk as his father: "Yes, very well. I'm one of you. You win" (*SC*, 171).

But despite this realization of his ties to his father and the fact that he, too, finds himself unable to accept the death-in-life of modern existence, Will also sees that his father did not look for any alternative other than death: "It dawned on him that his father's suicide was *wasted*. It availed nothing, proved nothing, posed no questions let alone answered any questions, did nobody good. It was no more than an exit, a getting up and a going out, a closing of a door" (*SC*, 182). Though Will does not rule out suicide for himself, he says that he will first test the possibility of another option: Christian faith. He devises an experiment, which he says will settle once and for all the question of God's existence. He will descend into a cave, and there wait for a sign from God. If none comes, he will stay in the cave to die; if he does see a sign, he will emerge knowing that Christ's words are true and that there does exist a way for him to live. "Can you discover a single flaw in this logic?" he writes to Sutter Vaught, who long ago gave up his own quest for truth (settling down instead to practice medicine and watch television). "I've got him!" Will writes, referring to God. "No more tricks! No more *deus absconditus!*" (*SC*, 192).

Will's experiment, however, proves inconclusive. After spending seven or eight days in the cave in drugged consciousness (he has taken with him a thirty-two-day supply of Placidyl), he develops a toothache so severe "that every heartbeat feels like a hot ice pick shoved straight up into the brain." To make matters worse, waves of nausea rush over him, making him so sick from vomiting that he ultimately decides to abandon his experiment. As the narrative consciousness points out, "There is one sure cure for cosmic explorations, grandiose ideas about God, man, death, suicide, and such—and that is nausea. . . . A nauseated man is a sober man. A nauseated man is a disinterested man" (*SC*, 213). So it is with Will. "Let me out of here," he says in his sickness, "with no thought of God, Jews, suicide, tigers, or the Last Days" (*SC*, 223). He now begins his perilous quest—he is so weak that he falls down a shaft and gets lost—to get out of the cave. The possibility that the toothache could be God's sign, forcing Will to return to the world above, where he belongs, never crosses his mind.

After floundering around the cave, Will sees a small square of light. Pushing through the opening he slips and falls, landing with a crash on the concrete floor of a greenhouse that has been built into the mountain. In the greenhouse lives Allison Huger, the nineteen-year-old daughter of Kitty Vaught Huger (Will's old flame in *The Last Gentleman,* who went on to marry a dentist). Allison's story comprises close to half of *The Second Coming,* presented in alternating chapters with Will's, until their stories merge at the end of the novel.

Allison is a recent escapee from a mental institution, where, diagnosed as a schizophrenic, she underwent a series of electric-shock treatments. She now lives, a fugitive, in the old greenhouse on some land she inherited; disoriented and given to fits of forgetfulness, she is trying hard to establish a place for herself. Like Will, Allison is on a search of sorts, trying to discover a way to order her life and be happy. Particularly puzzling to her is how to relate to people. In a note to herself, written while at the institution in anticipation of some guidance she will need after her escape, she writes: "What about people? Men? Do you want (1) to live with another person? (2) a man? (3) a woman? (4) no one? (5) Do you want to make love with another person? (6) 'Fall in love'? (7) What is 'falling in love'? (8) Is it part of making love or different? (9) Do you wish to marry? (10) None of these? (11) Are people necessary?" (*SC*, 239).

Allison knows the answers to few of these questions. While living at the greenhouse, she does discover, however, that she can be fairly happy by herself, except during the late afternoons when she yearns for companionship. This afternoon letdown disturbs her, because it suggests that she needs someone in her life. Also unsettling is the question of sex, which keeps plaguing her as men try, unsuccessfully, to pick her up. She wonders if having sex (or, as she says, "doing it") is the same thing as "falling in love." "What did she want?" she asks herself at one point. "Was she supposed to want to 'do it'? If she was supposed to, who was doing the supposing? Was it a matter of 'falling in love'?" (*SC*, 241).

Predictably, Will and Allison find happiness together. With "Allie," Will becomes strong enough to exorcise once and for all his father's ghost, which tempts him to commit suicide. In a climactic moment, as the tempter whispers in his ear, trying to make him take "the one quick sure exit of grace and violence and beauty" (*SC*, 336–37), he tosses his father's shotgun and his own pistol down an overlook. Will is now free to live. And so is Allie, who finds that having sex with Will is more than just "doing it": it is, rather, the joyous expression of their newfound unity. "Oh my," she says to Will. "It is now evident that whatever was wrong with me is now largely cured. Quel mystery" (*SC*, 340).

Together Will and Allie plan their new life: marriage, a child, a job for Will in a modest law office; Allie will work on the greenhouse and build more cabins and greenhouses on her land. Will arranges for some friends he met at the local rest home—old people, still fit for work, but whose lives at the home are filled with nothing but boredom and television—to help Allie with her projects.

At the very end of the novel (*SC*, 358–60), Will visits Father Weatherbee, an old emaciated priest whose two interests are the Seaboard Air Line Railroad and the Apostolic Succession. Will wants Father Weatherbee to perform his and Allie's marriage ceremony. He senses that he can learn from the old priest something that will help in his ongoing investigation into God's existence. "Accordingly," he tells Father Weatherbee, "I am willing to be told whatever it is you seem to know and I will attend carefully to what you say." Father Weatherbee then launches into a speech about the contradictions in modern society: "How can we be the best dearest most generous people on earth, and at the same time so unhappy? How harsh everyone is here! How restless! How impatient! How worried! How sarcastic! How unhappy! How hateful! How pleasure-loving! How lascivious! Above all, how selfish!" "Why can't we be grateful for our great blessings and thank God?" he asks. He describes an isolated and poverty-ridden village where he once worked as a missionary. The people there were happy and content, and, what's more, he says, "They believed me! They believed the Gospel whole and entire, and the teachings of the church."

"Right!" answers Barrett, sensing the truth of Father Weatherbee's words and realizing that the life of this village in many ways resembles what he envisions for himself and Allie and his collection of society's castoffs. He grabs the priest's wrists, thinking about Allie at the same time. And then, in the final words of the novel, Will realizes that God has indeed sent him a sign: "His heart leapt with a secret joy. What is it I want from her and him, he wondered, not only want but must have? Is she a gift and therefore a sign of a giver? Could it be that the Lord is here, masquerading behind this simple silly holy face? Am I crazy to want both, her and Him? No, not want, must have. And will have."

Walker Percy has said that he considers *The Second Coming* his "first unalienated novel," and that "there's a definite advance, a resolution of the ambiguity with which some of my other novels end: the victory, in Freudian terms, of eros over thanatos, life over death."[56] Though it is indeed the clearest expression of his vision of life's victory with Christ's love, the ending of *The Second Coming* resonates with echoes from *The Moviegoer* and *Love in the Ruins,* where Binx and Thomas More also settled down to live with love and faith. But how sharply this novel differs from *Lancelot,* in which Percy dealt so sternly with his readers! With *The Second Coming,* Percy has switched from a strategy of fierce assault to one of easygoing sentimentality (with touches of satire thrown in here and there). "It's a very ordinary, conventional story," Percy has said of *The Second Coming,* "that could even be seen in Hollywood terms: Boy meets girl, boy loses girl, and boy gets girl."[57] While much of the story line is very conventional, the message behind it certainly is not, and the two elements do not merge wholly successfully. The sentimentality of the conclusion weakens the point Percy is making about Will's movement towards the Church. We sense little effort or struggle as Will and Allie plan their new life; after all their previous anguish, the ease with which they start afresh seems artificial and unduly romantic. Particularly saccharine is the scene where Will frees the old folks from the confines of their rest home. No mention is made of the frailties of human nature; all is rosy, as the deserving elderly help the new lovers with their idealistic projects.

While flawed by its sentimentality, *The Second Coming* remains an effective novel, and its happy ending resolves many of the disturbing issues Percy has raised here and in his other works about man's existential dilemmas. With this novel, Percy concludes the story of Will Barrett, exorcises the spirit of the Stoic tradition, points almost directly to Catholicism as its replacement, and celebrates Christian marriage as one solution to the modern malaise.

Percy continues, however, to probe the ongoing questions surrounding man's fate. His recent work of nonfiction, *Lost in the Cosmos: The Last Self-Help Book,* spoofs the structure and intent of the myriad self-help books currently available. He uses a series of loaded questions and "thought experiments" (hypothetical situations to which readers are asked to imagine a response); these are designed to unsettle his readers and make them realize the many searing contradictions that the human condition entails. Percy's overriding theme here is that man is able to explain the workings of almost every element of the universe—except himself. Percy has wrestled with this problem from the beginning of his career; his struggles to articulate an approach to meaning and fulfillment, along with his efforts to persuade us to join with him in this search, have passed through several stages and still continue today.

# Epilogue

In his essay "Postmortem on a Rebirth: The Catholic Intellectual Renaissance," James Hitchcock points out that an unusually high number of distinguished Catholic philosophers and writers in the twentieth century have been converts. He notes that the conversion phenomenon—which brought with it a flourishing of intellectual endeavor—occurred roughly during the years between Pope Pius X's condemnation of Modernism in 1907 (when he issued *Lamentabili Sani Exitu* and *Dominici Gregis*) and the early 1960s when, during the pontificate of Pope John XXIII (1958–63) and the term of Second Vatican Council (1962–65), Pius X's strictures limiting intellectual dissent and historical inquiry were loosened. Though recognizing that many Catholics prefer to see these intervening years as a reign of terror, marked by the stifling of free expression and the smudging of the Church's image, Hitchcock goes on to say that "the remarkable fact is that the distinguished converts of the twentieth century were attracted to the Church, not in spite of the condemnation [by Pope Pius X of Modernism], but almost, in some cases, because of it. What they found attractive and credible in it were precisely those things which Pius X sought to protect with his condemnation, and they found the characteristic doctrines of Modernism either false or uninteresting."[1] "Intellectual converts," Hitchcock adds later in his essay, "are almost always attracted to rather traditional and even rigorous versions of religion, probably because liberalized religion merely confirms the skeptic's suspicion that the traditional faith was false."[2]

Although Hitchcock's essay focuses primarily on European Catholics, without mentioning Allen Tate, Caroline Gordon, or Walker Percy, it nonetheless comes very close to summarizing their reasons for turning to the Church. As we have seen, these three writers all were attracted to the Church because of its steadfast traditions and rigorous definitions of order. Raised in the predominately anti-Catholic South amidst conservative Old South traditions, these three converts came to see the Church as a way to reestablish an order they lost when, as adults, they entered the modern world. Other systems—such as social and economic theories based on a belief in humanity's infinite potential—they found both false and unappealing. As Caroline Gordon has pointed out, growing up in the South meant imbibing a profound knowledge of human weakness and evil, a knowledge that cut against the grain of liberal social philosophy.

Both Tate and Gordon, early in their careers, sought to create order through art, and both came to realize that the creation of artifacts—a momentary and fragmented assertion of unity—ultimately failed to fulfill their longings. As Tate was to discover during his involvement with the Agrarians, a secular historical identity also fell short, even when grounded in the ideals of the Old South. After leaving the South, Walker Percy initially believed that science and medicine offered a way to comprehend and master the complexities of life; later, during his years of self-education while he lay sick with tuberculosis, he discovered that a crucial element was unaccounted for: man himself. Science, he came to see, could not explain the human condition and its seemingly inexplicable infirmities and pain. Armed with the realization that they craved both a religious view of man and a strictly structured tradition, Tate, Gordon, and Percy came to believe that only Roman Catholicism could fulfill their needs.

For Tate and Gordon, both of whom had pursued long and distinguished writing careers before they became Catholics, joining the Church greatly affected the direction and shape of their art and their vision. (Percy, in contrast, did not begin his writing career until after he was converted.) Admitting that most of his preconversion poetry was about his suffering from unbelief, Tate virtually ceased writing poetry after his conversion. After writing the three terza-rima poems, "The Maimed Man," "The Swimmers," and "The Buried Lake," in the early 1950s, through which he reevaluated his past in the light of his Catholic vision, Tate became primarily an essayist and lecturer—and a staunch defender of the Church. His struggles with unbelief, together with the poetry they gave rise to, were over.

Caroline Gordon's artistic vision, too, suffered with her conversion, at least in those works written soon after her entry into the Church. Her best work was done before her conversion, when she used her art to wrestle with the problem of man's tragic destiny in a chaotic world. After her acceptance of the faith, those wrenching questions of man's identity and purpose, which she once saw embodied in man's heroic struggle to assert a private dignity, were put to rest—too easily, it seems, at least as evidenced in her fiction. As a Catholic, Gordon came to see art as the "handmaiden of the Church."[3] Unfortunately, this description proved all too accurate of her own writing; it became true to the Church, but false to experience, manipulated towards a theological goal. After her conversion, Gordon wrote less out of a struggle within herself and more from a wish to move people towards the Church. Her attempt was overly blatant and heavy-handed; much of her work from this period is too obviously didactic. After those initial years of her conversion, however, Gordon took a new path in her writing, returning to explore some of those old problems of heroism and struggle with which she was still concerned. Rather than belittling those problems, as she had been doing since her conversion, Gordon now sought to merge them with her Christianity; a stronger and more forceful body of art resulted, though it still lacked the depth of her work from the 1930s.

Walker Percy, like Gordon, has been acutely aware of his identity as Catholic writer facing a hostile audience, and he, too, has developed strategies to bridge the gap. Several of his works, particularly *Love in the Ruins* and *Lancelot*, resemble Gordon's (in method though not in style) in that they use an underlying strategy to shock and disorient secular readers. In his other novels, Percy speaks with a quieter, gentler voice, relying more on suggestion and ambiguity to communicate with a more enlightened, or consciously alienated audience. Like Gordon, Percy sometimes overplays his Catholic bias and lets his theological message take precedence over his artistic judgment. In his best work, though, Percy draws also on his secular consciousness, which is firmly rooted in the southern landscape and in traditional Stoic ideals. The tension created between Old South Stoicism and Catholicism gives several of his novels great power and depth.

According to Flannery O'Connor, Catholic writers possess two sets of eyes: their own, which observe the world, and the Church's, which peer through the material world to the larger realm of Christian truth. "It would be foolish to say there is no conflict between these two sets of eyes," wrote O'Connor. "There is a conflict, and it is a conflict which we escape at our peril, one which cannot be settled beforehand by theory or fiat or faith."[4] At their best, O'Connor said, Catholic writers work with and draw from this tension. At their worst, they avoid it, either by writing only through the perspective of the Church (thereby creating what she called "pious trash") or by using only their personal vision (thereby fashioning works merely "in the fashion of a camera").[5] O'Connor's words speak tellingly of the southern Catholic writers looked at in this study, for all of them needed some underlying tension working against the Church—usually derived from their southern allegiances—to compel them to remain true to their own eyes and to restrain them from becoming unconvincingly moralistic. Out of this tension, these writers brought forth their best art; without it, their work was flat and predictable, usually designed primarily to convert the heathen, as we can see in certain instances in the fiction of Gordon and Percy. Once Tate no longer wrestled with the contradictions between the Church and the world, he turned away from writing introspective poetry (after writing the three terza-rima poems immediately following his conversion).

As a result of their struggles with belief and craft, these writers produced a significant body of literature. They wrote from a region which, at first glance, seems unlikely and unfertile ground for such a flowering. Ironically, though, as we have seen, the peculiarities of the modern South—America's Protestant Bible Belt and the heartland of an eroding tradition of life based on Stoic ideals and strong community bonds—inspired intellectuals searching for a lost order to turn towards the Church. The South also provided rich material for their work as artists, so much so that Flannery O'Connor was prompted to write that "the opportunities for the potential Catholic writer in the South are so great as to be intimidating."[6] The South, Modernism, the literary priesthood, Agrarianism—many forces of twentieth-century culture come together in the lives and works of Allen Tate, Caroline Gordon, and Walker Percy, three southern writers who as adults embraced the faith and traditions of the Roman Catholic Church.

# Notes

## Introduction

1. Flannery O'Connor, "The Catholic Novelist in the Protestant South," in *Mystery and Manners: Occasional Prose,* ed. Sally and Robert Fitzgerald (New York: Farrar, Straus & Giroux, 1969), pp. 200–201.

2. Flannery O'Connor, *The Habit of Being: Letters,* ed. Sally Fitzgerald (New York: Farrar Straus Giroux, 1979), p. 374. All further citations to O'Connor's letters are from this edition and will be cited parenthetically *(HB)* in the text.

3. Jackson Lears, *No Place of Grace: Antimodernism and the Transformation of American Culture 1880–1920* (New York: Pantheon, 1981), p. 43.

4. Lewis P. Simpson, *The Brazen Face of History: Studies in the Literary Consciousness in America* (Baton Rouge: Louisiana State University Press, 1980), pp. 4–6.

5. Simpson, *The Brazen Face of History,* p. 27.

6. Simpson, *The Brazen Face of History,* p. 184.

7. Allen Tate, "One Escape from the Dilemma," *Fugitive* 3 (April 1924): 35.

8. Quoted in Simpson, *The Brazen Face of History,* p. 165.

9. Walker Percy, "From Facts to Fiction," *Writer* 80 (October 1967): 27.

10. Allen Tate, "The Profession of Letters in the South," in his *Essays of Four Decades* (Chicago: Swallow Press, 1968), p. 533.

## Chapter 1
### (Allen Tate)

1. Allen Tate, "The Profession of Letters in the Modern South," in his *Essays of Four Decades* (Chicago: Swallow Press, 1968), p. 529. All further references to Tate's essays, unless otherwise indicated, are from this edition and will be cited parenthetically *(EFD)* in the text.

2. Allen Tate, "Religion and the Intellectuals," *Partisan Review* 17 (1950): 250.

3. Biographical material on Tate comes from the following sources: Ferman Bishop, *Allen Tate* (New York: Twayne, 1967); Radcliffe Squires, *Allen Tate: A Literary Biography* (New York: Pegasus, 1971); Louise Cowan, *The Fugitive Group: A Literary History* (Baton Rouge: Louisiana State University Press, 1959); Louis D. Rubin, Jr., *The Wary Fugitives: Four Poets and the South* (Baton Rouge: Louisiana State University Press, 1979); Robert Buffington, "Young Hawk Circling," *Sewanee Review* 87 (1979): 541–56; Robert Buffington, "Allen Tate: Society, Vocation,

Communion," *Southern Review* 18 (1982): 62–72; and Willard Thorp, "Allen Tate at Princeton," *Princeton University Library Chronicle* 41 (1979): 1–21.

4. Allen Tate, "Several Thousand Books," *Sewanee Review* 75 (1967):380.

5. Allen Tate, "A Lost Traveller's Dream," in his *Memoirs and Opinions, 1926–1974* (Chicago: Swallow Press, 1975), pp. 7–8.

6. Tate, "A Lost Traveller's Dream," p. 7.

7. Allen Tate, "Mere Literature and the Lost Traveller" (Nashville, Tenn.: George Peabody College for Teachers, 1969), p. 3.

8. Tate, "Mere Literature," p. 3.

9. Tate, "Mere Literature," p. 3.

10. John Crowe Ransom, "In Amicitia," in *Allen Tate and His Work: Critical Evaluations,* ed. Radcliffe Squires (Minneapolis: University of Minnesota Press, 1972), p. 14.

11. Allen Tate, "Whose Ox," *The Fugitive* 1 (December 1922):99.

12. Tate, "Whose Ox," p. 99.

13. Tate, "Whose Ox," p. 99.

14. Tate, "Whose Ox," p. 99.

15. Tate, "Whose Ox," p. 100.

16. Allen Tate, "One Escape from the Dilemma," *Fugitive* 3 (April 1924):35.

17. Tate, "One Escape from the Dilemma," p. 35.

18. Tate, "One Escape from the Dilemma," p. 35.

19. Squires *Allen Tate,* p. 44.

20. Allen Tate, *The Literary Correspondence of Donald Davidson and Allen Tate,* ed. John Tyree Fain and Thomas Daniel Young (Athens: University of Georgia Press, 1974), p. 58. All further references to letters between Tate and Davidson are from this edition and will be cited parenthetically *(LCDT)* in the text.

21. Tate, "One Escape from the Dilemma," p. 36.

22. Tate, "Mere Literature," p. 3.

23. Tate, "Mere Literature," p. 3.

24. Andrew Lytle, "Allen Tate: Upon the Occasion of His Sixtieth Birthday," in *Allen Tate and His Work,* p. 24.

25. Quoted in Buffington, "Young Hawk Circling," p. 544.

26. Squires, *Allen Tate,* p. 60.

27. Lewis P. Simpson, *The Brazen Face of History: Studies in the Literary Consciousness in America* (Baton Rouge: Louisiana State University Press, 1980), p. 203.

28. Tate, "A Lost Traveller's Dream," p. 17.

29. Allen Tate, *Collected Poems, 1919–1976* (New York: Farrar Straus Giroux, 1977), p. 19. All further references to poems by Tate are from this edition and will be cited parenthetically *(CPT)* in the text.

30. Allen Tate, "Introduction to *White Buildings* by Hart Crane," in Tate's *Memoirs and Opinions, 1926–1974,* p. 174.

31. Tate, "Introduction to *White Buildings* by Hart Crane," p. 112.

32. Quoted in Irv Broughton, "An Interview with Allen Tate," *Western Humanities Review* 32 (1978):329.

33. Lytle, "Allen Tate: Upon the Occasion of His Sixtieth Birthday," p. 24.

34. Rubin, *The Wary Fugitives*, p. 96.

35. Allen Tate, *Stonewall Jackson: The Good Soldier* (New York: Minton, Balch & Co., 1928), p. 25.

36. Robert S. Dupree, *Allen Tate and the Augustinian Tradition* (Baton Rouge: Louisiana State University Press, 1983), pp. 36, 37.

37. Allen Tate, "A Symposium: The Agrarians Today," *Shenandoah* 3 (Summer 1952): 28–29.

38. Quoted in Buffington, "Young Hawk Circling," pp. 552–53.

39. Buffington, "Young Hawk Circling," pp. 552–53.

40. Allen Tate, *Jefferson Davis: His Rise and Fall* (New York: Minton, Balch & Co., 1929), p. 301. All further references to this book are from this edition and will be cited parenthetically *(JD)* in the text.

41. Quoted in Buffington, "Young Hawk Circling," p. 552.

42. I am indebted in my reading of "The Cross" to Louis D. Rubin, Jr.'s fine discussion of the poem in his book *The Wary Fugitives*, pp. 127–30.

43. Wallace Fowlie, *Aubade: A Teacher's Notebook* (Durham, N.C.: Duke University Press, 1983), p. 157.

44. Quoted in Daniel Joseph Singal, *The War Within: From Victorian to Modernist Thought in the South, 1919–1945* (Chapel Hill: University of North Carolina Press, 1982), p. 246.

45. Allen Tate, "Remarks on the Southern Religion," in *I'll Take My Stand: The South and the Agrarian Tradition* by Twelve Southerners, Harper Torchbooks (New York: Harper & Row, 1962), p. 163. All further references to this essay are from this edition and will be cited parenthetically *(ITMS)* in the text.

46. Allen Tate, *The Republic of Letters in America: The Correspondence of John Peale Bishop and Allen Tate,* ed. Thomas Daniel Young and John J. Hindle (Lexington: University Press of Kentucky, 1981), p. 45. All further references to Tate's letters to Bishop are from this edition and will be cited parenthetically *(RL)* in the text.

47. Quoted in Squires, *Allen Tate*, p. 108.

48. Allen Tate, *The Fathers* (New York: G. P. Putnam's Sons, 1938), p. 5. All further references to this novel, unless otherwise noted, are from this edition and will be cited parenthetically *(F)* in the text.

49. Allen Tate, *The Fathers*, rev. ed., in his *The Fathers and Other Fiction* (Baton Rouge: Louisiana State University Press, 1977), pp. 306–7.

50. Allen Tate, "Note on 'The Migration' and 'The Immortal Woman,' with a Glance at Two Scenes in *The Fathers*," in *The Fathers and Other Fiction*, p. 314.

51. Dante Alighieri, *The Inferno*, trans. J. A. Carlyle (London: J. M. Dent & Sons, 1932), p. 137.

52. Allen Tate, "Introduction to *Land of Unlikeness* by Robert Lowell,"

in *The Poetry Reviews of Allen Tate, 1924–1944,* ed. Ashley Brown and Frances Neel Cheney (Baton Rouge: Louisiana State University Press, 1983), p. 210.

53. Jacques Maritain, *The Dream of Descartes,* trans. Mabelle L. Andison (New York: Philosophical Library, 1944), p. 179.

54. Maritain, *The Dream of Descartes,* p. 180.

55. Squires, *Allen Tate,* p. 199.

56. Augustine's influence on Tate is discussed fully in Robert S. Dupree, *Allen Tate and the Augustinian Imagination* (Baton Rouge: Louisiana State University Press, 1983). My short discussion here is indebted to Dupree's book.

57. Dupree, *Allen Tate and the Augustinian Imagination,* p. 136.

58. Quoted in Squires, *Allen Tate,* p. 183.

59. Tate, "A Lost Traveller's Dream," p. 12.

60. Allen Tate, "Christ and the Unicorn," *Sewanee Review* 63 (1955):178.

61. Tate, "Christ and the Unicorn," p. 180.

## Chapter 2
### (Caroline Gordon)

1. Caroline Gordon, "Notes on Hemingway and Kafka," *Sewanee Review* 57 (1949):220.

2. Biographical material on Gordon comes from the following sources: William J. Stuckey, *Caroline Gordon* (New York: Twayne, 1972); Frederick P. McDowell, *Caroline Gordon,* University of Minnesota Pamphlets on American Writers (Minneapolis: University of Minnesota Press, 1966); Louise Cowan, *The Fugitive Group: A Literary History* (Baton Rouge: Louisiana State University Press, 1959); and *The Southern Mandarins: Letters of Caroline Gordon to Sally Wood, 1924–1937,* ed. Sally Wood (Baton Rouge: Louisiana State University Press, 1984).

3. Caroline Gordon, "Cock-Crow," *Southern Review,* n.s. 1 (1965):554.

4. Caroline Gordon, "Always Summer," *Southern Review,* n.s. 7 (1971):430.

5. Gordon, "Cock-Crow," p. 557.

6. Gordon, "Cock-Crow," p. 557.

7. Caroline Gordon, "A Narrow Heart: The Portrait of a Woman," *Transatlantic Review* 3 (1960):18.

8. Gordon, "A Narrow Heart," p. 18.

9. Caroline Gordon, "Letters to a Monk," *Ramparts* 3 (December 1964):8.

10. Quoted in Cowan, *The Fugitive Group,* p. 98.

11. Caroline Gordon, *The Southern Mandarins: Letters of Caroline Gordon to Sally Wood, 1924–1937,* ed. Sally Wood (Baton Rouge: Louisiana State University Press, 1984), p. 31. All further references to Gordon's

letters to Wood are from this edition and will be cited parenthetically *(SM)* in the text.

12. Gordon, "Cock-Crow," p. 558.

13. Willard Thorp, "The Way Back and the Way Up: The Novels of Caroline Gordon," *Bucknell Review* 6 (1953):3.

14. Caroline Gordon, *Aleck Maury, Sportsman* (New York: Cooper Square, 1971), p. 60. All further references to this novel are from this edition and will be cited parenthetically *(AM)* in the text.

15. Louise Cowan, "Aleck Maury, Epic Hero and Pilgrim," in *The Short Fiction of Caroline Gordon*, ed. Thomas H. Landess (Dallas: University of Dallas Press, 1972), p. 16.

16. Caroline Gordon, "The Last Day in the Field," in *The Collected Stories of Caroline Gordon* (New York: Farrar Straus Giroux, 1981), p. 102. All further references to short stories by Caroline Gordon are from this volume and will be cited parenthetically *(CSCG)* in the text.

17. Caroline Gordon, *The Garden of Adonis* (New York: Cooper Square, 1971), pp. 54–55. All further references to this novel are from this edition and will be cited parenthetically *(GA)* in the text.

18. Thomas H. Landess, "The Function of Ritual in Caroline Gordon's *Green Centuries*," *Southern Review*, n.s. 7 (1971):507.

19. Caroline Gordon, *Green Centuries* (New York: Cooper Square, 1971), p. 469.

20. Caroline Gordon, *The Women on the Porch* (New York: Cooper Square, 1971), p. 130. All further references to this novel are from this edition and will be cited parenthetically *(WP)* in the text.

21. Caroline Gordon, "The Art and Mystery of Faith," *Newman Annual*, 1953, p. 58.

22. Gordon, "The Art and Mystery of Faith," p. 58.

23. Gordon, "Letters to a Monk," p. 6.

24. Flannery O'Connor, *The Habit of Being: Letters*, ed. Sally Fitzgerald (New York: Farrar Straus Giroux, 1979), p. 114.

25. Caroline Gordon, "Flannery O'Connor's *Wise Blood*," *Critique*, 2 no. 2 (1958):7.

26. Caroline Gordon and Allen Tate, *The House of Fiction* (New York: Charles Scribner's Sons, 1950), p. 178.

27. Caroline Gordon, *How to Read a Novel* (New York: Viking Press, 1957), pp. 224, 225. All further references to this volume are from this edition and will be cited parenthetically *(HTRN)* in the text.

28. Gordon, "Letters to a Monk," p. 10.

29. Flannery O'Connor, "The Fiction Writer and His Country," in *Mystery and Manners: Occasional Prose*, ed. Sally and Robert Fitzgerald (New York: Farrar, Straus & Giroux, 1969), p. 34.

30. Quoted in Brainard Cheney, "Caroline Gordon's *The Malefactors*," in *Rediscoveries*, ed. David Madden (New York: Crown, 1971), pp. 241–42.

31. Caroline Gordon, *The Strange Children* (New York: Cooper

Square, 1971), p. 108. All further references to this novel are from this edition and will be cited parenthetically *(SCh)* in the text.

32. O'Connor, *The Habit of Being,* p. 202.

33. Caroline Gordon, *The Malefactors* (New York: Harcourt, Brace, 1956), p. 86. All further references to this novel are from this edition and will be cited parenthetically *(Mal)* in the text.

34. Quoted in Caroline Gordon, "Some Readings and Misreadings," *Sewanee Review* 61 (1953): 384.

35. Gordon, "Some Readings and Misreadings," p. 385.

36. Gordon, "Some Readings and Misreadings," p. 386.

37. Caroline Gordon, "On Learning to Write," *Four Quarters* 12 (January 1963): 15.

38. Gordon, "Letters to a Monk," p. 10.

39. Quoted in Donald E. Stanford, "Caroline Gordon: From *Penhally* to *A Narrow Heart*," *Southern Review,* n.s. 16 (1980): 282.

## Chapter 3
### (Walker Percy)

1. Biographical material on Percy comes from the following sources: Ellen Douglas, *Walker Percy's "The Last Gentleman": Introduction and Sources* (New York: Seabury Press, 1969); Martin Luschei, *The Sovereign Wayfarer: Walker Percy's Diagnosis of the Malaise* (Baton Rouge: Louisiana State University Press, 1972); Robert Coles, *Walker Percy: An American Search* (Boston: Atlantic-Little, Brown, 1979); and Lewis Baker, *The Percys of Mississippi* (Baton Rouge: Louisiana State University Press, 1983).

2. Walker Percy, "Introduction," to William Alexander Percy, *Lanterns on the Levee: Recollections of a Planter's Son* (Baton Rouge: Louisiana State University Press, 1973), p. vii.

3. Walker Percy, "Introduction," *Lanterns on the Levee,* p. vii.

4. Quoted in John Carr, "Rotation and Repetition: Walker Percy," in *Kite-Flying and other Irrational Acts: Conversations with Twelve Southern Writers,* ed. John Carr (Baton Rouge: Louisiana State University Press, 1972), pp. 35–36.

5. Walker Percy, "Introduction," *Lanterns on the Levee,* p. x.

6. William Alexander Percy, *Lanterns on the Levee: Recollections of a Planter's Son* (New York: Knopf, 1941), p. 95. All further references to this work are from this edition and will be cited parenthetically *(LL)* in the text.

7. Quoted in Carr, "Rotation and Repetition," p. 37.

8. Walker Percy, "Introduction," *Lanterns on the Levee,* p. xi.

9. Walker Percy, "From Facts to Fiction," *Writer* 80 (October 1967): 27.

10. Walker Percy, "From Facts to Fiction," p. 27.

11. Walker Percy, "From Facts to Fiction," p. 28.

12. Quoted in Coles, *Walker Percy,* p. 65.

13. Walker Percy, "From Facts to Fiction," p. 28.

14. Walker Percy, "From Facts to Fiction," p. 28.

15. Quoted in Coles, *Walker Percy,* p. 67.

16. Coles, *Walker Percy,* p. 68.

17. Quoted in Carr, "Rotation and Repetition," p. 46.

18. Quoted in Bradley R. Dewey, "Walker Percy Talks about Kierkegaard: An Annotated Interview," *Journal of Religion* 54 (1974): 282.

19. Sören Kierkegaard, "Of the Difference between a Genius and an Apostle," in *The Present Age and Two Minor Ethico-Religious Treatises,* trans. Alexander Dru and Walter Lowrie (London: Oxford University Press, 1940), p. 158.

20. Quoted in Coles, *Walker Percy,* p. 67.

21. Walker Percy, "Stoicism in the South," *Commonweal* 64 (1956): 343.

22. Walker Percy, "Stoicism in the South," p. 343.

23. Walker Percy, "The Failure and the Hope," *Katallagete,* Journal of the Committee of Southern Churchmen, Nashville (Winter 1967–68): 19.

24. Walker Percy, "The Failure and the Hope," p. 20.

25. Walker Percy, "Why I Live Where I Live," *Esquire,* April 1980, p. 35.

26. Walker Percy, "Why I Live Where I Live," p. 35.

27. Quoted in Ashley Brown, "An Interview with Walker Percy," *Shenandoah* 18 (Spring 1967): 4.

28. Quoted in Carr, "Rotation and Repetition," pp. 42–43.

29. Quoted in Carlton Creemans, "Walker Percy, the Man and the Novelist: An Interview," *Southern Review,* n.s. 4 (1968): 282.

30. Walker Percy, "From Facts to Fiction," p. 46.

31. Walker Percy, *The Moviegoer* (New York: Farrar, Straus & Giroux, 1967), p. 54. All further references to this novel are from this edition and will be cited parenthetically *(Mg)* in the text.

32. Walker Percy, Introduction to "*The Last Gentleman:* Two Excerpts from the Forthcoming Novel," *Harper's,* May 1966, p. 54.

33. Walker Percy, *The Last Gentleman* (New York: Farrar, Straus & Giroux, 1966), p. 22. All further references to this novel are from this edition and will be cited parenthetically *(LG)* in the text.

34. Louis D. Rubin, Jr., "The Boll Weevil, the Iron Horse, and the End of the Line: Thoughts on the South," *Virginia Quarterly Review* 55 (1979): 208.

35. Walker Percy, "From Facts to Fiction," p. 46.

36. Walker Percy, "From Facts to Fiction," p. 46.

37. Walker Percy, "The Delta Factor," in *The Message in the Bottle: How Queer Man Is, How Queer Language Is, and What One Has to Do with the Other* (New York: Farrar, Straus & Giroux, 1975), p. 20. All further references to essays from this collection are from this edition and will be cited parenthetically *(MB)* in the text.

38. Walker Percy, "From Facts to Fiction," p. 46.

39. Walker Percy, "The State of the Novel: Dying Art or New Science?" *Michigan Quarterly Review* 16 (1977): 360.

40. Walker Percy, "The State of the Novel," p. 361.

41. Walker Percy, "The State of the Novel," p. 361.

42. Quoted in Zoltan Abádi-Nagy, "A Talk with Walker Percy," *Southern Literary Journal* 16 (Fall 1973): 12.

43. Quoted in Abádi-Nagy, "A Talk with Walker Percy," p. 12.

44. Walker Percy, "The State of the Novel," p. 363.

45. Quoted in Dewey, "Walker Percy Talks about Kierkegaard," p. 295.

46. Quoted in Charles T. Bunting, "An Afternoon with Walker Percy," *Notes on Mississippi Writers* 4 (1971): 49.

47. Quoted in "The Authors that Bloom in the Spring," *Publishers Weekly*, 22 March 1971, p. 23.

48. Quoted in "The Authors that Bloom in the Spring," p. 23.

49. Walker Percy, *Love in the Ruins: The Adventures of a Bad Catholic at a Time near the End of the World* (New York: Farrar, Straus & Giroux, 1971), pp. 28–29. All further references to this novel are from this edition and will be cited parenthetically *(LR)* in the text.

50. Quoted in "The Authors that Bloom in the Spring," p. 23.

51. Walker Percy, *Lancelot* (New York: Farrar Straus Giroux, 1977), p. 177. All further references to this novel are from this edition and will be cited parenthetically *(L)* in the text.

52. Coles, *Walker Percy*, pp. 213–16.

53. Lancelot Andrewes, *The Devotions of Bishop Andrewes*, trans. John Henry Newman (London: S.P.C.K., 1920), 1:21.

54. Flannery O'Connor, "Some Aspects of the Grotesque in Southern Fiction," in *Mystery and Manners: Occasional Prose*, ed. Sally and Robert Fitzgerald (New York: Farrar, Straus & Giroux, 1969), p. 50.

55. Walker Percy, *The Second Coming* (New York: Farrar Straus Giroux, 1980), p. 124. All further references to this novel are from this edition and will be cited parenthetically *(SC)* in the text.

56. Quoted in James Atlas, "A Portrait of Mr. Percy," *New York Times Book Review*, 29 June 1980, p. 30.

57. Quoted in Atlas, "A Portrait of Mr. Percy," p. 30.

### Epilogue

1. James Hitchcock, "Postmortem on a Rebirth: The Catholic Intellectual Renaissance," *American Scholar* 49 (1980): 212.

2. Hitchcock, "Postmortem on a Rebirth," p. 213.

3. Caroline Gordon, "Letters to a Monk," *Ramparts* 3 (December 1964): 6.

4. Flannery O'Connor, "Catholic Novelists and Their Readers," in *Mystery and Manners: Occasional Prose*, ed. Sally and Robert Fitzgerald (New York: Farrar, Straus & Giroux, 1969), p. 180.

5. O'Connor, "Catholic Novelists and Their Readers," in *Mystery and Manners*, pp. 180, 181.

6. Flannery O'Connor, "The Catholic Novelist in the Protestant South," in *Mystery and Manners*, p. 208.

# Selected Bibliography

*Primary Sources*

## Works by Caroline Gordon

*Aleck Maury, Sportsman.* New York: Cooper Square, 1971.
"Always Summer." *Southern Review*, n.s. 7 (1971): 430–446.
"The Art and Mystery of Faith." *Newman Annual*, 1953, pp. 55–61.
"Cock-Crow." *Southern Review*, n.s. 1 (1965): 554–69.
*The Collected Stories.* New York: Farrar Straus Giroux, 1981.
"Flannery O'Connor's *Wise Blood.*" *Critique* 2 (1958): 3–10.
*The Forest of the South.* New York: Charles Scribner's Sons, 1945.
*The Garden of Adonis.* New York: Cooper Square, 1971.
*The Glory of Hera.* New York: Doubleday, 1972.
*Green Centuries.* New York: Cooper Square, 1971.
"Heresy in Dixie." *Sewanee Review* 76 (1978): 293–97.
*How to Read a Novel.* New York: Viking Press, 1957.
"Letters to a Monk." *Ramparts* 3 (December 1964): 4–10.
*The Malefactors.* New York: Harcourt, Brace, 1956.
"A Narrow Heart: The Portrait of a Woman." *Transatlantic Review* 3 (1960): 7–19.
"Notes on Chekhov and Maugham." *Sewanee Review* 57 (1949): 401–10.
"Notes on Hemingway and Kafka." *Sewanee Review* 57 (1949): 215–26.
*Old Red and Other Stories.* New York: Cooper Square, 1971.
"On Learning to Write." *Four Quarters* 12 (January 1963): 8–15.
*Penhally.* New York: Cooper Square, 1971.
"Some Readings and Misreadings." *Sewanee Review* 61 (1953): 384–407.
*The Southern Mandarins: Letters of Caroline Gordon to Sally Wood, 1924–1937.* Ed. Sally Wood. Baton Rouge: Louisiana State University Press, 1984.
"Stephen Crane." *Accent* 9 (1949):153–57.
*The Strange Children.* New York: Cooper Square, 1971.
"The Strangest Day in the Life of Captain Meriwether Lewis as Told to His Eighth Cousin, Once Removed." *Southern Review*, n.s. 12 (1976):387–97.
"To Ford Madox Ford." *Transatlantic Review* 3 (1960):5–6.
"A Walk with the Accuser." *Southern Review*, n.s. 13 (1977):597–613.
*The Women on the Porch.* New York: Cooper Square, 1971.

## Works by Walker Percy

"The Coming Crisis in Psychiatry." Parts 1, 2. *America*, 5 and 12 January 1957, pp. 391–93, 415–18.

"The Culture Critics." *Commonweal* 70 (1959):247–50.
"The Failure and the Hope." *Katallagete,* Journal of the Committee of Southern Churchmen (Winter 1967–68):16–21.
"From Facts to Fiction." *Writer* 80 (October 1967):27–28.
"Introduction," to William Alexander Percy, *Lanterns on the Levee: Recollections of a Planter's Son.* Baton Rouge: Louisiana State University Press, 1973.
*Lancelot.* New York: Farrar Straus Giroux, 1977.
*The Last Gentleman.* New York: Farrar, Straus & Giroux, 1966.
*"The Last Gentleman:* Two Excerpts from the Forthcoming Novel." *Harper's Magazine,* May 1966, pp. 54–61.
*Lost in the Cosmos: The Last Self-Help Book.* New York: Farrar, Straus & Giroux, 1983.
*Love in the Ruins: The Adventures of a Bad Catholic at a Time near the End of the World.* New York: Farrar, Straus and Giroux, 1971.
*The Message in the Bottle: How Queer Man Is, How Queer Language Is, and What One Has to Do with the Other.* New York: Farrar, Straus & Giroux, 1975.
*The Moviegoer.* New York: Farrar, Straus & Giroux, 1967.
"Naming and Being." *Personalist* 41 (Spring 1960):148–57.
"Questions They Never Asked Me." *Esquire,* December 1977, pp. 170–72, 184–94.
"Random Thoughts on Southern Literature, Southern Politics, and the American Future." *Georgia Review* 32 (1978):499–511.
*The Second Coming.* New York: Farrar Straus Giroux, 1980.
"The Southern Moderate." *Commonweal* 67 (1957):279–82.
"The State of the Novel: Dying Art or New Science?" *Michigan Quarterly Review* 16 (1977):359–73.
"Stoicism in the South." *Commonweal* 64 (1956):342–44.
"Virtues and Vices in the Southern Literary Renascence." *Commonweal* 76 (1962):181–82.
"Why I Live Where I Live." *Esquire,* April 1980, pp. 35–37.

**Works by Allen Tate**

"Allen Tate on *The Fathers.*" Letter to Philip Rahv. *Partisan Review* 6 (1939):125–26.
"Christ and the Unicorn." *Sewanee Review* 63 (1955):175–81.
*Collected Poems, 1919–1976.* New York: Farrar Straus Giroux, 1977.
*Essays of Four Decades.* Chicago: The Swallow Press, 1968.
*The Fathers.* New York: G. P. Putnam's Sons, 1938.
*The Fathers and Other Fiction.* Rev. ed. Baton Rouge: Louisiana State University Press, 1977.
*Jefferson Davis: His Rise and Fall.* New York: Minton, Balch & Co., 1929.
"Last Days of the Charming Lady." *Nation,* 28 October 1925, pp. 485–86.
*Memoirs and Opinions, 1926–1974.* Chicago: Swallow Press, 1975.

"Mere Literature and the Lost Traveller." Nashville, Tenn.: George Peabody College for Teachers, 1969.

"One Escape from the Dilemma." *Fugitive* 3 (April 1924):34–36.

*The Poetry Reviews of Allen Tate, 1924–1944.* Ed. Ashley Brown and Frances Neel Cheney. Baton Rouge: Louisiana State University Press, 1983.

"Religion and the Intellectuals." *Partisan Review* 17 (1950):250–53.

"Several Thousand Books." *Sewanee Review* 75 (1967):377–84.

"Speculations." *Southern Review*, n.s. 14 (1978):226–33.

*Stonewall Jackson: The Good Soldier.* New York: Minton, Balch & Co., 1928.

"Whose Ox." *Fugitive* 1 (December 1922):99–100.


*Secondary Sources*


Abádi-Nagy, Zoltan. "A Talk with Walker Percy." *Southern Literary Journal* 61 (Fall 1973):3–19.

Alighieri, Dante. *The Inferno.* Trans. J. A. Carlyle. London: J. M. Dent & Sons, 1932.

Andrewes, Lancelot. *The Devotions of Bishop Andrewes.* 2 vols., trans. from the Greek by John Henry Newman. London: S.P.C.K., 1920.

Atlas, James. "A Portrait of Mr. Percy." *New York Times Book Review*, 29 June 1980, pp. 1, 30–31.

"The Authors that Bloom in the Spring." *Publishers Weekly*, 22 March 1971, pp. 22–24.

Bain, Robert, Joseph M. Flora, and Louis D. Rubin, Jr., eds. *Southern Writers: A Biographical Dictionary.* Baton Rouge: Louisiana State University Press, 1979.

Baker, Howard. "The Strategems of Caroline Gordon; or, The Art of the Novel and the Novelty of Myth. *Southern Review*, n.s. 9 (1973):523–49.

Baker, Lewis. *The Percys of Mississippi.* Baton Rouge: Louisiana State University Press, 1983.

Berrigan, J. R. "An Explosion of Utopias." *Moreana* 38 (1973):21–26.

Bishop, Ferman. *Allen Tate.* New York: Twayne, 1967.

Broughton, Irv. "An Interview with Allen Tate." *Western Humanities Review* 32 (1978):317–36.

Brown, Ashley. "The Achievement of Caroline Gordon." *Southern Humanities Review* 2 (1968):279–90.

———. "An Interview with Walker Percy." *Shenandoah* 18 (Spring 1967):3–10.

———. "Caroline Gordon's Short Fiction." *Sewanee Review* 81 (1973):365–70.

Buckley, William F., Jr. "The Southern Imagination: An Interview with Eudora Welty and Walker Percy." *Mississippi Quarterly* 26 (1973):493–516.

Buffington, Robert. "Allen Tate: Society, Vocation, Communion." *Southern Review,* n.s. 18 (1982):62–72.

———. "Young Hawk Circling." *Sewanee Review* 87 (1979):541–56.

Bunting, Charles T. "An Afternoon with Walker Percy." *Notes on Mississippi Writers* 4 (1971):43–61.

Carr, John, ed. *Kite-Flying and Other Irrational Acts: Conversations with Twelve Southern Writers.* Baton Rouge: Louisiana State University Press, 1972.

Cheney, Brainard. "Caroline Gordon's Ontological Quest." *Renascence* 16 (1963):3–12.

———. "Caroline Gordon's *The Malefactors.*" *Sewanee Review* 79 (1971):360–72.

Coles, Robert. *Walker Percy: An American Search.* Boston: Atlantic-Little, Brown, 1979.

Colquitt, Betsy, ed. *Medieval, Renaissance, [and] American Literature: A Festschrift.* Forth Worth: Texas Christian University Press, 1971.

Cowan, Bainard. "The Serpent Coils: How to Read Caroline Gordon's Later Fiction." *Southern Review,* n.s. 16 (1980):281–98.

Cowan, Louise. *The Fugitive Group: A Literary History.* Baton Rouge: Louisiana State University Press, 1959.

Creemans, Carlton. "Walker Percy, the Man and the Novelist: An Interview." *Southern Review,* n.s. 4 (1968): 271–90.

Davidson, Donald. *Southern Writers in the Modern World.* Athens: University of Georgia Press, 1958.

Dewey, Bradley R. "Walker Percy Talks about Kierkegaard." *Journal of Religion* 54 (1974):273–98.

Douglas, Ellen. *Walker Percy's "The Last Gentleman": Introduction and Sources.* Religious Dimensions in Literature. New York: Seabury Press, 1969.

Dupree, Robert S. *Allen Tate and the Augustinian Imagination.* Baton Rouge: Louisiana State University Press, 1983.

Eisinger, Chester. *Fiction of the Forties.* Chicago: University of Chicago Press, 1963.

Fain, John Tyree, and Thomas Daniel Young. *The Literary Correspondence of Donald Davidson and Allen Tate.* Athens: University of Georgia Press, 1974.

Fitzgerald, Sally. "A Master Class: From the Correspondence of Caroline Gordon and Flannery O'Connor." *Georgia Review* 33 (1979):827–46.

Fowlie, Wallace. *Aubade: A Teacher's Notebook.* Durham, N.C.: Duke University Press, 1983.

Gordon, Caroline, and Allen Tate, eds. *The House of Fiction: An Anthology of the Short Story with Commentary.* New York: Charles Scribner's Sons, 1950.

Hemphill, George. *Allen Tate.* University of Minnesota Pamphlets on American Writers. Minneapolis: University of Minnesota Press, 1964.

Hill, Samuel S., Jr. *Religion and the Solid South.* Nashville, Tenn.: Abingdon Press, 1972.

————. *Southern Churches in Crisis.* Boston: Beacon Press, 1968.
Hitchcock, James. "Postmortem on a Rebirth: The Catholic Intellectual Renaissance." *American Scholar* 49 (1980):211–25.
Horsford, Howard C. "Letters of Caroline Gordon Tate to Sally Wood Kohn." *Princeton University Library Chronicle* 44 (Autumn 1982):1–24.
Kazin, Alfred. "The Pilgrimage of Walker Percy." *Harper's,* June 1971, pp. 81–86.
Kierkegaard, Sören. *The Present Age and Two Minor Ethico-Religious Treatises.* Trans. Alexander Dru and Walter Lowrie. London: Oxford University Press, 1940.
Landess, Thomas H. "The Function of Ritual in Caroline Gordon's *Green Centuries.*" *Southern Review,* n.s. 7 (1971):495–508.
————, ed. *The Short Fiction of Caroline Gordon.* Dallas: University of Dallas Press, 1972.
Lawson, Lewis. "Walker Percy: Physician as Novelist." *South Atlantic Bulletin* 37 (April 1972):58–63.
————. "Walker Percy's Indirect Communications." *Texas Studies in Literature and Language* 11 (1969):869–900.
Lears, Jackson. *No Place of Grace: Antimodernism and the Transformation of American Culture 1880–1920.* New York: Pantheon, 1981.
Luschei, Martin. *The Sovereign Wayfarer: Walker Percy's Diagnosis of the Malaise.* Baton Rouge: Louisiana State University Press, 1972.
Lytle, Andrew. "The Forest of the South." *Critique* 1 (Winter 1956):3–9.
————. *The Hero with the Private Parts.* Baton Rouge: Louisiana State University Press, 1966.
————. "The Passion of Alex [*sic*] Maury." *New Republic,* 2 January 1935, pp. 227–28.
Maritain, Jacques. *The Dream of Descartes.* Trans. Mabelle L. Andison. New York: Philosophical Library, 1944.
Mathews, Donald G. *Religion in the Old South.* Chicago: University of Chicago Press, 1977.
McDowell, Frederick P. *Caroline Gordon.* University of Minnesota Pamphlets on American Writers. Minneapolis: University of Minnesota Press, 1966.
Meiners, R. K. *The Last Alternatives: A Study of Allen Tate.* Denver, Colo.: Allan Swallow, 1963.
Millgate, Michael. "An Interview with Allen Tate." *Shenandoah* 12 (Spring 1961):27–34.
O'Connor, Flannery. *The Habit of Being: Letters.* Selected and edited by Sally Fitzgerald. New York: Farrar Straus Giroux, 1979.
————. *Mystery and Manners: Occasional Prose.* Edited by Sally and Robert Fitzgerald. New York: Farrar, Straus & Giroux, 1969.
————. *Wise Blood.* New York: Harcourt, Brace, 1952.
Percy, William Alexander. *Lanterns on the Levee: Recollections of a Planter's Son.* New York: Knopf, 1941.
Purdy, Rob Roy, ed. *Fugitives Reunion: Conversations at Vanderbilt.* Nashville: Vanderbilt University Press, 1959.

Rocks, James E. "The Christian Myth as Salvation: Caroline Gordon's *The Strange Children.*" *Tulane Studies in English* 16 (1968):149–60.

———. "The Mind and Art of Caroline Gordon." *Mississippi Quarterly* 21 (1967–68):1–16.

Rubin, Louis D., Jr. "The Boll Weevil, the Iron Horse, and the End of the Line: Thoughts on the South." *Virginia Quarterly Review* 55 (1979):193–221.

———. *The Wary Fugitives: Four Poets and the South.* Baton Rouge: Louisiana State University Press, 1979.

———. "What to Do about Chaos." *Hopkins Review* 5 (1951):65–68.

Serebnick, Judith. "First Novelists—Spring 1961." *Library Journal* 86 (1961):597.

Simpson, Lewis P. *The Dispossessed Garden: Pastoral and History in Southern Literature.* Athens: University of Georgia Press, 1975.

———. *The Brazen Face of History: Studies in the Literary Consciousness in America.* Baton Rouge: Louisiana State University Press, 1980.

Singal, Daniel Joseph. *The War Within: From Victorian to Modernist Thought in the South, 1919–1945.* Chapel Hill: University of North Carolina Press, 1982.

Smith, Marcus. "Talking about Talking: An Interview with Walker Percy." *New Orleans Review* 5 (1976):12–18.

Squires, Radcliffe. *Allen Tate: A Literary Biography.* New York: Pegasus, 1971.

———, ed. *Allen Tate and His Work: Critical Evaluations.* Minneapolis: University of Minnesota Press, 1972.

———. "Allen Tate and the Pastoral Vision."*Southern Review*, n.s. 12 (1976):733–43.

Stanford, Donald E. "Caroline Gordon: From *Penhally* to *A Narrow Heart.*" *Southern Review*, n.s. 7 (April 1971):xv–xx.

Stuckey, William J. *Caroline Gordon.* New York: Twayne, 1972.

"A Symposium: The Agrarians Today." *Shenandoah* 3 (Summer 1952):14–31. "A Symposium on Fiction." *Shenandoah* 27 (Winter 1976):3–31.

Thorp, Willard. "Allen Tate at Princeton." *Princeton University Library Chronicle* 41 (1979):1–21.

———. "The Way Back and the Way Up: The Novels of Caroline Gordon." *Bucknell Review* 6 (1956):1–15.

Twelve Southerners. *I'll Take My Stand: The South and the Agrarian Tradition.* New York: Harper & Bros., 1930.

Walker, William E., and Robert L. Walker, eds. *Reality and Myth: Essays in American Literature in Memory of Richmond Croom Beatty.* Nashville, Tenn.: Vanderbilt University Press, 1964.

Williamson, Alan. "Allen Tate and the Personal Epic." *Southern Review*, n.s. 12 (1976):714–32.

Young, Thomas Daniel, and John J. Hindle. *The Republic of Letters in America: The Correspondence of John Peale Bishop and Allen Tate.* Lexington: University Press of Kentucky, 1981.

# Index

Agar, Herbert, 32–33
Agrarianism: and Caroline Gordon, 79, 86–87; and Allen Tate, xiv, 22–24, 28, 31–39, 79, 86, 125, 158, 170, 172
Agrarians (Nashville group). *See* Agrarianism
*Allen Tate and the Augustinian Imagination: A Study of the Poetry* (Dupree), 63
Andrewes, Lancelot, 161
Aquinas, Saint Thomas, 124
Arnold, Matthew, 135
*Art and Scholasticism* (Maritain), 112–13
Augustine, Saint, 57–58, 61, 63–64

Baldwin, James, 99
Barr, Stringfellow, 79
Baudelaire, Charles, 6, 49
Belloc, Hillaire, 32
Benet, Stephen Vincent, 120
Bishop, John Peale, 41, 60–61. *See also* Tate, Allen: letters to John Peale Bishop
*The Brazen Face of History: Studies in the Literary Consciousness of America* (Simpson), xii–xiii
*The Bridge* (Crane), 108
Brooke, Rupert, 120
Brown, John, 17
Buffington, Robert, 23
Burke, Kenneth, 10

*Carolina Magazine,* 127
Catherine of Siena, Saint, 108
Catholicism: and Caroline Gordon, xv–xvi, 73–75, 89, 169–71, 172; and Modernism, 169–72; and Walker Percy, xv–xvi, 119, 123–27, 133, 138–41, 145–50, 152, 154–55, 157–61, 166–68, 169–72; and William Alexander Percy, 120–21; and

the South, ix–x, 171–72; and Allen Tate, xiv–xvi, 3, 5–6, 24–28, 30–33, 42–43, 45–48, 61–73, 96, 169–70, 172
Chesterton, G. K., 32
Coles, Robert, 123, 160
*Confessions* (Augustine), 57–58, 63
Cowan, Louise, 83
Cowley, Malcolm, xiii, 10. *See also* Tate, Allen: letters to Malcolm Cowley
Crane, Hart, 10, 11, 15, 108
Cummings, E. E., 78

Dante, 53 –54, 61, 63–65, 69–70, 92, 93
*Das Kapital* (Marx), 78
Davidson, Donald, 6, 33. *See also* Tate, Allen: letters to Donald Davidson
de Gourmont, Remy, 6
Deism, 75
Descartes, René, xiii, 61–62, 153
*Devotions* (Andrewes), 161
Dickens, Charles, 144
Distributism, 32–33
*The Divine Comedy* (Dante), 63–64
*Divino Dialogo* (Saint Catherine), 108
*Dominici Gregis,* 169
Dostoevski, Fyodor, 122
"Dover Beach" (Arnold), 135
Dupree, Robert S., 18, 63

Eliot, T. S., 25
Existentialism, xv, 119, 122–23, 124–25, 128, 133

Faulkner, William, xiii, 120
Fitzgerald, Robert, 116
Foote, Shelby, 123
Ford, Ford Madox, xiv, 35, 76–77
Fowlie, Wallace, 27
*Fugitive,* 7, 75
Fugitives (Nashville group), 6–10, 76

*Oedipus at Colonus* (Sophocles), 116
"Of the Difference between a Genius and an Apostle" (Kierkegaard), 124
Owsley, Frank, 33

*Paradiso* (Dante), 70
*Partisan Review,* 3
Percy, LeRoy, 119
Percy, Walker, ix, x–xiii, xv–xvi, 119–68, 169–72; and Catholicism, xv–xvi, 119, 123–27, 133, 138–41, 145–50, 152, 154–55, 157–61, 166–68, 169–72; and existentialism, xv, 119, 122–23, 124–25, 128, 133; and Modernism, xiv; and Stoicism, 119–21, 124–27, 129–30, 132–33, 134–36, 163–64, 168, 171. Works: *The Charterhouse* (unpublished), 127–28; "The Delta Factor," 143, 145; "The Failure and the Hope," 125–26; "From Facts to Fiction," 121–22, 123, 129, 142, 143–44; "Introduction" to *Lanterns on the Levee* (William Alexander Percy), 119–21; *Lancelot,* 155–61, 167, 171; *The Last Gentleman,* 129, 133–42, 145–47, 155, 162, 163, 165; *Lost in the Cosmos: The Last Self-Help Book,* 168; *Love in the Ruins,* 148–55, 158, 167, 171; "The Message in the Bottle," 142–43, 145, 149; *The Moviegoer,* 129–33, 141–42, 145–46, 155, 162, 167; "Notes for a Novel about the End of the World," 145, 147–48, 151, 159; *The Second Coming,* 161–68; "The State of the Novel: Dying Art or New Science?" 144–45, 147; "Stoicism in the South," 127, "Symbol as Hermeneutic in Existentialism: A Possible Bridge to Empiricism," 127; "Symbol as Need," 127; "Why I Live Where I Live," 127
Percy, William Alexander, 119–21, 124, 125
Picasso, Pablo, 7
*Pisan Cantos* (Pound), 59
Pius X, 169
Plato, 52, 57
Poe, Edgar Allen, 62, 64
Pope, Alexander, 16–18
Porter, Katherine Anne, xv

Pound, Ezra, 59
Powers, J. F., ix
Protestantism: and Catholic writers, ix; and Caroline Gordon, 75; and Allen Tate, 5, 24, 25, 30–31
Proust, Marcel, xii

*Queste del Saint Graal,* 160

Ransom, John Crowe, 6, 75
Read, Herbert, 11
Richards, I. A., 11
Roman Catholic Church. *See* Catholicism
Rubin, Louis, 16, 136

Sanborn, Herbert, 20
Sandburg, Carl, 120
Santayana, George, 11
Second Vatican Council, 169
*Sewanee Review,* 49, 112
Shakespeare, William, 120
*Shenandoah,* 22
Simons, John W., 100
Simpson, Lewis P., xii–xiii, 12, 80
Spengler, Oswald, 9
Squires, Radcliffe, 9, 11, 62
Stanford, Donald, 116
Stoicism: and Caroline Gordon, 80–85; and Walker Percy, 119–21, 124–27; 129–30, 132–33, 134–36, 155–61; 163–64, 168, 171; and William Alexander Percy, 120–21, 124; and Allen Tate, 66
Sullivan, Harry Stack, 120

Tate, Allen, ix, x–xii, xiii–xvi, 3–72, 73, 74, 76–77, 80, 83, 86, 90, 95, 119, 124, 125, 127, 128, 154, 158, 169–70, 172; and Agrarianism, xiv, 22–24, 28, 31–39, 79, 86, 125, 158, 170, 172; and Catholicism, xiv–xvi, 3, 5–6, 24–28, 30–33, 42–43, 45–48, 61–73, 96, 169–70, 172; and Modernism, xiii–xiv, 6–16; and Protestantism, 5, 24–25, 30–31; and Stoicism, 66. Works: "Aeneas at Washington," 35, 37–39; "The Angelic Imagination," 61–62, 64; "The Buried Lake," 65, 69–71, 170; "Causerie," 13–14, 21–22, 39, 53; "Christ and the Unicorn," 71–72; "The Cross," 25–27, 29; "The